Polar Science and Global Climate

An International Resource
for Education and Outreach

We thank the following organizations for support for the printing of this book:

Alfred Wegener Institute for Polar and Marine Research
British Antarctic Survey
European Polar Board
Government of Canada IPY Program
International Arctic Science Committee
International Council for Science
Ministry of Science and Innovation, Spain
NSF Office of Polar Programs
Netherlands IPY National Committee
Research Council of Norway
Research Council and Polar Research Secretariat of Sweden
Scientific Committee for Antarctic Research
UK Natural Environment Research Council
University of the Arctic
WWF International Arctic Programme

To find out more about the International Polar Year, visit www.ipy.org.

Polar Science and Global Climate
An International Resource
for Education and Outreach

General Editor:
Bettina Kaiser

Associate Editors:
Becky Allen and Sandra Zicus

PEARSON
Custom
Publishing

Pearson Education Limited
Edinburgh Gate
Harlow
Essex CM20 2JE

And associated companies throughout the world

Visit us on the World Wide Web at:
www.pearsoned.co.uk

First published 2010

This Custom Book Edition © 2010 Published by Pearson Education Limited

Cover photo credit: Christian Morel / www.ourpolarheritage.com

ISBN 978 1 84959 593 3

Printed and bound in Great Britain by Ashford Colour Press, Gosport,
Hampshire.

Brief Contents

Contents

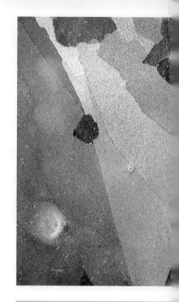

Chapter 3

Chapter 4

Foreword

A recent paper, published in October 2009, shows that the area of the Arctic Ocean covered by thick multi-year ice has decreased precipitously in only three years. The average annual mass loss from a global reference set of 30 mountain glaciers has accelerated dramatically over the same time span. Mass loss from the Greenland ice sheet has tripled since the last major assessment by the Intergovernmental Panel on Climate Change in its Fourth Assessment Report (AR4) in 2007. As I write this, a new paper already shows faster loss and greater sea level rise than a very thorough overview published only a few months earlier. The huge Antarctic ice sheet, considered stable or in slight decline in AR4, now shows clear signs of deterioration. Because of rapid change, and because of increased attention during IPY, new information about polar systems appears monthly, in some cases even weekly, in science journals as well as in the public media.

This rapid staccato of harsh messages—the first rumblings of a forthcoming avalanche of IPY results (if I may use that analogy)—presents severe internal challenges to science itself and a grim picture to the interested public. For science the challenges lie in revising our cautious and philosophic communication processes to match swift changes in polar environments, and particularly, in more quickly transforming new knowledge into predictive skill. For the public the latest announcements of disappearing snow and ice raise concern, but also confusion. Have such changes occurred in the past? Do we know the causes? What relevance do the changes have to daily lives? How, if at all, should we react—individually or collectively?

I find reason for optimism in this book, for science and for the public. Herein, on the occasion of IPY, we observe science interacting directly with a large audience through interviews, blogs, web videos, interactive exhibits and live events, exposing the full challenges, complexities and uncertainties of our research processes to public scrutiny. Science and the public learn from this dialogue; science begins to recognise and respond directly to its 'users', and the processes of direct communication with the public become (we hope) recognised (and rewarded) responsibilities of scientists. Herein as well, educators and the general public discover the energy and commitment of an international network of fellow educators and communicators engaged in creative, fun and informative advocacy for the health of our planet. I hope the book motivates every reader, as it does me, with the strength and wisdom of the words of Grand Chief Gerald Antione of the Dehcho First Nation, who credited IPY with "connecting the worlds that we work in." In these connections, demonstrated and documented by this book, we can discover purpose and optimism.

8 November 2009
David J. Carlson

NEEM Camp, Greenland: observing seasonal snow deposit layers and summer melting in the snow wall at the entrance to the science trench.

Polar Science in the Context of Global Citizenship

*P*olar Science and Global Climate: An International Resource for Education and Outreach is the product of a group of international polar researchers and educators with a shared commitment to outreach and education. It is a response to continual requests from teachers, early career and senior scientists worldwide wishing to raise awareness of the importance of polar science. This book is a direct result of education and outreach projects carried out during the International Polar Year (IPY).

The book is written for a multidisciplinary and international audience including educators, undergraduate and graduate students; as well as experts from the natural, physical and social sciences, the humanities, and the arts, who wish to present their work in the classroom or public arena.

Polar Science and Global Climate introduces readers to basic ideas of education and outreach as well as key aspects of polar research. The book combines science teaching in schools with public education and outreach.

In the Prelude you will become familiar with six basic themes of polar science: Atmosphere, Ice, Ocean, Land, People and Space; and in Chapter 1 we show you how these themes can be implemented in the classroom. Chapter 2 explains how polar scientists can present their field of expertise in public. Chapter 3 focuses on how polar research can be addressed in large- and small-scale education and outreach initiatives. Finally, the concluding chapter, an essay on capacity building among reindeer herding peoples in the circumpolar north, introduces you to the variety of indigenous voices in the Arctic regions.

We, the contributors to this book, believe that it serves as a crucial IPY legacy product, capturing the energy and enthusiasm of IPY education and outreach, as well as being a practical handbook for both researchers and educators to raise awareness of environmental issues in general and polar science in particular. Its preparation has benefited from direct financial support from the Canadian IPY Federal

Program Office, the Polar Research Board of the United States National Academy of Sciences and Engineering, and the organising committee for the flagship IPY Science Conference in Norway, 2010. It has been endorsed by the United Nations Environment Programme (UNEP), the World Meteorological Organization (WMO), the International Council for Science (ICSU), the IPY Polar Books Project, and the Association of Polar Early Career Scientists (APECS).

Being published by Pearson, *Polar Science and Global Climate* will become part of an educational initiative driven by the UK company Edexcel, part of the Pearson Education group, to introduce new qualifications in climate change proficiency—termed 'Global Citizenship'. Edexcel is currently developing IGCSE (International General Certificate of Secondary Education for students aged 14 to 16) and AS level (for students aged 16 to 18) qualifications in Global Citizenship and will be working with a range of international NGOs and publishers who provide materials in this area to support the qualifications. They will cover a wide range of related areas, including climate change as well as other global issues. Edexcel will provide more information about the qualifications in the near future. Further information is available from Dr David Davies, International Business Manager, Edexcel (david.davies@edexcel.com) and Tom Eats, International Strategic Development Manager (tom.eats@edexcel.com).

How to Use this Book

You have several options using the assembled material. Here, we outline the content and useful tools to navigate through the chapters according to your specific interests. You can use the book by consulting specific chapters or by browsing to find what is relevant for your particular education and outreach purpose. The first part of this section gives you an overview of the content structure, while the second part lists the function of features like icons, cross-references, glossary and CD-ROM.

CONTENT STRUCTURE

IPY and Six Themes of Polar Science

The *Prelude* gives you an introduction to polar science and the history of the International Polar Year. It provides important background on six polar research themes: Atmosphere, Ice, Ocean, Land, People and Space. We explain why and how we study them, and what further questions are being asked in these research fields to determine the effects of global climate change. This chapter also provides background information for further use in Chapter 1.

Teaching Resources for Teachers

Chapter 1 contains teaching resources for use in the classroom, lab or during a field trip. An Icon indicates whether it is a lab, field or classroom activity. Resources are grouped under the book's six polar themes. We give you a list of activities under each polar theme to help you find specific resources. Each resource contains background information, a description of the activity, a list of necessary material, estimates of preparation and classroom time, objectives, graphics, and suggestions for extensions. The resources are not laid out for students of a certain age group; we leave it to the teacher and educator to adapt them to particular age levels. Activities include student worksheets and visuals that you can also find on the CD-ROM. The CD-ROM further contains background material on indigenous communities in the circumpolar north and additional web links for each activity.

Presentation Guide for Scientists

Chapter 2 lists 'do's and don'ts' of successful public engagement for polar scientists. This unit helps you understand how presentations should be planned and structured when going into a classroom or a community. We tell you what to expect from certain age groups, how to present inclusively to all audiences, and what you should know when presenting to the Inuit communities of Nunavut.

Outreach Initiatives for Educators

Chapter 3 provides you with an overview of successful education and outreach initiatives in polar science during IPY. It begins with a list of education and outreach categories, which is followed by a one-page list of school level, university level, and public level initiatives. The rest of the chapter showcases successful initiatives in these three groups. Each project description lists the country, key aspects, keys to success, and their relevant education and outreach categories.

IPY and Local Competence Building in the Circumpolar North

Chapter 4, written by Ole Henrik Magga (politician and Sámi linguist), Svein D. Mathiesen (Advisor at the International Centre for Reindeer Husbandry [ICR] and veterinary scientist), Anders Oskal (Director of ICR), and Johan Mathis Turi (Secretary General of the Association of World Reindeer Herders on the Arctic Council), discusses the role of IPY for indigenous communities in the circumpolar north and the significance of Traditional Knowledge in polar science.

TOOLS FOR EASY USAGE

Icons

There are four icons used in the book to help identify activities in Chapter 1, and CD-ROM material used in the book.

classroom activity

lab activity

field activity

CD-ROM

Cross References

Teaching resources, outreach descriptions and tips and tricks for science presentations occasionally relate to one another. When this is the case, we tell you where you can find more information.

Contributing Polar Institutions

There is a list of 'Contributing Polar Institutions' at the end of the book. It contains the acronym, full name, country and website of each listed polar research institution. The list is in alphabetical order. If you are not sure, for example, what country an institution belongs to, you can use this list to find further information.

Glossary

There is a Glossary at the end of the book. It is arranged in alphabetical order and lists key terms that are critical for understanding aspects of polar science.

Abbreviations and Acronyms

Throughout the book you will come across a number of abbreviations and acronyms. We give you a complete list with short explanations at the end of the book. Acronyms that are also part of 'Contributing Polar Institutions' are highlighted in italics.

References

Each chapter contains a number of interesting references to further online and print material. You find a list of full references at the end of the book.

CD-ROM

The Prelude and Chapter 1 contain references to additional CD-ROM material. At the beginning of each of these chapters you find a list with the relevant features; in addition, Chapter 1 lists CD-ROM material for each activity. The CD-ROM icon highlights additional material in the text.
The CD-ROM contains:

- Material on indigenous communities in Arctic regions
- Chapter 1 student worksheets and visuals
- Chapter 1 additional web links

Index

The Index at the end of the book helps you find information on a particular term or area of polar research.

Acknowledgements

We would like to thank the international group of enthusiastic educators and young polar scientists who developed the vision of this project. Mieke Sterken from Belgium brought the idea to the attention of the IPY Programme Office. Mélianie Raymond from New Zealand, chair of the APECS Education and Outreach committee; Bettina Kaiser from Germany, chair of Polarjugend; and Rhian A. Salmon from the United Kingdom, Education and Outreach Coordinator at the IPY IPO, stirred the interest in this book, created the Resource Book Steering Group, and refined the vision of this project.

This project would not have been possible without the skilful coordination of hundreds of submissions, reviews and international conference calls by Karen Edwards from Canada. Without Sandra Zicus from Australia, the quality and structure of the book, in particular of Chapter 1, would have been unthinkable. We also thank Becky Allen from the United Kingdom for her editing support on Chapter 3 and the Glossary. Sandy Riel of Studio X Design put the material into its final form and was an invaluable support during the final stages of the project. We also thank Melissa Deets for creating the web-presentation of the project.

The authors of this book also wish to thank Pearson Custom publishing, in particular, Debbie Cole and Tom Eats for their assistance with this project.

Without the ceaseless support of the IPY Resource Book Steering Group, this project would not have come to fruition. We thank Khadijah Abdul Rahman-Sinclair, Jenny Baeseman, Lucette Barber, Miriam Hebling Almeida, Louise Huffman, Bettina Kaiser, René Malherbe, Nicola Munro, Liz Murphy, Mélianie Raymond, Mieke Sterken, Elena Bautista Sparrow, Rhian A. Salmon and Sandra Zicus.

We benefited greatly from the advice of our science reviewers:
Nicola Blake, Jody W. Deming, Cindy Dickson, Marianne Douglas, James Drummond, Steven Ferguson, Susanne Fietz, Duane Froese, Gerlis Fugmann, Ken Golden, Jose A. Gonzalez, Barry Goodison, Daniela Haase-Liggitt, David Herring, Haylay Hung, Kim Jochum, Loïc Jullian, René Malherbe, Mark McCaffrey, Cameron McNaughton, Stephanie Meakin, Klaus Meiners, Nazune Menka, Charlene Nielsen, Joan Nymand Larsen, Stig Petersen, Jason Roberts, Ursula Schauer, Christian Spiering, Colin Summerhayes, Barbara J. Thompson, Roland Warner, Peter Wasilewski, Kirsten Werner, Scott Williamson, Cameron Wobus, Thomas Woodruft, Anthony Worby and José Xavier.

We also wish to express our gratitude to our numerous professional educators for their reviews:
Sheena Adamson, Elke Bergholz, Anne Briggs, Anica Brown, Christina Ciarametaro, Tanya Connors, Elizabeth Eubanks, Lollie Garay, Kathleen M. Gorski, Mike Hansen, Patricia Janes, Rainer Lehmann, Tim Martin, James P. McGinn, Mark McKay, Janet Nadeau, Jason Petula, Gunnar Sandvik, Dave Shoesmith, Walter Staveloz, Mats Svensson, Betsy Wilkening and Jillian Worssam.

We extend our deep appreciation to our two professional photographers who gave us permission to use their work.

Christian Morel: For 25 years, the French professional photographer has focused on the polar regions. During IPY, he began the Our Polar Heritage project. As a result, for two years he joined many international teams of scientists in the field, and created an exceptional set of innovating and surprising pictures to stir people's interest in the significance of the Poles for the Earth system. His work has been display at the UNO in Geneva during the closing ceremony of IPY.
Contact: http://www.ourpolarheritage.com, http://www.morel-photos.com.

Douglas Yates: In semi-arid interior Alaska, Douglas Yates pays attention to the coming and going of water. His photography of this valued resource informs the heart and mind. See more of his work in the Arctic at www.arcticrefugeart.org.
Contact: dayates@mosquitonet.com.

Fundamentally, this book represents the ideas, energy and enthusiasm of hundreds of researchers, students, teachers, journalists, and outreach professionals who voluntarily developed, implemented and supported the education and outreach impact of IPY. Their talent and dedication created the opportunity and the content for this book.

All contributors to this book wish to thank David J. Carlson, head of the IPY International Programme Office (IPO), for making this project a reality, for believing in the importance of education and outreach, and for recognising and respecting the dedication and commitment of volunteers from around the world. This book would not have been possible without him.

Finally, the IPO, the contributors to this book, and the IPY community owe a substantial debt to the general editor Bettina Kaiser, who provided a compelling vision, unique talent and vital energy to the daunting tasks of assembling and editing the final product. From so many sources, across languages and specialities, in such a short time, with grace and skill, Bettina has given us an integrated, attractive and effective book, one that exceeds our most optimistic expectations.

Preparation of light measurements in and below the sea ice: the sensor head of a radiometer measures the solar spectra at levels below the sea ice. The swivel arm ensures that observations are conducted under undisturbed ice away from the 5 cm diameter hole drilled through the sea ice.

Authors: David J. Carlson and Rhian A. Salmon
Contributors: Bettina Kaiser and Elena Bautista Sparrow

Introduction

To this present day, polar regions continue to spark our curiosity and imagination. The Arctic and Antarctic still cause a fascination that is coupled with a sense of adventure and fear of the unknown. With this book, we hope to capture this feeling of awe that characterises our attitude towards these two remote regions. Here we begin by introducing the past and present of polar science.

First, we give you a brief description of the history of the International Polar Years that have been landmarks of polar research since their inception in the nineteenth century and had an impact on the planning of the most recent IPY. Throughout the decades, polar research has shown that the Poles need to be seen in the context of global connectivity, that is, as part of the Earth system in which a disruption of balance leads to long-term consequences, and in which

humans no longer stand outside this system. The story of the Polar Years has also been one of unprecedented international collaboration and of gradual acceptance of the necessity for interdisciplinary research. To make clear the interdisciplinary nature of polar science, the second part of the chapter outlines six themes that have emerged as key fields of polar study since the extraordinary beginnings of Arctic and Antarctic scientific exploration. The chapter concludes with a personal view on polar regions.

Negotiating Research Relationships with Inuit Communities: A Guide for Researchers

The Significance of the International Polar Year in Communicating Polar Science

Since their initiation in the nineteenth century, International Polar Years have instigated pioneer research in the polar regions and have regularly shifted the focus of science. From the beginning, the Polar Years were anticipated as bi-polar endeavours. In 1875 an Austrian explorer and naval officer, Karl Weyprecht, called for an international and collaborative focus on the polar regions. He proposed that in order to properly study the Arctic, countries should work together rather than mount independent national expeditions. A multi-national scientific effort, focussed largely on meteorology, grew from Weyprecht's suggestions and became the first 'International Polar Year' and one of the first examples of modern global scientific cooperation.

The realisation of Weyprecht's vision eventually involved 700 researchers from 11 nations. Between 1881 and 1884 they maintained 12 major research stations in the Arctic and two in the sub-Antarctic. Difficulties and delays in sharing data (often hand-written) limited pan-Arctic synthesis of the results, but preservation of major portions of data from the first IPY has allowed modern researchers to show its continued relevance. A worldwide public had followed the news of explorers of various nations to the Arctic and the Antarctic between 1820 and 1880. During the first IPY, the polar regions entered the public mind mostly through public lectures, expedition reports and newspaper articles, which,

for example, fed on a general public interest in the Northwest Passage where men could simply disappear, like Sir John Franklin and his crew who set off for the passage in 1845—never to return. The tragic element of polar exploration was underscored in the first IPY by a serious accident, the unexpected wintering over of the Greely expedition on Pim Island in the Arctic, and the subsequent loss of eighteen men out of twenty-five in the party (Barr, 1983, 465).

The collaborative scientific concept initiated in the first polar year inspired a second IPY in 1932–33. Occurring during a global economic depression, between world wars, and shortly after the invention of rocketry, the second IPY focused on meteorology, magnetism, auroras and radio science, leading to an early understanding of the role of the ionosphere in the Earth system. Once again, and reflecting the straightened economic circumstances of the times, the focus was on the Arctic. Wartime disruptions prevented full analysis of data from the second IPY but it has been estimated that the information gathered was worth "hundreds of millions of dollars worldwide for telecommunications alone" (Arktowski, 1931).

Fifty years later, need and enthusiasm for a third International Polar Year stimulated a geographically broader International Geophysical Year (IGY) in 1957–58. Global scientific (and military) attention shifted to the unknown regions of the Antarctic. Twelve nations conducted Antarctic research during IGY, deploying people, equipment and supplies in long-term coastal and interior stations and in many temporary ice camps. Several nations conducted difficult expeditions across the Antarctic ice sheets, producing some of the first

First IPY
1881–84

Bi-polar: **13 Arctic expeditions, 2 sub-Antarctic expeditions**

11 nations

Scientific Focus on:
Meteorology and geophysics

Data-Sharing Processes:
Limited, mostly hand-written records
US records of the first IPY:
www.arctic.noaa.gov/ipy-noaa.html
National Oceanic and Atmospheric Administration (NOAA)

Second IPY
1932–33

Bi-polar: **40 permanent observation stations (Arctic), one winter-long research station (Antarctic)**

40 nations

Scientific Focus on:
Meteorology, magnetism, atmospheric science, 'mapping' of ionospheric phenomena

Data-Sharing Processes:
Not fully analysed
Partly lost in the war

measurements of ice sheet thickness. Several younger members of those expeditions like Behrendt (1998) have recently published accounts of the tasks and challenges of crossing unknown expanses of the Antarctic surface, while French IGY scientists Schlich and Lorius have participated in a film of the first ever wintering on the polar plateau (*Enterrés Volontaires*, 2008).

The Soviet Union launched the first earth-orbiting satellite, Sputnik-1, on the fourth of October in 1957 as part of IGY activities. Sputnik signalled a technological revolution during which earth-observing satellites became essential components of national and international Earth science. Other IGY explorations led to discoveries of the Van Allen radiation belts, to new understanding of solar processes and auroras, to new theories about the Earth's magnetic field, and to early hints at the circulation systems of the oceans. IGY stimulated the formation of several international scientific committees (on space, the oceans, and the Antarctic, for example) to preserve and extend valuable international cooperation, and prompted an international political agreement, the Antarctic Treaty System (ratified in 1961), which preserves Antarctica as a continent for peaceful scientific collaboration. As such, the IGY became a major step forward in creating public awareness of the polar regions and in gradually exciting more general public interest for the complex scientific and political processes in and around the Poles.

The international committees responsible for organising and coordinating the activities of the IGY enabled the planning of the fourth International Polar Year (2007–08). Major advances in remote sensing from space and global warming leading to larger changes in the polar environments than elsewhere on the planet called for another collaborative scientific effort. Polar research still required both coordinated international cooperation, as envisioned by Weyprecht, and systems for data sharing and preservation such as the World Data Centres that evolved from IGY. During this fourth IPY, approximately 10,000 scientists from 63 nations worked together to better understand the Arctic and Antarctic regions and their connections to global processes. Like earlier Polar Years, this scientific cooperation also involved a sense of discovery. Unlike earlier Polar Years, it was driven by a sense of urgency because of the significant environmental changes occurring at the Poles. IPY embraced the geophysical disciplines of the previous Polar Years, but also biology, ecology, anthropology, economics, linguistics, history, physiology and many other specialties—all the talents and skills needed to understand the integrated physical, chemical, biological and social systems of the polar regions. Another major strength of this IPY has been the focus on education and outreach, involving collaboration with a large community of educators into classrooms and public spaces. The international dimension of this Polar Year went beyond its predecessors as it made scientific research accessible to diverse audiences, with almost the same immediacy the public had come to expect from the moon landings and space exploration. As such, the IPY community made polar science one of the first scientific fields that communicated its relevance across age groups, disciplines and national boundaries to raise awareness for the current dramatic changes occurring at the Poles.

Third IPY
1957–58

Bi-polar: **Arctic and Antarctic research**

67 nations

Scientific Focus on:
Geomagnetism, glaciology, gravity, ionospheric physics, precision mapping, meteorology, oceanography, seismology, solar activity and many more

Data-Sharing Processes:
World Data Centres

Fourth IPY
2007–08

Bi-polar: **Arctic and Antarctic research**

63 nations

Scientific Focus on:
Geophysical, ecological and human dimensions of polar regions

Data-Sharing Processes:
Polar Information Commons
IPY Data and Information Service
(www.ipydis.org)

The significance of the International Polar Year to the global community, with intense and collaborative research in the circumpolar regions as well as education, outreach and communication, becomes evident when viewed in the context of studying and understanding the Earth as a system. Components of the Earth system such as the cryosphere, atmosphere, hydrosphere, pedosphere, biosphere and lithosphere are immediately connected through cycles of matter and energy. Understanding how the Earth system works requires appreciation of scientific findings from all of these fields and of the interactions between them—a complex and demanding challenge. In a similar way, the six polar research themes that we introduce here are inseparably connected. For each theme, we explain *why* we study the polar regions, *how* we conduct our research, and *what* key scientific questions are being asked. Central to these fields is the current awareness of rapid changes taking place in the Arctic and Antarctic and the need to communicate these changes to a wide audience. Although effects of climate change are appearing sooner and more dramatically at the Poles, the impacts in these remote places are predicted to extend beyond their borders into non-polar regions. International Polar Years continue to urge us to comprehend the implications of these global transformations, and to come up with ways of preparing for, adapting to and/or mitigating them. Thus, the following disciplines are different parts of one goal—to understand the Earth system.

ATMOSPHERE

Why study the atmosphere?

Air consists of much more than just nitrogen and oxygen. It also contains trace molecules in tiny concentrations: parts per million (ppm), billion (ppb) or trillion (ppt). Today's sophisticated scientific instruments allow us to measure such tiny quantities. Several of these molecules, the greenhouse gases, absorb outgoing infrared radiation and thereby keep the Earth warm enough to sustain life. Air travels across the Earth's surface as wind, carrying heat (or cold), moisture, and natural and contaminant materials. This large-scale movement is driven by the temperature gradients between the tropics and the Poles, between the ocean and land, and by the influence of the Earth's rotation. In this way, air provides connections between oceans, deserts, forests, ice and people.

Large-scale atmospheric circulations produce polar weather systems that result in spring thaws, sea ice movement and severe winter storms. Changes in storm frequency and intensity accelerate erosion of polar coastlines. Long-range atmospheric transport

Figure P.1 Virga, appearing as hanging curtains of rain, sweeps across Alaska's boreal forest zone.

processes deliver pollutants to Arctic and Antarctic environments. Transport of remote aerosols and local emissions from the open ocean play a major role in polar cloud formation and in polar precipitation as rain or snow.

During the IPY period, ozone-depleting pollutants reached peak concentrations. At the same time scientists observed changes in circulation, temperature and moisture in the stratosphere, where the ozone depletion occurs. It was therefore a key time to study this area of the atmosphere, including polar stratospheric clouds, chemistry, meteorology as well as radiation, and discover how these processes interact and influence each other.

Figure P.2 Jumping with a weather balloon with radiosondes before launching it into the atmosphere from aboard the *CCGS Amundsen* as part of the Circumpolar Flaw Lead system study.

How are we investigating the polar atmosphere?

We study the global atmosphere by using observations from satellites, weather balloons, aircraft and automated weather stations. Powerful computers process and integrate these data and use them to simulate and guide global circulation models as the basis for forecasting changes in weather and projecting likely changes in climate. Polar regions have many fewer observations compared to temperate, non-polar regions, and the models often contain components, such as cloud modules, optimised for temperate conditions. Comparison of models for the polar regions is helping researchers refine them to produce more accurate outputs. Because several research centres run large-scale models and because atmospheric researchers have a good system for worldwide data sharing, researchers from around the world can cooperate in the study of polar atmospheres and in the improvement of polar climate models.

Other atmospheric researchers make careful measurements of trace chemicals at remote field stations in Antarctica and on ships in the Arctic. Some of these chemical studies involve ultra-clean collection techniques, storage and transport, and extensive measurements in specialised laboratories. Other chemical information comes from measuring changes in selected frequencies of light as they pass through the atmosphere.

During IPY, many of these atmospheric measurements occurred simultaneously, in many locations in both hemispheres and allowed extensive inter-comparisons: between observations, observations and models, and among models. These inter-comparisons stimulated rapid improvements in both observations and models. Improved models also allow more accurate predictions of what will happen in the future.

Figure P.3 Wind studies above sea ice in the harsh Antarctic environment.

What key questions are being asked about the polar atmosphere?

How do global atmospheric components, such as desert dust, volcanic or oceanic aerosols, get delivered to and stored in ice sheets? What local photochemical processes occur in the upper sunlit layers of the snow?

Have atmospheric circulations changed in polar regions? In the Arctic, have average storm tracks moved, and have storm intensities or frequencies changed? In the Antarctic, have the winds around Antarctica strengthened? How might changes in polar weather link to global weather changes?

How do biological processes in the upper ocean, physical processes over ice, and chemical processes in the atmosphere produce or influence clouds, especially in the Arctic? How do these local processes interact with regional processes? How does daytime and night-time cloudiness influence incoming and outgoing heat budgets?

Will the polar ozone holes recover as predicted? Why do recovery processes take so long? What other man-made chemicals do we detect in the polar regions and what does their presence and abundance tell us about global atmospheric transport processes?

ICE

Why study ice?

At its present average temperature, our Earth holds water in three phases: as a gas (water vapour in the atmosphere), as a liquid (low clouds and rain, oceans, lakes and rivers) and as ice (snow, sea ice, ice sheets, glaciers and high cold clouds). Cooling of the Earth shifts these types of water from gas and liquid towards solid ice, while warming moves the water types from ice towards liquid and gas. As the geological records of ice ages show, quantitatively small changes in phases of water can have profound impacts on Earth's climate and life.

An enormous amount of fresh water is frozen in the great ice sheets of Greenland and Antarctica. The Greenland ice sheet stores enough water to raise global sea level by more than five metres—were it to melt! Antarctic ice sheets store enough water to raise global sea level by more than

Figure P.4 The speed of light: what was once an exhalation from a lake bottom, these trailing discs are now embedded in a block of ice more than two feet thick. Cut and lifted from the ice and stacked horizontally at the Fairbanks ice festival, they now resemble sci-fi technology.

60 metres! In addition, large areas of highly reflective snow and ice cover the land and ocean of polar regions, at least seasonally, helping to keep these areas cold. We need to understand the processes occurring within and around ice sheets in order to understand their current and future contributions to sea level change. We also need to study the processes determining the annual and long-term changes in snow and ice cover to understand future warming.

This IPY occurred amidst abundant evidence of changes in extent of snow and ice, including reductions in extent and mass of most glaciers, reductions in area, timing and duration of snow cover, and reductions in extent and thickness of sea ice. These changes show steady downward trends of snow and ice coverage over recent years and decades. As the coverage (area) and duration (time) of snow cover and sea ice decrease, the underlying relatively dark surfaces of land and ocean become exposed, absorbing the energy that snow or ice would have reflected. This additional warming of land and ocean, and the effect of both in warming surface air temperatures, causes more rapid decreases in snow and ice, which in turn lead to further land and ocean warming. This positive feedback cycle, where small changes lead to additional similar changes, has immediate consequences for land geography and hydrology, for ocean mixing and circulation, and for terrestrial and marine ecosystems. In other parts of the world, the disappearance of mountain snow packs and glaciers will increase water supplies—due to enhanced melting—in the short term but eventually cause a substantial decrease in water available for personal, agricultural and commercial use.

Northern snow and sea ice show significant decreases, and glaciers worldwide show clear downward trends in extent and mass. Net changes of the massive Greenland and Antarctic ice sheets show increasing evidence of mass loss. On Greenland, increased precipitation and snow accumulation in central areas does not keep up with surprisingly rapid melting and erosion at the edges; the Greenland ice sheet appears to have lost mass over the past decade *(Figure P.5)*. Melt water at the surface percolates through the Greenland outflow glaciers, causing erosion of the ice sheet and enhancing melting and ice flow at the base. The major Antarctic ice sheets seem more stable than in Greenland, although they are also more difficult to measure, with small increases in some areas balanced by small decreases in others. The most recent measurements suggest a present-day net loss of mass from the Antarctic ice sheet, mostly from West Antarctica. In just the last decade or so, researchers have discovered water beneath the Antarctic ice: lakes

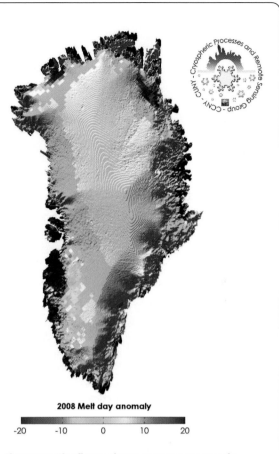

2008 Melt day anomaly

-20   -10   0   10   20

Figure P.5 The figure shows extreme snowmelt during summer in 2008 over the northern part of the Greenland ice sheet. Colours indicate the 2008 melt day anomaly for Greenland, that is, the number of days in 2008 with surface melt minus the average melt number for 1979–2007. Red areas in northern Greenland indicate where extreme melting occurred and new records were set. Green colours represent areas where melt days were close to the seasonal average, with no large anomalies. Updates on recent climate science at http://www.copenhagendiagnosis.org

and large scale water drainage systems under several kilometres of ice. An understanding of how these sub-glacial systems form and where the water flows is critical for understanding the stability of ice sheets.

How are we investigating ice?

Studing of ice involves everything from individuals climbing up glaciers with measuring sticks to large-scale observations from space. Some of the most challenging but useful data comes from the combination of local measurements with satellite observations. The latter include visible images of snow on land, microwave images of sea ice extent, laser measurements of ice sheet

Figure P.6 Striped iceberg in Antarctica.

height and sensitive measurements of changes in gravity influenced by changes in ice mass.

Water drainage systems beneath the ice are investigated using a combination of air-borne geophysical instruments that can map geomagnetic variations and ground-based investigations that pull radars across the snow surface. Some of these surveys occur in areas where ice cores exist, to allow direct comparisons between ice changes with depth and the

retrieved signals of density and thickness.

New shallow and medium-depth ice cores are drilled to increase the number and geographic ranges of these unique records of past climates. Ice cores from high accumulation regions with lots of snowfall show seasonal detail on short timescales. Additional ice cores from low accumulation areas show longer time records with less resolution, but allow us to build more accurate pictures of the geographic variability of past climate change.

What key questions are being asked about ice?

How quickly will summer Arctic sea ice disappear? As ice extent decreases, what happens to ice thickness? How will larger areas free of ice in the summer influence ice formation and accumulation in the following winters? Has the Arctic summer-time sea ice reached a tipping point? Will sea ice in Antarctica show a similar decline?

What are the precise balances between accumulation and erosion in Greenland and Antarctica? How does water in lakes and channels below the ice influence the ice flows? Is there a critical point at which ice sheets melt and erode quickly? How fast will sea level rise?

OCEANS

Why study the polar oceans?

Cooling and freezing processes in polar regions produce dense and cold ocean water. These cold waters flowing towards the equator from the Poles at depth, coupled with warm equatorial waters flowing towards the Poles at the surface, represent the Earth's primary mechanism for redistributing heat. The balance of these processes, heating in the tropical oceans and cooling in the polar oceans, influences the overall climate of our planet. In addition, an upwelling process, the rising of deep, cold, nutrient-rich waters to the surface, determines the overall productivity of the oceans on several levels.

Marine ecosystems in polar regions play key roles as downward biological pumps in the global carbon cycle. Polar waters capture carbon dioxide from the atmosphere because cold water holds more carbon dioxide than warm water. Cold water sinking at the Poles thus represents an important 'sink' for carbon dioxide. Oceanic micro-organisms use sunlight and carbon dioxide in polar surface water to increase their biomass. Part of that biomass, passing through intermediate organisms like krill or fish and higher organisms like seals or penguins, sinks to the bottom, thus transferring or 'pumping' carbon from the atmosphere through the surface ocean into ocean sediments. In polar oceans, and particularly in the Southern Ocean surrounding Antarctica, favourable combinations of sunlight and vertical mixing of water masses, often enhanced by atmospheric transport of dust from temperate regions containing iron and other biologically essential trace elements, produce very strong episodes of this biological pumping.

Polar oceans also contain remarkable species adapted to constant cold, to ice cover and to long seasons of light and dark. Warmer waters, changes in mixing, loss of sea ice, invading species and contaminants delivered from lower latitudes will affect polar marine ecosystems, particularly top polar predators such as polar bears, seals and whales. Both polar regions also support substantial fisheries. We therefore need new combinations of climate, ecosystem and economic information, along with advanced numerical models, to develop strategies for sustainable use of current and future polar marine resources.

Within the ocean basin, ocean sediments contain important records of past conditions. At the edges of ocean basins, those records help to establish histories of the opening or closing of oceanic gateways and to understand past polar ocean current systems. The open ocean sediments hidden under sea ice contain records of the extent and duration of ice cover, while ocean sediments in coastal regions record the glaciation history of the adjacent land.

How are we investigating the polar oceans?

Most ocean data comes from ships. Unfortunately, ships travel slowly, cover only small areas of the ocean, generally work only in seasons of favourable weather, and are extremely limited in what they can do where sea ice is widespread. During IPY, oceanographers tried to operate a large number of ships in coordinated explorations, and to maximise the types of measurements (physical, chemical and biological) made from each research vessel *(Figure P.8)*. Some ships worked along predetermined routes called 'transects'

Figure P.7 Fishing for zooplankton using plankton net offshore from Ny-Ålesund in Spitsbergen. The Svalbard archipelago is increasingly influenced by Atlantic currents, thus being one of the first places to be affected by climate change in the Arctic. It is important to gain a better understanding of how plankton function so as to try and predict how this ocean will change as it warms up.

to ensure continuity with past measurements and often to service moored instruments deployed along those transect lines. Other ships made measurements across the transect lines, around the Arctic basin and along the Antarctic coastline, to understand how ocean properties evolve along the major currents. Several ships deliberately entered the Arctic prepared to be frozen into the ice throughout the winter, to act as floating laboratories. Other ships worked summer seasons in both the Arctic and Antarctic, and made measurements of global circulation processes during their long trips between the Poles.

Oceanographers also deployed unattended systems on the sea ice, placed moorings under the sea ice and used new remotely-operated and autonomous glider vehicles to make measurements far under the ice shelves adjacent to the continent. They used advanced high-resolution mapping systems and special tools for sampling and coring the sea floor to understand geological histories of ocean gateways and climate cycles in polar regions. Many of these shipboard explorations of the sea floor occurred near and within the relatively thin sea ice. Other groups develop new technologies to work through the thick Antarctic ice shelves to reach the underlying sea floor.

As part of IPY, many ships were involved in a census of marine life and explorations of marine ecosystems. Census activities covered life of all sizes, from microbial communities and phytoplankton to fish, sea birds and marine mammals. They included organisms in the water column, on the sea floor, and in as well as under sea ice. Many studies took an ecosystem approach, to understand how plankton, krill, fish, bird and mammal systems respond to changes in ocean circulation, to warmer ocean temperatures and to changes in sea ice. All these biological explorations included new tools of genetic and protein analysis, to understand not only the taxonomic diversity, but also which organisms can most efficiently use various nutrients or possess various cold-adapted enzymes.

What key questions are being asked about the polar oceans?

How will changes in cooling and freezing processes, related to changes in sea ice, glacier discharge, river run-off and polar weather, affect global ocean circulation patterns? Will the speed and intensity of circulation processes of deep cold flows towards the equator and warm surface flows towards the Poles change?

What will happen to endemic (local) polar marine species? How and how fast will marine species from lower latitudes migrate towards the Poles? What will happen to species and ecosystems that depend on sea ice if it disappears?

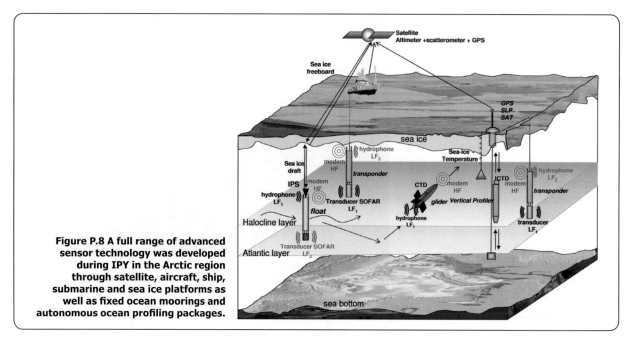

Figure P.8 A full range of advanced sensor technology was developed during IPY in the Arctic region through satellite, aircraft, ship, submarine and sea ice platforms as well as fixed ocean moorings and autonomous ocean profiling packages.

LAND

Why study land?

The land of polar regions contains many clues to the history of the Earth's environment, for example, the development of its vegetation or the unique structure and evolution of its soil. In the polar regions, ice and land come together in a frozen mixture called permafrost that influences nearly 25 per cent of the landmass of the northern hemisphere. Studying permafrost constitutes a major field in understanding polar landmasses. Permafrost is any rock or soil remaining at or below 0°C for two or more years. It often contains large quantities of ice, known as 'ground ice.' The soil is frozen to depths of many tens to hundreds of metres and to over one thousand metres in some parts of Siberia. These soils generally have a shallow active layer at the top that thaws in the warm season but refreezes in the winter. At the southern edge of northern permafrost, the entire permafrost depth may show an annual cycle of thawing and freezing. At many places along its northern edge, northern permafrost extends into the coastal sediments below the Arctic Ocean. Permafrost can be thousands of years old and often exists close to its melting point.

Northern permafrost has recently been showing substantial change, mostly in the form of thermal decomposition due to warming air temperatures. The area of northern hemisphere seasonal permafrost has decreased by seven per cent in the past century. In the past 50 years, the depth of the active thawing layers on northern permafrost has increased by 20 centimetres. Researchers monitor permafrost by drilling holes, analogous in some ways to ice cores. Temperatures at different soil and rock depths in these bore holes below the active layers are the result of a slow integration of many seasonal changes. Measurements show that the temperatures in most northern hemisphere boreholes have increased.

Degrading permafrost affects soil stability. Roads, pipelines and buildings become unstable as permafrost thaws. Trees growing over permafrost start to tilt. Hydrology also changes. Ice masses become ponds, ponds connect to other ponds through new drainage channels, and new run-off systems develop over substantial areas of previously frozen ground. Decomposition of permafrost mobilises reserves of frozen carbon stored in the permafrost. Some of this carbon, in the form of methane, will escape into the atmosphere and increase the global greenhouse effect. Land carbon will wash into the Arctic Ocean, changing the local coastal sedimentation and ecology.

Land vegetation also shows substantial alterations, in many areas undergoing a change from grasses to shrubs. In other areas, fire becomes a more frequent stress as vegetation dries out during warm seasons. Grazing animals, such as caribou that rely on summer grasses and winter trees, will experience a shortage of food resources throughout the year. Migrations of plants, grazers, predators and diseases will alter the polar terrestrial ecosystems.

Studying the land and vegetation of both polar regions on a geological timescale, when continents were of different shapes and occupied different places on the

Figure P.9 Boreal canopy: during autumn when the hardwoods change colour, it is easy to spot aspen clones in the canopy. Clones are clusters of individual trees that are actually the same organism.

Earth's surface, leads to fascinating insights into the history of the Earth. Fossilised leaves from Antarctica, for example, demonstrate that it was once a forested continent, with vegetation similar to that found in fossils from Africa and South America. Rock samples from exposed mountains and radar mapping of the ice-covered Gamburtsev Mountain Range in Antarctica help us understand factors that initiated and guided formation of Antarctic ice sheets. Sediments from below the Southern Ocean help us understand processes that led to the separation of continents and the glaciation of the polar regions. These scientific clues unveil the world of thousands to millions of years ago. They help us to understand early human migration patterns, because about 12,000 years ago, the Bering Land Bridge connected Asia and North America and enabled human migration to the Americas from Asia until the sea broke through to form the Bering Strait.

How are we investigating land?

Polar research on land often involves long treks and careful personal observations and measurements, conducted during polar summers. Encampments of small teams of people over months during the brief Antarctic summer are the basis of land research in the few accessible regions of Antarctica. Scientists measure microbial abundance and activities in soils, identify vegetation types and changes, and measure the influences of light, wind, moisture and warmth on the condition of permafrost and the exchange of gases between soils below and atmosphere above. Hydrologists observe and record rain- and snowfall, water quality, seasonal and annual melting, and surface and subsurface water migration routes and rates.

Geologists sample rocks where they can and use ground-penetrating radar and airborne geomagnetic measurements to understand the shape and composition of mountains below the ice. Others will measure the travel paths and times of sound waves to understand deep densities and heat flows beneath the Antarctic continent. Geologists and geographers use ultra-precise GPS measurements to understand regional movements of pieces of Antarctica relative to large-scale movements of Earth's crustal plates. They will also drill into the ocean floor to retrieve records from millions of years ago in the Arctic and Southern Oceans.

Permafrost researchers combine detailed measurements at surface sites with data from instrumented boreholes and build local information into larger-scale composite maps using satellite imagery. Chemists and biologists use small chambers or other enclosures on natural ground to simulate or manipulate the effects of warming or drying, increased atmospheric carbon dioxide or UV irradiation. Where glaciers retreat scientists study local soil and biology in de-glaciated regions.

Figure P.10 Survey of the snow water equivalent, which is crucial for the water budget of the permafrost. During IPY, the Sensitivity of Permafrost in the Arctic (SPARC) programme studied the two major cycles (water and heat) in the complex Arctic landscape system at scales from metres to kilometres. The goal was to close the gap between small-scale process understanding and the large scale that is accessible to satellite remote sensing.

Polar Science and Global Climate

What key questions are being asked about the land?

Will degradation of permafrost continue? How quickly, and how extensively? What will happen to the carbon, especially the methane in shallow coastal ocean sediments, trapped in permafrost?

What will happen to northern biodiversity and to Arctic ecosystems? What temperate plants and animals will replace polar species? What organisms will colonise the bare rocks and soils uncovered by retreating glaciers?

What can we learn from mountains hidden under the Antarctic ice? Did the great Antarctic ice sheets start in those high remote regions, millions of years ago?

Figure P.11 Glacial outwash on Baffin Island in the Arctic.

PEOPLE

Why study people?

Previous Polar Years focussed exclusively on geophysical sciences: astronomy, glaciology, geology, meteorology, oceanography and many others. IPY 2007–08 differed substantially in its inclusion of a wide range of biological and ecological sciences. Over the past 50 years, this broader range of science developed from the expanded appreciation and understanding that Earth's climate and ecological systems interact in many ways and on many time scales. The inclusion of both geophysical and ecological sciences seemed natural, essential and unsurprising, especially in view of the necessity to develop a comprehensive understanding of, and predictive capability for, the Earth's integrated physical-chemical-biological systems.

The reality of climate change urged science to identify new methods and approaches to further our understanding of rapid changes in polar regions. The inclusion of people, their well-being and their cultures in polar regions, arises from two essential facts. First, an understanding of the Arctic requires understanding how Arctic people, including indigenous communities, perceive the Arctic. A comprehensive, accurate, useful and relevant understanding of the integrated Arctic system requires engagement with northern people

as partners in planning and conducting of research, and in the evaluation, dissemination and assessment of results and legacies. Second, understanding polar regions requires an understanding and assessment of human activities that affect those regions. In the Arctic as well as the Antarctic, this includes harvesting of natural resources, exploitation of mineral and energy resources, transportation developments, tourism, and production and dispersion of pollutants. We cannot understand change in the polar regions, their climate and ecosystems, without assessing the roles of humans as agents, moderators and recipients.

To a large extent, researchers in social sciences focus on northern human well-being, particularly on impacts of pollution on humans and their food sources, on contaminants and parasites in traditional foods and on many aspects of health: existing and emerging infectious diseases (such as active tuberculosis, *(Figure P.13)*, chronic diseases and unhealthy behaviours. Arctic health issues are a consequence of local and global changes in climate, ecosystems, economies and culture. Scientists therefore explore many aspects of an integrated Arctic social system to determine community resiliency to internal and external change and the ability of communities to adapt and prepare for change. These investigations include studies of social and environmental interactions, studies of language as a cultural resource and of unique uses of language, studies of how legal systems protect the value and integrity of Traditional Knowledge (TK), and economic and social assessments of the impacts and opportunities related to oil and gas, mineral and transportation developments.

Northern people live at the forefront of climate change. For them changes in weather, soils and vegetation, and in food availability coincide with

Figure P.12 Seal bladder in Gambell on St. Lawrence Island: seals are hunted for food and products. A seal bladder can be used to store food or as a fishing gear float.

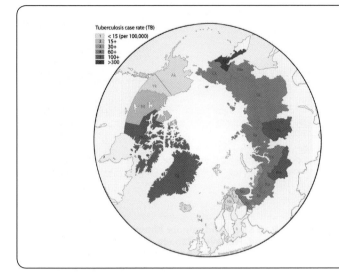

Tuberculosis case rate (TB)
< 15 (per 100,000)
15+
30+
60+
100+
>300

Figure P.13 The figure shows variation in incidence rates of active tuberculosis cases among northern regions. For comparison, much lower rates for the same period (2000–04) were recorded for the full populations of Sweden (4.9 per 100,000), the USA (5.3) and Canada (5.4). The tuberculosis case rate in the Arctic is very high. The study and possible reduction of incidence of respiratory diseases like tuberculosis is a priority in human health studies in polar regions.

substantial alterations of economic circumstances, of means of information and concepts of self-determination and governance. There are also urgent, immediate issues of housing, education and jobs to be considered. Those of us occupying warmer regions of the planet have much to learn from, and would do well to pay close attention to, the ways in which northern societies confront climate change issues. We should also regard the northern cultures, developed with remarkable success over thousands of years in the inhospitable Arctic environment, as a global cultural resource, valuable for their inherent skills, wisdom and Traditional Knowledge. Traditional Knowledge is as diverse as its peoples but it is often holistic and based on the belief that land and life are interconnected and that humans are part of nature. To give but a few examples, the Sámi language knows numerous terms for reindeer, landscape and snow; for centuries Inuvialuit and other Inuit people have lived in close proximity to the ocean and their understanding of marine environment is kept alive in important stories, art and music. Traditional ways of life and their cultural pools of knowledge can offer new perspectives on how to address climate change issues. Just as climate change threatens polar global biodiversity, it likewise threatens polar and global cultural diversity.

How are we investigating people?

All studies of people must involve the people themselves, to determine not only the methodology of social studies but also the value and evaluation systems used to analyse social data collections in survey, interviews or health assessments.

Health and social sciences involve surveys, interviews, physiological and epidemiological studies, and studies of markets, population statistics and demographics. Many of these surveys and studies include Traditional Knowledge, often gained by talking with Elders and contributing to the field of oral social study and history. New analysis tools and thinking patterns will help all partners discover the value gained by combining quantitative data (such as weather data) with qualitative data (such as records of hunting conditions). This

Figure P.14 Inuit from Clyde River pulling a sled on the west coast of Baffin Island in Nunavut, Canada.

combination of quantitative and qualitative data leads to a perception of life in the polar regions that is both complex and realistic. Moreover, social and historical research of the people will preserve Traditional Knowledge that, in view of the recent changes in the polar regions, might disappear. In all cases, Traditional and local knowledge must be obtained and shared respectfully in accordance with ethic research guidelines and with the support of the communities involved. Polar scientists increasingly recognise the potential of Traditional Knowledge for their own efforts to understand the role of polar regions in the Earth system. They are also encouraged to do so and the CD-ROM of this book contains one of many examples of practical advice for researchers working in northern Canada, *A Guide for Researchers* prepared by Inuit Tapiriit Kanatami and the Nunavut Research Institute.

Figure P.15 Small and remote Kimmirut community on Baffin Island, Nunavut, Canada, has only around 400 inhabitants. While hunting is an important part of the local economy, tourism also provides income for residents.

What key questions are being asked about people?

What are the key human health and medical issues in polar regions? What are the new or persistent health challenges unique to polar communities and polar regions? What do polar societies contribute to global cultural diversity and the political status of indigenous people worldwide?

What factors contribute to an overall sense of well-being among northern people? How does the sense of well-being vary by region, by age, by education level? How do the challenges of climate and ecosystem change affect real and perceived well-being?

What unique aspects of behaviour and culture, including language, food traditions, and intergenerational connections, have developed to allow humans to survive in polar regions? Which of those aspects most helps individuals and communities to adapt and survive in the face of transformations of traditional social systems,

of the natural habitat as well as of economic contexts? How does, for example, tourism impact on the social, economical and ecological structures of both polar regions.

What has been the effectiveness of remote and local governance regimes in polar regions, and how can or should these respond to rapidly evolving cultural and socio-economic systems? Who will make difficult future decisions about natural resource conservation and management? Where will northern people receive training, and how can they develop pan-Arctic connections and perspectives?

How do researchers in the Antarctic respond to polar winter, biologically and psychologically? What can we learn from these polar experiences about the human body clocks, our relationship with sunlight and community-building strategies under extreme circumstances?

SPACE

Why study space?

Space research during IPY focused on space between the Earth and the Sun, particularly solar processes that impact Earth's outer atmosphere, on making measurements of distant space from polar regions, and on the use of satellite sensors in space to monitor polar conditions and processes.

As Earth rotates about its geographic Poles, rotation of its inner core induces a magnetic dipole with magnetic poles very near the geographic Poles. Imaginary lines tracing the strength of Earth's magnetic field far into space converge at the Poles. Many geoelectric phenomena such as the auroras occur in these polar magnetic convergence zones. Sun-induced disturbances cause geomagnetic storms, a form of space weather, near the Earth. Severe space weather can harm satellites and disrupt global communication and energy systems. IPY researchers measured global geoelectric circuits and auroras, exploring global electric connections between Northern and Southern Hemispheres, and relationships of these geoelectric systems to solar variations and to weather that we experience at the Earth's surface.

Polar regions, particularly the high central regions of Antarctica, offer some of the best 'viewing sites' on Earth for antennas, telescopes and other detection systems looking far out into space. Because of their predominantly dry, clear and generally very stable atmospheres, because of long periods of darkness and because of the relative absence of human-caused light and radio noise, polar regions offer ideal conditions for visual examination of the cosmos. During IPY, researchers made observations of the outer space across a wide part of the electromagnetic spectrum to discern, for example, hints of the early universe recorded in the polarisation of incoming cosmic microwave radiation.

Figure P.16 In polar regions, auroras are the most obvious visual indication of the interaction of the Earth's magnetosphere and upper atmosphere.

How are we investigating space?

Measurements of auroras and geoelectric circuits come from visible and infrared detectors and magnetic field detectors, often deployed in large arrays and from satellites. Monitoring of solar processes such as flares and ejections occurs through the use of specialised telescopes and detectors tuned to visible or UV radiation and even X-ray outputs of the sun.

Polar space observatories consist of telescopes, large dish antennas, antenna arrays, and large 3-D neutrino detection arrays deployed within a very large, one kilometre wide cube of Antarctic ice. Some space detection systems operate automatically with remote control. Others require human operators. All space observing systems in polar regions require enormous care and effort in set-up and maintenance.

What key questions are being asked about space?

How does the field strength and orientation of the Earth's magnetic field and its projection into space vary on short and long time scales? How do the Earth's fields interact with particles and energy arriving from the Sun?

Do processes such as auroras occur in a coordinated fashion at both Poles? Can observing these geoelectric processes help us predict space weather?

What can optical, microwave, or X-ray signals detected at the Poles tell us about the formation and evolution processes of galaxies and stars, and about the history of the universe?

Figure P.17 The EISCAT radar systems at Tromsø (Norway), Kiruna (Sweden), Sodankylä (Finland) and Svalbard (Spitsbergen) are used to study disturbances in the magnetosphere and atmosphere.

A Personal View: The Wonder of the Polar Regions

The Arctic and Antarctic are two of the greatest treasures of our planet. The changing night sky, that heavenly clock of stars that lasts for months, reminds us of our place in the universe and teaches us about other galaxies. The strange optical effects during months of sunlight: sundogs, fogbows, mirages and angel dust show us not only beauty in the simple interaction of light and ice, but are also a keyhole to understanding atmospheric processes. Animals in these areas are also unique: polar bears, arctic hares and arctic foxes in the North; penguins, albatrosses and giant sea spiders in the South. Again, they are wonderful to observe but also teach us about adaptability, evolution and survival in extreme environments.

In the oceans, you will discover giant squid and the coldest, densest ocean water. From the oceans, we also learn about the great conveyer belt of energy around the world and what drives this circulation—a fine balance between two simple factors: temperature and saltiness, that obtain critical conditions in the polar regions.

The ice will crack and grumble. It is dangerous and beautiful. Working on glaciers and ice sheets, you will discover both how to walk across a crevassed ice field and what the chemistry and climate of Earth might have looked like in past millennia. The land will also teach you about the past. Fossils and rock structures lead us back to a time when trees and forest covered Antarctica. The land is also home to shrubs and animals that depend on its resources, food, water and shelter, for survival.

People who live in the polar regions will both engage you with stories and teach you about the ice, the snow, the land, the sky and the animals that are so important to the local food and economy. Communities in the Arctic will also inform you through their culture, language, music and art.

All of these treasures are both interesting and important. They affect us all and can inform how we live. Understanding our planet will help us to take greater care of it for future generations, to heed warning signs and observe when a system is failing or recovering. The polar regions are changing quickly at the moment but models suggest that the ultimate course for the planet is not yet decided. It depends on us, and how we treat the Earth system over the next few decades. To invest in the next generation of scientists around the world and to help educators and scientists increase awareness of the polar regions and our planet amongst the public is the intention of this book.

Figure P.18 Adelie Penguins in the Antarctic.

Figure P.19 The transient union of ocean, ice, land and sky in the Arctic.

In the Bering Sea: the cutting blades of a saw are used for sectioning ice cores into 2 to 10 cm long segments while being on the sea ice.

Author: Sandra Zicus

Contributors: Jenny Baeseman, Lucette Barber, Jerry Brown, David J. Carlson, Matteo Cattadori, Jane Dobson, Laurent Dubois, Isabelle Du Four, Karen Edwards, Uta Fritsch, Claudia V. Garcia, Anne Giangiulio, Robin Gislason, Tamsin Gray, Bill Grosser, Turtle Haste, Alain Hubert, Louise Huffman, Andrea Kaiser, Jessica Kotierk, Vanessa Lougheed, Eric Muhs, Isla Myers-Smith, Nancy Nix, Nancy Pearson, Caroline Pellaton, Clémentine Rasquin, Philipp Rastner, Bill Robertson, Torsten Sachs, Rhian A. Salmon, Kristi Skebo, Elizabeth Hodges Snyder, Mieke Sterken, Christian Steurer, Steve Stevenoski, Francesca Taponecco, Josep Marlés Tortosa, Alexandre Trinidade Nieuwendam, Craig Tweedie, Anton Van de Putte, Sandra Vanhove, Agathe Weber and José Xavier

Introduction

There are lots of easy, fun ways to introduce polar science concepts to students in the classroom. We have collected a number of learning activities, grouped under the six themes outlined in the previous chapter. Each section begins with an example of a specific field of polar research, followed by activities that address this and other aspects of the same theme. There is a choice of short and simple as well as longer and more complicated activities. These are listed at the beginning of each section to make it easy for you to find an appropriate activity for your particular needs.

The activities are not designed for any particular school curriculum or any specific age group. They were developed by an international group of educators and scientists, and are intended for an international audience. We trust that teachers worldwide will be able to select and adapt those resources that fit their particular goals. Each resource can be used on its own,

or can form part of a module on the polar regions.

All the activities have been tested in the classroom, so we hope you will find the instructions logical and easy to follow. Each activity includes the following information:

Lesson at a Glance: One or two sentences describing the lesson and its purpose. An icon indicates whether it is a classroom, laboratory or field-based activity.

Background: A short introduction to the concept or concepts illustrated and the basic information needed to conduct the activity.

Time: An estimate of the amount of time needed to prepare materials for the activity, and the average classroom time to complete the activity.

Materials: A list of materials and resources needed for the activity.

Activity Directions: Step by step instructions on how to proceed.

Discussion: Questions to encourage discussion, reflection and deeper thinking.

Extensions: Ways to adapt or extend the activities.

Some activities also include personal accounts and observations of the polar regions from researchers and educators. We hope they will inspire you and your students to communicate your own experiences of polar science beyond your classroom and share them with a community of like-minded polar enthusiasts.

We hope you will enjoy digging for treasure in this assortment of classroom activities created by an enthusiastic group of polar aficionados!

Figure 1.1 A scientist removes last pieces of ice from a hole cut in the pack ice before she will deploy sediment tracks for the Circumpolar Flaw Lead (CFL) system study in the southeast of the Beaufort Sea in the Arctic.

Activity Icons

    classroom activity

    lab activity

    field activity

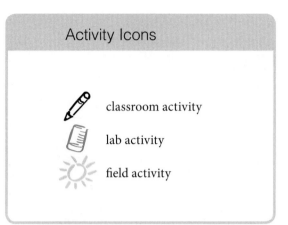

CD-ROM Resources

The accompanying CD-ROM provides more resources to supplement those in the book.

- **Visuals:** Maps and photographs needed for some of the book activities.
- **Worksheets:** Worksheets and data sheets needed for some of the book activities are provided in a format that will make it easier for you to use them in the classroom.
- **Links:** Web links and links to other media related to the activity topics.

Introductory Activities

FROM POLE TO POLE

POLAR COMPARISONS

FROM POLE TO POLE

(Thanks to Sandra Zicus, Australia)

Lesson at a glance

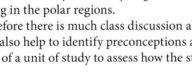 *Students draw pictures of the polar regions and compare their ideas to build a community of knowledge and develop questions for further investigation.*

Background

How do the Arctic and Antarctic regions differ? What features do they share? Some major differences are:

- The Arctic is mostly water, surrounded by land; Antarctica is a continent surrounded by water.
- Polar bears live in the Arctic; penguins live in the Antarctic.
- There are no land mammals in the Antarctic; the Arctic has numerous land mammals including musk ox, reindeer, caribou, foxes, wolves and hares.
- There are no trees and no tundra in Antarctica; the Arctic has vast stretches of tundra with areas of shrubby trees.
- More than 4 million people live in the Arctic; there are no permanent human inhabitants in Antarctica.

When starting a unit of study about the polar regions, you may find that students have very different perceptions depending on their backgrounds and interests. You can help them develop a broader base of understanding by having them draw, and then compare and discuss their ideas.

The objects that students include in their drawings and the subsequent discussion serves as an initial assessment of their level of knowledge. Some students may focus on the physical setting and geography of the Poles. Others might draw pictures of plants and animals they think they might see. Still others may think primarily of the human aspect of people living and working in the polar regions.

If the students do the activity before there is much class discussion about the polar regions (so you do not bias their thinking beforehand), it can also help to identify preconceptions and misconceptions they may have. The activity can be repeated at the end of a unit of study to assess how the students' knowledge has changed.

Time

Class time: 30–40 minutes

Materials

(can be done individually or in small groups)

- drawing supplies
- paper

Polar Map Projection

Polar Comparisons: True or False?

Activity Directions

1. Divide the class into small groups and give each group a piece of newsprint or other large paper and some coloured markers or crayons.
2. Ask half of the groups to draw a picture of the Arctic and the other half to draw the Antarctic. Tell them to include as many features as they can think of.
3. While the students are drawing, post a large Venn diagram with two circles at the front of the room *(Figure 1.2)*. Label one circle 'Arctic' and the other 'Antarctic'.
4. When the students have completed their drawings, have the groups post their drawings on either side of the Venn diagram.
5. As a whole class, discuss the students' work. Ask them to decide which features the two regions share and which are specific to either the Arctic or the Antarctic. Add them to the proper categories on the Venn diagram.
6. In cases where the students disagree, start a separate list of questions for investigation. This can serve as a basis for a student-directed investigation of the polar regions and students can add to or modify questions as their investigations progress.

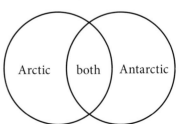

Figure 1.2 After discussion, students decide which features are specific to each polar region and which features are shared, and then place them in the proper position in a Venn diagram.

Extensions/Adaptations

1. For younger students, give them a selection of pictures showing Arctic and Antarctic animals, plants and geographic features. Have them work in groups to place the pictures into the proper place on a large Venn diagram (made of yarn circles or drawn on large sheets of paper).

2. The polar regions are often distorted (or missing altogether) on many standard map projections. Give the students copies of the *Polar Map Projections* sheet *(Figure 1.3)*. Show them other maps such as a standard world map (usually a Mercator or modified Mercator projection) and have the students compare them.

   - Which projection shows the polar regions most accurately? *(The polar projections. A good way to illustrate this is to ask the students to look at the world map and rank the following by apparent size from largest to smallest: Greenland, Australia, India and Brazil. Now look at a globe and compare the apparent sizes. Then tell them the actual areas: Brazil—8,506,663 km²; Australia—7,682,300 km²; India—3,287,588 km²; and Greenland—2,175,600 km².)*

   - Why are most world maps so inaccurate in the polar regions? *(The Earth is roughly spherical in shape, so large physical features such as oceans or continents can be represented with reasonable accuracy on a globe. However, trying to represent a sphere on a flat surface [e.g., when making a flat map] has been a universal problem for cartographers. Many different approaches have been used but all of these different projections have limitations and inaccuracies. Common world maps found in classrooms generally are most accurate in the equatorial region and the features become increasingly distorted as you move towards the Poles. You can illustrate this with the students by giving them large round heavy-weight balloons. After the balloons are inflated, have the students mark the equator and sketch the positions of the major continents. Deflate the balloons and challenge the students to turn them into flat maps. They will notice that if they stretch the part of the balloon that was near the 'Poles' to make it as large as the part near the 'equator', the continents near the Poles will appear to become much larger.)*

3. Assess the students' understanding of the differences between the Arctic and Antarctic using the pre- and post-lesson *Polar Comparisons: True or False?* sheet.

Figure 1.3 Polar map projections of the Arctic and the Antarctic.

POLAR COMPARISONS: TRUE OR FALSE?
(Thanks to Louise Huffman, USA)

Directions:
Answer the questions with a T (true) or an F (false) before the presentation or unit of study. Then, answer the questions again at the end. If you answer F in the 'Post' section, reword the statement to make it true.

	NAME:_____	Pre	Post	**After completing the 'post' section, reword any false statements to make them true.**
1	Penguins make delicious polar bear prey.			
2	Most of the world's fresh water is frozen in Antarctica's ice.			
3	Antarctica is the highest, driest, windiest, coldest, cleanest place on Earth.			
4	The largest land animal in Antarctica is only about 12 mm long.			
5	The Arctic is frozen land surrounded by ocean.			
6	The Antarctic is frozen ocean surrounded by land.			
7	The only direction you can go from the North Pole is south.			
8	There are candy striped barber poles to mark both the North and South Poles.			
9	There are more than 3 million permanent residents in the Arctic.			
10	More fish live in the coastal waters of the Arctic Ocean than anywhere else on Earth.			
11	The male emperor penguin incubates one egg on his feet for nine weeks, moving very little and eating nothing.			
12	People have been in the Antarctic since prehistoric times.			
13	The Arctic Ocean is the world's largest ocean.			
14	If you want to find meteorites, Antarctica provides the best hunting grounds.			
15	There are only six sunrises and six sunsets each year at the Poles.			

Polar Comparisons: True or False? Answer Key

1. False—Polar bears live in the Arctic, but no penguins live north of the equator (except in zoos).

2. True

3. True—And it is the iciest!

4. True—It is a wingless midge or colombola.

5. False—The Arctic is frozen ocean surrounded by land.

6. False—The Antarctic is frozen land surrounded by ocean.

7. True—And from the South Pole, the only direction you can go is north.

8. False—There is a red and white 'barber pole' that marks the South Pole at the Amundsen-Scott base. It has to be moved about 10 metres each year because the ice sheet is constantly moving toward the sea. The North Pole does not have such a marker because it would drift on the moving sea ice.

9. True—But only visitors and scientists live and work in Antarctica.

10. True

11. True

12. False—There are no native populations on the continent of Antarctica, unlike the Arctic where native populations have thrived since prehistoric times.

13. False—It is the smallest ocean.

14. True—Meteorites are carried to the Antarctic Mountains by the movement of the ice sheet, where they can be found more easily than in many other places on Earth.

15. False—The sun rises and sets once a year at the Poles.

ATMOSPHERE

Ozone depletion and its impact on Earth systems was a major focus of atmospheric research during IPY. In order to respond to effects of global climate change, we need to understand these complex atmospheric processes.

10,000 km

Exosphere

690 km

Thermosphere

Shuttle

Aurora

100 km
(Kármán line)

85 km

Mesosphere

Meteors

50 km

Stratosphere

Weather balloon

6 – 20 km

Troposphere

Mount Everest

Figure 1.4 Schematic drawing of the Earth's atmosphere.

The stratospheric ozone holes over both Poles provide a clear example of human impacts on polar systems. The ozone holes are caused by complex atmospheric interactions involving both chlorofluorocarbons (CFCs) and other greenhouse gases.

CFCs were first used on a large-scale in the 1950s as agents in refrigeration, propellant for aerosols, fire retardants and cleaning agents. In the 1980s, scientists found that CFCs catalysed the destruction of stratospheric ozone in the polar vortex over Antarctica. By 1990, the use and distribution of CFCs worldwide was restricted and monitored by the Montreal Protocol. CFCs emitted over the past decade, however, continue to deplete the ozone layer.

Increased greenhouse gas concentrations that warm the *troposphere* (the lowest section of the atmosphere) also tend to cool the *stratosphere,* just above it. These temperature changes affect the formation and strength of large-scale vortices in the polar stratosphere, which in turn affect the rate of the ozone depletion.

Understanding recovery trends of the ozone holes requires an in-depth knowledge of local and global atmospheric chemistry and physics, local measurements from the Poles, and satellite observations of upper atmosphere circulation and composition, all integrated into models that simulate these multifaceted interactions in the past, present and future.

Knowledge of 'local and global atmospheric chemistry and physics,' however, requires understanding how the atmosphere interacts with oceans, land and ice. It also requires knowledge of past emissions from human activities, as well as predictions for the future. This is a compelling example of how understanding the polar regions requires a coordinated, global, interdisciplinary campaign, and the study of our environment as an integrated system.

The activities in this section introduce students to the complex nature of atmospheric processes.

Atmosphere Activities

WEATHER OR CLIMATE?

WHY IS IT COLD IN THE POLAR REGIONS?

A SPIN ON OZONE

WEATHER OR CLIMATE?

(Thanks to Agathe Weber, Clémentine Rasquin, Sandra Vanhove and Isabelle Du Four, IPF, Belgium and Switzerland)

Lesson at a glance

 Students record and graph daily weather measurements over a period of time and discuss how weather relates to climate.

Background

Understanding the difference between weather and climate is necessary for a good comprehension of climate change. *Weather* is what you experience daily—the day-to-day atmospheric conditions such as temperature, precipitation, wind and humidity. *Climate* is a long-term average of weather. According to the World Meteorological Organization (WMO), weather conditions should be averaged over 30 years or more to determine climate.

Climate varies naturally on both short and long timescales. Natural climate variability results from internal atmospheric processes as well as from interactions among different components of the climate system, such as between the atmosphere, the oceans and/or the land. *Climate variability* refers to fluctuations in these systems on timescales ranging from months to decades.

Climate change, or changes in the average state of the atmosphere over timescales ranging from decades to millions of years. The impacts of climate change may be felt through changes in climate variability—for example, El Niño-Southern Oscillation (ENSO) events may become more common under a warmer climate.

It is impossible to attribute any single weather event to climate change because these events are based on statistical probabilities. This makes it extremely difficult to predict the probable effects of climate change without long-term historical data.

The following activity will help students realise that the information they hear about climate and climate change is based in part on thousands and thousands of precise meteorological measurements that scientists have been making for centuries.

Time

Preparation: Several hours (to borrow or buy the instruments for a weather station, plus 10 minutes to copy or print out the student sheet)
Class time: 15 minutes (for daily measurements) and 2–3 class periods (for the activity)

Materials

(per class)
- 1 thermometer *(to measure temperature)*
- 1 hygrometer *(to measure relative humidity)*
- 1 anemometer *(to measure wind speed)*
- 1 bucket or glass *(to measure precipitation)*
- 1 wind sock or flag *(to measure the wind direction)*

(per student)
- *Weather and Climate* worksheet

Weather and Climate Worksheet

Activity Directions

Part 1—Gathering weather data
1. Install all the weather instruments somewhere outside. Try to find a site in an open area away from trees, buildings and other tall objects, but close enough that the students can access it daily. You may want to do this in advance, or have the students assist.
2. Show the students the different instruments. Discuss the purpose of each instrument and how to read it. Emphasise the importance of using a standard protocol—i.e., all students should use the same method for reading the instruments and recording the data.
3. Have groups of students take daily instrument readings (for example, a different group each week) and record the results in Part 1 of their *Weather and Climate* worksheet. To limit the variables and allow comparison, the weather readings must be made at the same time each day. At the end of the week, the students should graph their data.

Part 2—Graphing and interpreting the data

1. After all groups have done the measurements, combine their graphs to summarise the results. This will illustrate what happened over the course of a month or more, depending on how many groups were involved.
2. Show the graphs to the students and discuss how weather varies on different timescales. Discuss the seasons and what causes them. *(See the activity 'Why is it cold in the polar regions?' for more information.)*
3. Read aloud the definitions of weather and climate from the student sheet. Ask the students to explain the difference between weather and climate in their own words.
4. Ask them to find which climatic zone they live in, using the climate map on the student sheet.
5. Compare the students' meteorological observations with the region's climate as shown on the map. Do they correspond to one another? How many readings are needed to determine the climate of a region?

Part 3—Predicting the future

1. Give a brief introduction to the potential consequences of current climate change *(see web links to this activity on the CD-ROM for more information)*. Have the students write their own 'weather forecasts' for a day in the year 2020 in their region.
2. Ask the students if their region will still be in the same climate zone in 2020. If they do not think so, ask them which zone it might be in and why.

Discussion

1. How do you react to your local weather? Do you wear different clothing? Do you choose certain types of transportation? Do you change the heating or cooling of your home?
2. What do these observations tell you about seasonal effects? About local effects? About differences between your location and polar locations?

Extensions/Adaptations

1. If you cannot set up a weather station at your school, have the students gather the daily data through online sources (e.g., your local meteorology office) or the local media.
2. Use the WMO world weather map (http://www.worldweather.org/) to compare your local weather to weather in the Arctic and elsewhere on the planet.
3. Between the meteorological measurements and the climate discussion, visit a regional weather station or invite a meteorologist to come and speak to the class.
4. Link up with a classroom in another part of the country or world to compare the weather at different times of the year.

WEATHER AND CLIMATE WORKSHEET

1) Weather Readings

Meteorology is the science that studies variations in weather events (clouds, rain, snow, wind, etc.). The aim is to understand how these events develop by using precise data taken in the field.

Date and time										
Temperature										
Humidity										
Precipitation (in cm)										
Wind speed										
Wind direction										
Cloud cover										
Type of weather										

Figure 1.5 Weather data table.

2) The Climate in my Region: Today and Tomorrow

Climatology is the science that studies weather conditions over extended periods of time in a particular region using statistics based on at least 30 years of readings. This enables us to define the climate of a region.

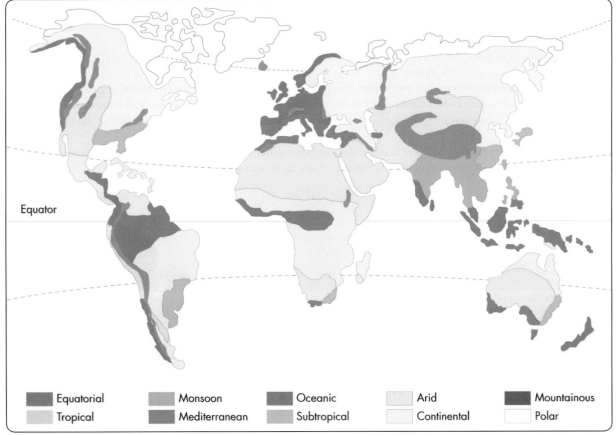

Equatorial	Monsoon	Oceanic
Tropical	Mediterranean	Subtropical
		Arid
		Continental
		Mountainous
		Polar

Equator

Figure 1.6 Broad scale global climatic regions.

WHY IS IT COLD IN THE POLAR REGIONS?

(Thanks to Alexandre Trindade Nieuwendam and José Xavier, Portugal)

Lesson at a glance

Students conduct a simple experiment that illustrates how the angle of solar rays affects the temperature in polar regions.

Background

To understand why it is cold in the polar regions, we need to consider what causes the Earth's seasons and why, when it is summer in the Arctic, it is winter in the Antarctic (and vice versa):

- The total amount of solar radiation reaching the Earth is essentially constant throughout the year. However, this energy is not distributed evenly around the globe and the distribution changes through the year.
- The Earth revolves around the Sun on a flat plane, known as the *plane of the ecliptic*. One revolution equals a year.
- The Earth also rotates on its axis once every 24 hours, creating day and night. (Imagine a pole through the centre of the Earth that extends out at the North and South Poles—this is the axis.)
- Earth's axis is not perpendicular to the plane of the ecliptic—it is tilted at an angle of about 23½°. This angle remains constant throughout the Earth's revolution around the Sun. This is called *parallelism (Figure 1.7)* and is the key to the seasons.
- At two points during the year, the noon sun shines directly on the equator. These dates (roughly 21 March and 23 September) are known as the *equinoxes*. At the equinox, all parts of the planet have 12 hours of daylight and 12 hours of darkness.

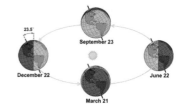

Figure 1.7 Parallelism and the seasons.

- At two other points in the year (21 June and 22 December), because of tilt of the Earth's axis, the noon sun falls directly at 23½° North latitude in June (known as the Tropic of Cancer) and at 23½° South in December (the Tropic of Capricorn). These dates are called the *solstices*. During the solstices, one Pole (as far north or south as 66½°) has 24 hours of light, while the other Pole has 24 hours of darkness.

Since the amount of energy received from the Sun is constant throughout the year, the angle of the Sun's rays as they reach the Earth's surface affects how much energy is received at any one spot. Because of the tilt of the Earth's axis, the polar regions never receive as much solar energy as the lower latitudes or the equatorial regions. In addition, in the polar regions the Sun's energy travels farther through the Earth's atmosphere so more of it may be absorbed, scattered or reflected before reaching the surface. These are a couple of the reasons why it is colder at the Poles.

Note: Winter temperatures are not lower because the Earth is farther from the Sun. The Earth's orbit is not circular, but slightly elliptical (oval). Because of this, Earth is actually farthest from the Sun around the time of the northern summer solstice!

Time
Preparation: 20 minutes
Class time: 30 minutes

Materials
(per small group of students)
- 1 piece of black cardboard
- 2–3 thermometers
- 1 lantern (or a 100w lamp)

Activity Directions
1. Cut the cardboard in half and attach a thermometer to each piece.
2. Stand one piece of cardboard vertically or at an angle. Lay the other one flat.

Figure 1.8 Setting up the experiment.

3. Aim the light in the direction of the cardboard, making sure both are the same distance from the light.
4. If you have a third thermometer, place it away from the light as a control, so that you can compare the ambient temperature in the room with the readings you get under the light.
5. Wait 10 minutes, and then check the thermometers to see which cardboard is warmer.

Discussion

1. Imagine you are at the North Pole. At what time of the year is it daylight for 24 hours? *(There is only one sunrise and one sunset per year at the Poles. If you are standing directly on the Pole, dawn begins in early March and you will see sunrise on 21 March, the spring equinox. The Sun then gets higher in the sky each day until the summer solstice in June. It sets on 23 September, the autumnal equinox. The opposite is true for the South Pole.)* When would it be dark for 24 hours? *(After the Sun sets in September, the Pole is in twilight until early October, then completely dark until the spring equinox.)*
2. What other factors besides the angle of the Sun's rays might affect the temperature in the polar regions? *(Earth's atmosphere and oceans hold heat that would otherwise be lost to space. Circulation in both the atmosphere and the oceans redistributes heat around the planet, making the polar regions warmer and the equatorial region cooler than they would be otherwise.)*
3. Which has a colder average temperature—the Arctic or the Antarctic? *(the Antarctic)* Why? *(Antarctica, being a land mass with high mountains and thick ice sheets, has a much higher average elevation than the Arctic. Antarctica is also surrounded by ocean and the powerful Antarctic Circumpolar Current prevents warm ocean currents from reaching the continent.)*
4. Would you get different results if your cardboard was white rather than black? Why or why not? *(See 'Investigating albedo' in the Ice section of this chapter.)*

Extensions/Adaptations

1. Try changing the angle of the tilted cardboard and repeat the experiment. Do you notice any difference?
2. In a darkened room, shine a torch (flashlight) directly at a wall so that the rays of light hit the wall at a right angle (90°). Measure the circle of illumination. Standing the same distance from the wall, now tilt the torch so that the rays of light reach the wall at a different angle. You will notice that the area illuminated is now larger and oval-shaped. Note that the torch is still emitting the same amount of energy, but that energy is now spread over a larger area. Discuss how this might affect the temperature at a given spot.
3. Shine the torch or a lamp on a globe in a darkened room. (Make sure that the torch is large enough or far enough away to illuminate the entire side of the globe that is facing it.) Keeping the light and globe in the same spots and the angle of inclination of the globe's axis parallel, repeat the experiment for the solstices and the equinoxes. Compare parts of the globe that are illuminated in each case and discuss.

Figure 1.9 Use a globe and a lamp to show how the Earth's angle of inclination affects the amount of solar radiation received by different regions at different times of the year.

A SPIN ON OZONE
(Thanks to Tamsin Gray, BAS, UK)

Lesson at a glance

*Students act out the formation of the polar vortex
and the destruction of the ozone layer above Antarctica.*

Background

The ozone layer is located around 20 kilometres above us in a layer of the atmosphere called the *stratosphere*. Each year above Antarctica, a dramatic destruction of ozone takes place resulting in levels of ozone in the atmosphere dropping to around one-third of their usual value.

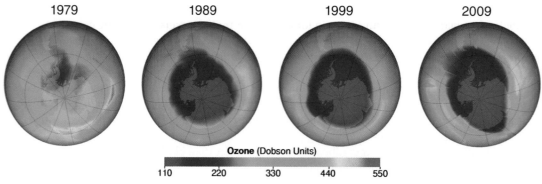

| 1979 | 1989 | 1999 | 2009 |

Ozone (Dobson Units)

110   220   330   440   550

**Figure 1.10 The maximum extent of the ozone hole above Antarctica over the past 40 years.
Violet shows the area of lowest ozone concentrations, with red indicating the highest.**

Chlorofluorocarbons (CFCs) are a family of chemical compounds that were developed in the 1930s as safe alternatives for refrigeration and spray can propellants. CFCs are highly stable. They accumulate in the stratosphere where they can last for up to 100 years. During that time, they can do a lot of damage to the ozone layer. In the presence of ultraviolet radiation from the Sun, CFCs break up and release their chlorine atoms. The chlorine then reacts with ozone (O_3), removing one oxygen atom to form chlorine monoxide (ClO) and leaving an oxygen molecule (O_2).

During the Southern Hemisphere winter, a *vortex* forms in the Antarctic stratosphere, preventing warmer air from lower latitudes from reaching the centre of the vortex. Inside the polar vortex, the air is extremely cold and *polar stratospheric clouds* (PSCs) made of ice crystals often form when temperatures drop below –75°C.

These ice clouds provide a surface where the chemical reaction that destroys ozone can take place. Since sunlight is needed for this reaction, the ozone hole does not start to form until light returns at the end of the long dark Antarctic winter. The combination of extremely cold temperatures (which allow PSCs to form), sunlight, and the presence of CFCs results in the formation of an ozone hole over Antarctica in the austral spring time. The vortex breaks down at the end of spring and ozone-rich air from outside moves in to refill the hole.

Time

Preparation: 5–10 minutes
Class time: 15–20 minutes

Materials

(per class)
- 10 inflated balloons
- bowl or plate (plastic or metal recommended)
- 1 straightened paperclip or toothpick
- several willing volunteers

Figure 1.11 Polar stratospheric clouds are ice clouds formed high up in the atmosphere (around 20 km) when the temperature drops below –75°C. Chemical reactions that destroy ozone gas take place on the surfaces of these beautiful and unusual looking clouds.

Activity Directions

1. Pick four or five volunteers to hold hands in a circle and walk around in one direction—they are the polar vortex.
2. Choose one volunteer to be the Sun. The Sun begins the activity crouched in the middle of the polar vortex, holding a paperclip or toothpick to represent the CFCs.
3. Place a bowl or plate of inflated balloons inside the polar vortex—the balloons are molecules of ozone, and the bowl or plate is a polar stratospheric cloud.
4. The Sun rises and begins to destroy the ozone using the CFCs (i.e., breaks the balloons).
5. Other volunteers try to bring more balloons in from outside but cannot due to the barrier of the polar vortex.
6. The polar vortex breaks up (it is now Antarctic summer) and outside volunteers succeed in bringing in new ozone to replace that which was destroyed.

Note: Do not let the polar vortex continue to spin for too long or the volunteers may suffer!

Discussion

1. Does an ozone hole form over the Arctic? *(Small holes can form over the Arctic but it is not usually cold enough there to form the ice clouds on which reactions take place. There is no polar vortex isolating the Arctic stratosphere, so warmer air from lower latitudes can flow in.)*
2. Why is the ozone hole a problem for us? *(Ozone is currently being destroyed faster than new ozone is being made. This not only raises the risk of skin cancer in humans; it can also have a negative effect on other animals and plants. The ozone layer also plays an important role in global climate and is now thought to be largely responsible for the rapid warming of the Antarctic Peninsula region over the past few decades. This warming has caused floating ice shelves to disintegrate, allowing glaciers to flow faster into the sea and contributing to global sea level rise.)*
3. What will happen to the ozone hole in the future? *(Although the use of CFCs has slowed down dramatically since the Montreal Protocol came into force, they remain in the atmosphere for a long time. The ozone layer is recovering slowly but it probably will not have fully recovered until at least 2070.)*
4. What is the difference between the ozone in the stratosphere and ground level, or tropospheric, ozone? *(Chemically, there is no difference—it is just where it is located. Ozone in the stratosphere helps protect us from dangerous levels of ultraviolet radiation. Ozone in the air we breathe is a pollutant that results from human activities such as industrial emissions and automobile exhaust, especially during hot weather. It is corrosive and can damage people's lungs, as well as harming other animals and plants.)*

Extensions/Adaptations

1. Instead of balloons, use two different colour building blocks that snap together (e.g., green to represent chlorine from the CFCs and yellow for oxygen). The Sun would then start with a number of 'ozone' molecules (3 yellow blocks snapped together). When the reaction begins, the Sun would break apart the ozone molecules, then attach one of the oxygen atoms to the chlorine atom (to form ClO) and rejoin the two other oxygen atoms (to form O_2).
2. For high school chemistry students, make the chemical reactions more accurate and complicated. Have the students research the process *(see web links to this activity on the CD-ROM for more information)* and challenge them to create more accurate models using materials such as building blocks, or through an interactive medium such as drama or interpretive dance.

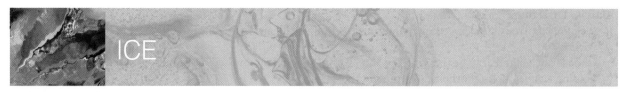

ICE

Understanding ice—how it forms; how ice sheets grow, flow and eventually melt; and how sea ice influences global ocean circulation—is crucial to understanding how natural and human-driven changes may affect our future climate.

The cryosphere, from the Greek word 'kryo' meaning cold, refers to all of the frozen water on the Earth's surface. This can be in the form of snow, mountain glaciers, ice caps, ice sheets, sea ice, lake and river ice and frozen ground, including permafrost. Any change in the cryosphere can have a direct and profound impact on other Earth systems such as the atmosphere, the hydrosphere and the biosphere.

The most recent Intergovernmental Panel on Climate Change (IPCC) report shows that snow and ice have been declining on a global scale. This decline has been especially great since 1980, and the rate of decline has increased dramatically during the past decade. On the Antarctic Peninsula, for example, the Larsen Ice Shelf broke off in two dramatic events in 1995 and 2002.

Ice and snow are important climate regulators because they increase the Earth's surface reflectivity *(albedo)* and reduce the amount of solar radiation absorbed by the ocean or land. For example, sea ice generally has a high albedo, reflecting from 25% to 85% of the solar radiation that reaches it, depending on the state of the ice and the snow cover on it. Open water, on the other hand, has a low albedo, reflecting less than 10%.

Global ocean circulation is also closely connected to sea ice processes. Sea ice forms in both the north and the south polar regions during the winter when ocean water temperatures drop below –1.8°C. When it is winter in the Arctic, it is summer in the Antarctic, so when ice is forming in one polar region, it is melting in the other. On average, between 16 and 23 million square kilometres of the ocean are covered by sea ice at any given time. Antarctic sea ice covers about 19 million square kilometres at its maximum extent in late winter, decreasing to about three to four million square kilometres at summer's end. In the Arctic, sea ice typically covers about 14 to 16 million square kilometres in late winter, decreasing to about seven million square kilometres at its minimum in September. Over the past several years, however, Arctic sea ice minima have been only four to six million square kilometres.

Sea ice is also important for marine ecosystems. New sea ice starts to form in autumn, when there are still substantial concentrations of microorganisms in the surface waters. Some of these organisms become trapped within the ice matrix and start growing, forming ice-associated communities that are dominated by algae. The algae and other organisms are released to the water column in the spring as the ice melts, contributing to algal blooms along the ice edges.

Ice sheets are also a very important part of the cryosphere. Large ice sheets covering Greenland and Antarctica hold about 75% of the world's fresh water. If all of this ice were to melt, the fresh water produced would be equivalent to about 70 metres of global sea level rise. Annual snowfall, compacted and compressed, builds the ice sheets, which can grow to a thickness of more than three kilometres.

Studying ice cores and ice crystals from polar ice sheets and sea ice can help us understand many aspects of past, present, and possible future changes in complex Earth systems as well as global climate. The following activities and experiments give you a chance to explore the cryosphere from several different perspectives.

Ice Activities

INVESTIGATING ALBEDO

GROWTH AND FLOW OF ICE SHEETS

WHEN ICE MELTS . . .

SEA ICE AND OCEAN CURRENTS

EXAMINING ICE CRYSTALS

PENGUIN REUNION

INVESTIGATING ALBEDO

(Thanks to Sandra Zicus, Australia; and José Xavier and Alexandre Trindade Nieuwendam, Portugal)

Lesson at a glance

 Students investigate the concept of albedo by using hand-held light meters to measure the amount of light reflected off different-coloured surfaces.

Background

The radiant energy from the Sun received by the Earth is called *insolation* (for *in*coming *sol*ar radi*ation*). The amount of this energy that is absorbed by the Earth's surface depends primarily on:

- its distance from the Sun.

  If the Earth were 5% closer to the Sun, the oceans would boil off and form a dense atmosphere; if it were 1% farther away, the oceans would permanently freeze. The reason for this is that the Sun's rays spread out over an ever-increasing area the further they travel outward from the Sun. This spreads the same amount of energy over a larger area, reducing the amount that is received at a given location. *(See extension activities in 'Why is it cold in the polar regions' in the Atmosphere section for more information.)*

- its *albedo* (the amount of sunlight reflected).

  About 6% of the insolation that reaches the upper atmosphere is reflected back into space by atmospheric gases and dust. Approximately another 20% is reflected back into space by clouds. Around 19% is absorbed by water droplets in the clouds and by the molecules of gases of the atmosphere, especially water vapour (H_2O), carbon dioxide (CO_2), methane (CH_4), ozone (O_3), and chlorofluorocarbons (CFCs).

This means that only a little more than half of the solar energy that strikes the Earth's outer atmosphere reaches the surface of the planet. Another 4% of this energy is reflected back into space, leaving about 51% to be absorbed by the Earth's surface rocks, soils, water and biota.

Albedo is one of the physical variables that influence the dynamics of polar systems. The albedo of an object is affected by the colour, texture and composition of its surface. The darker and duller the object, the more energy it absorbs. Conversely, the lighter-coloured or the shinier the object is, the less energy it absorbs. Rough objects also reflect less radiation than smooth ones.

The different reflective capacities of snow, ice, water or land exert a significant and interconnected control on global climate. For example, sea ice reflects from 25% to 85% of the solar radiation that reaches it, depending on the thickness of the ice and the amount of snow cover on it. Open water reflects less than 10%.

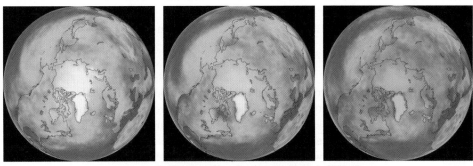

Reflected Shortwave Radiation (W/m²)

0   212.5   425

Figure 1.12 The globes show the amount of insolation (watts per square metre) reflected by Earth in June, July and August 2009 (from left to right), based on measurements collected by the CERES sensor on NASA's Terra satellite. The Arctic Ocean is in the centre, with North America in the lower left and Asia to the upper right. The most reflective areas are white, and the least reflective areas are deep blue.

INVESTIGATING ALBEDO continued

Changes in the extent of sea ice cover can lead to a *positive feedback loop*. Less ice cover means less solar energy is reflected and more is absorbed by the ocean, warming the water and leading to further melting and more open water. Water is very effective at storing heat, so greater-than-normal melting in one season could add enough heat to the system to limit ice formation the next season. This is known as the ice-albedo effect.

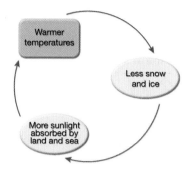

Figure 1.13 The sea ice-albedo effect—loss of sea ice can lead to a positive feedback loop resulting in increased climate change.

Time
Preparation: 30 minutes (to prepare materials if doing small group exercises)
Class time: 1–2 class periods (depending on students' prior knowledge)

Materials
(per group of students if done as a laboratory exercise, or per class if done as a demonstration)
- hand-held photographic light meter or a camera with a built-in light meter
- squares of white and black paper
- squares of aluminium foil and other materials with different colours or textures

Investigating Albedo Worksheet

Activity Directions
1. Discuss the concept of albedo with the students. Ask them if they think that dark- or light-coloured surfaces would reflect more light. You might relate this to the idea of wearing a white shirt or a black shirt in hot weather, and asking which is cooler.
2. Tell them that they are going to do an experiment to test the albedo of different-coloured surfaces. Show them the different-coloured papers and ask them to predict which ones will reflect the most light.
3. Show them the light meter and explain how it works. Explain that the light meter only measures light that is being reflected in the visible spectrum, so their results will not be completely accurate. (Models, in any case, are only a simplified representation of a much more complex reality.)
4. Discuss the variables that might affect the results of the experiment—e.g., the angle of the light shining on the surface, the distance of the light from the surface, the distance and angle at which they hold the light meter when taking their readings, etc. These are the things that need to be kept constant for every measurement if you want to compare them. If you are using a camera, a good way to control these variables is to put the camera on a tripod and point it down on a flat surface such as a table.
5. Give them a copy of the Investigating Albedo instruction sheet and time to carry out the investigation, or do the investigation as a whole class exercise.
6. Discuss the results.

Note: There are two different types of photographic light meters. One type measures only reflected light, which makes it the best type to use for this activity. Built-in camera meters are reflected light meters, so you can also use any camera that displays exposure options. Set your camera to 'aperture priority'—this will keep the size of the camera opening (called the F-stop) from changing. Press the shutter half-way down and hold it, and note the shutter speed information displayed. This will usually show as a fraction of a second (e.g., 1/60, 1/100, etc.) As you move the camera from a light object to a darker one, the shutter speed should change. A faster shutter speed indicates that more light is being reflected off the object.

The experiment also works best if there is enough light shining on the object. This is especially true if you are using a camera with a built-in meter because they may not be very sensitive in dim light.

It is important to explain to the students that the readings they get using the light meter will only be relative—in other words, they will give a general idea about how much light is being reflected from each object, but the actual numbers will not have a scientific meaning.

Light meters (and most cameras) are not waterproof, so be careful if using them around water.

Discussion

1. What happens to the energy that is not reflected from the surface of the object? *(It is absorbed, causing the object and what is below it to become warmer. Try the temperature extension activity to illustrate this.)*
2. How might decreasing sea ice extent in the Arctic affect the Earth's albedo? *(See background information above.)*
3. As the Arctic continues to warm, trees are starting to grow farther north replacing tundra vegetation. How might this affect albedo? *(Coniferous trees are darker in colour than the grasses, small shrubs and other vegetation of the current tundra. Therefore, large changes in tundra vegetation could substantially alter the albedo in the region.)*
4. How might clouds affect the Earth's albedo? *(This depends on the type and location of the clouds. For example, high and thin clouds will allow sunlight to pass through, whereas low, dense clouds will usually reflect the sunlight back to space.)*

Extensions/Adaptations

1. Try using the light meters outdoors. Have the students measure the reflectivity of various different surfaces such as different-coloured pavements, sand, soil, grass or other vegetation. (Remember, you must always take each reading at the same angle and the same distance from the surface if you want to compare them.) Discuss how land use patterns might affect your local and regional climate.
2. For younger students, introduce the concept through an experiment measuring the heat absorption capabilities of two different-colour objects:
   - Take 2 identical metal food cans with the labels removed. Paint one can with a matt black paint and leave the other one metallic and shiny. Half-fill the cans with room temperature water, and measure and record the water temperature (both should be the same). Place the cans under a hot lamp or in a sunny window. Check and record the temperature of each periodically over the next hour. Discuss the results.
   - An even simpler method is to place two flat thermometers under a light source. Cover one thermometer with a sheet of white paper and the other with a sheet of black paper. Check the thermometers after a couple of minutes and note the difference in temperature.

INVESTIGATING ALBEDO WORKSHEET

Investigation Question: How does the colour of a surface affect its albedo?

1. Predict which of the coloured papers will reflect the most light and which will reflect the least. Record your predictions in the form of a *hypothesis*.

    Hypothesis: _____

    _____

2. Use the light meter or camera to determine the relative amount of light being reflected off the different colours. First, determine your *independent* and *dependent variables,* and what things need to be kept *constant* to minimise the chance of other factors affecting the results of the experiment.

    Independent variable: _____

    Dependent variable: _____

    Constants: _____

    _____

3. Record the results in the table below.

Sample colour	Light meter reading		
	Trial 1	Trial 2	Trial 3

4. Discuss your results. What happened and why do you think it happened?_____

    _____

5. What happened to the energy that was not reflected from the surface? _____

    _____

6. If Arctic sea ice continues to disappear, how might this affect the Earth's albedo and the temperature in the region?

    _____

    _____

    _____

✳ GROWTH AND FLOW OF ICE SHEETS
(*Thanks to Rhian A. Salmon, UK; and Louise Huffman, USA*)

Lesson at a glance
Students build a continent from clay and use a cornstarch mixture to model the movement of polar ice sheets.

Background
Large ice sheets covering Greenland and Antarctica hold most of the world's fresh water. Annual snowfall, compacted and compressed, builds the ice sheets, which can grow to a thickness of more than three kilometres. Ice sheets can cover mountain ranges; in other places only the tops of mountains protrude. Ice sheets flow slowly, from plateaus to valleys and eventually to the ocean. Ice sheets can extend into the ocean as ice shelves. Once an ice sheet reaches the ocean, outlet glaciers and ice shelves can break off into icebergs, which melt as they drift in the sea.

Glaciers and ice sheets move by two main processes: *internal flow* and *basal sliding*. Internal flow, also called *creep*, occurs in the interior of a glacier where the downslope component of the weight of the ice deforms the crystal structure.

Basal sliding, on the other hand, results from lubrication of meltwater under the glacier. This is more common in mountain and outlet glaciers than under large polar ice sheets themselves.

In the experiment below, the cornstarch behaves somewhat like a real ice sheet: it flows around mountains; it will flow over an ocean and it can cover the whole landscape. The cornstarch does not show all aspects of a real ice sheet. Large ice sheets can have continuous flows from high point to low point and from surface to bottom. Ice at the bottom of an ice sheet is under the greatest stress and is warmest, so the flow is fastest there.

Figure 1.14 The southern portion of the Greenland ice cap captured by MODIS on 23 August 2006.

Time
Preparation: 30 minutes (to prepare clay and cornstarch mixture)
Class time: 20–30 minutes

Materials
(*per pair of students*)
• clay (*for continent*)
• small paper plate or tray on which to build the continent
• bowl or pan for mixing cornstarch
• ½ cup cornstarch mixture (*for ice sheet*)

Preparation
Clay: If you do not have modelling clay, you can make it by mixing 1 cup salt, 1½ cups flour, and ½ cup vegetable oil with enough water to give it the consistency of thick biscuit or cookie dough. Adjust the amounts of water and flour until it is easy to mould, as the humidity may affect the quantities needed. You can make it the day before, but keep the clay covered and moist

Figure 1.15 Prepare cornstarch and water to a consistency that runs off your fingers, but feels solid when tapped with your finger.

in an airtight container until you are ready to use it. (This recipe makes 3–4 'continents'.)

Cornstarch mixture: Stir about 7–8 tablespoons (120 mL) of water into ½ cup of dry cornstarch. Mix until you do not see any dry powder or water left. It should feel solid when the surface is tapped with the spoon, but still be able to flow off the end of the spoon when scooped up. Clean up is easy! Wipe up spills with a wet sponge or paper towel. The mixture can be washed down the sink when done and hands rinse clean in seconds. Be careful—with its properties between liquid and solid, this mixture can provide hours of fun!

Figure 1.16 Model 'ice sheet' flowing over clay mountain.

Activity Directions
1. Use clay to build a continent with features like mountains and valleys.
2. Place 5–6 tablespoons (80–90 mL) of cornstarch mixture in the location where the ice sheet will first form. Watch where the ice sheet moves.
3. Add more cornstarch mixture at the centre of the 'ice'.
4. Observe where the ice sheet moves.

Discussion
1. If your ice sheet ran into a mountain, what would happen? *(Build clay mountains and try it. Glaciers move from higher elevations to lower, but if a glacier meets an obstruction it will flow around it, or pile up until it flows over it, or it will scrape parts of it off and drag them with it.)*
2. What would happen if a real ice sheet flowed over a thin layer of liquid water? *(Do not try this with the corn starch because additional water will make the mixture too runny. On a slope, an ice sheet will flow faster because the water decreases the friction between the bottom of the ice and the land surface. This is known as basal sliding.)*

⟡ WHEN ICE MELTS . . .
(Thanks to Louise Huffman, USA; Isabelle Du Four, Belgium; and Sandra Zicus, Australia)

Lesson at a glance
Students compare and contrast the effects of melting icebergs or sea ice, with melting glaciers and ice sheets, on sea level.

Background
Scientists have shown that global average sea level rose by no more than 0.1 mm per year during the 3,000 years prior to 1950. Since 1950, sea level has risen by an average 1.8 mm per year. Recent satellite measurements have shown an overall increase of 3.3 mm per year since 1993—much faster than before! We are already seeing the consequences of this: humid coastal areas and mangrove forests are decreasing, while coastal erosion and flood-induced damage are increasing.

This recent sea level rise has two major causes:

Figure 1.17 Monitoring tide gauges over time is one way to gather data about sea level changes on local and regional levels.

- *Thermal expansion:* The current rise in global temperatures is warming the ocean surface waters. Water takes up more space as it warms (like mercury in a thermometer), which causes sea level to rise.

- *Melting glaciers, ice caps and ice sheets:* When land-based ice melts, the resulting water ultimately flows into the ocean, which also causes sea level to rise.

By contrast, when sea ice or icebergs melt, sea level will not rise. Water contracts as it cools until it reaches about 4°C. It then expands by up to 10% as it freezes, making it less dense than liquid water. (You can check this out by freezing a carefully measured volume of water in a plastic measuring cup, then checking the volume again after it is frozen.) Sea ice and icebergs will not raise sea level when they melt because they are already floating in the ocean and their volume contracts again when the ice melts.

Until recently, sea level rise has been due mostly to thermal expansion, and only mountain glaciers have melted significantly. In the past few years, however, polar ice caps and ice sheets (which hold 99% of land ice on Earth) have started melting, especially in the Arctic and around the Antarctic peninsula.

Time
Preparation: Several hours *(to freeze ice cubes)*
Class time: 20–30 minutes *(per part for ice to melt, plus extra for discussion)*

Materials
(per small group of students)
- deep dish pie or cake pan
- toothpick
- modelling clay *(enough to make a small 'continent' in the centre of the pan)*
- 8–10 ice cubes
- water
- clear plastic wrap *(enough to cover the pan)*

Activity Directions
Part 1—If sea ice or icebergs melt, will sea level rise?
Give each team of students a pan, a lump of clay and the following directions:
1. Mould the shape of a continent with the clay, pressing the edges flat against the bottom of the pan.
2. Pour in enough water to partially cover the clay continent.
3. Put 4–5 ice cubes in the water to represent sea ice or icebergs.

4. Trace the water level into the clay with a toothpick or pencil.
5. Cover the pan with clear plastic wrap to prevent evaporation of the water.
6. Observe the marked water line as the ice melts. Does the water level rise? Why or why not?

Part 2—If glaciers and icecaps melt, will sea level rise?
1. Use the same pan and continent from Part 1.
2. Place 2–3 new ice cubes on top of the clay continent to represent glaciers or icecaps.
3. Observe the marked water line as the ice melts. Does the water level rise? Why or why not?

Discussion
1. What can you figure out about the influence of melting ice on sea level? *(Sea level will only rise when land ice melts. The melting of sea ice or icebergs does not cause a rise because this ice is already displacing the mass of the water it contains.)*
2. What might be some consequences of significant sea level rise from melting land ice? *(Sea level rise might cause increased coastal erosion; more frequent and serious damage during extreme weather events; saltwater contamination of surface water and groundwater; and some low-lying island nations would be submerged.)*

Figure 1.18 The ice cubes on the right represent the land ice; the ones on the left represent sea ice.

Extensions/Adaptations
1. For younger students, try this as a simpler way to illustrate the concept *(Figure 1.18)*:
   a. Put 2 ice cubes in a cup and fill it to the rim with water. The ice cubes represent icebergs or sea ice.
   b. Fill a second cup with water and place a perforated plate on top of it. Be careful not to spill any water. Put 2 ice cubes on top of the perforated plate to represent land ice.
   c. Let the ice cubes melt and note what happens.
2. For older students, explore Archimedes' principle, which states that the buoyant force pushing up on an object submerged in a liquid is equal to the weight of the liquid the object displaces.
   See the video at http://www.youtube.com/watch?v=eQsmq3Hu9HA.

✳ SEA ICE AND OCEAN CURRENTS

(Thanks to Sandra Zicus, Australia; Louise Huffman, USA; and Begoña Vendrell-Simón, Spain)

Lesson at a glance

Students create 'sea ice' and investigate the effect on water density and the formation of ocean currents.

Background

The seasonal formation and melt of sea ice is the dominant factor controlling the salinity and thus the density of surface ocean waters in the polar regions. Salt is not included in the ice matrix as the ocean water freezes, so it accumulates in the surface waters. In Antarctica, this creates a dense brine that sinks and flows down the continental shelf of Antarctica to form *Antarctic Bottom Water*—the densest water in the open ocean. This water flows outward from the Southern Ocean and through other ocean basins as part of the global ocean circulation 'conveyor belt' that distributes heat, nutrients and gases around the world. There are only a few areas in the world, in Antarctica and in the Arctic, where such dense water is formed. *(See 'Deep water circulation' in the Ocean section for more information.)*

Time

Preparation: Several hours *(for freezing the water)*
Class time: 30–40 minutes

Materials

(per group of 3–4 students)
Part 1
- plastic 500–600 mL soft drink bottle with the top half cut off
- insulated drink cooler or other insulation to wrap around bottle
- fresh water
- salt water *(use 2 tsp salt per litre of water)*
- hydrometer or multimeter
- thermometer
- freezer

Part 2
- aquarium tank or clear plastic box
- salt water *(use 2 tsp salt per litre of water)*
- food colouring
- water remaining after you made your sea ice in Part 1

Activity Directions

Part 1—Making sea ice
1. Fill the cut-off soft drink bottle 2/3 full with plain water at room temperature.
2. Measure and record the water temperature.
3. Test the salinity of the water with the hydrometer* or the multimeter* and record the results.
4. Add 2 teaspoons salt per litre of water and stir until dissolved. Test the salinity again and record.
5. Put the bottle in the insulated cooler or other insulator and place it in the freezer.
6. Leave the bottle in the freezer until about 2 centimetres of ice has formed on the top of the water. Freezing time will vary, but should take between 4–6 hours.
7. Remove the bottle from the freezer, squeeze slightly and remove the 'sea ice'. Place the ice in a separate dish.
8. After you remove the ice, allow the remaining water to warm to room temperature. Test the salinity and record the results.
9. Allow the ice to melt and warm to room temperature, then test the salinity of the resulting water.

*Note: Neither a hydrometer nor a multimeter measures salinity directly.

A **hydrometer** measures the *density* of a liquid. Density is a measurement of the quantity of matter contained in a given volume and is usually expressed as grams per cubic centimetre. When salt is dissolved in water, the volume of the water does not change, but the density increases. *Buoyancy* is a function of density—it is the ability of an object to float on a liquid because of the greater density of the liquid. The higher the salinity, the denser the liquid and the higher the hydrometer will float. You can purchase hydrometers in stores that sell aquarium equipment.

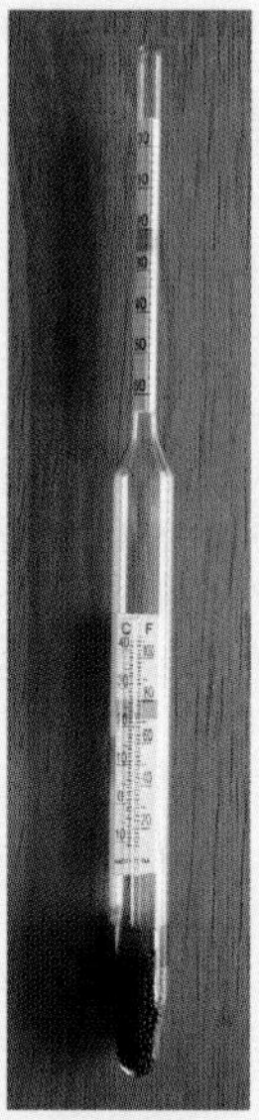

Figure 1.19
A hydrometer measures the density of a liquid. Salt increases water density, so the greater the salinity, the higher the hydrometer will float.

A **multimeter,** set on the ohm scale, measures *electrical resistance,* which is a measurement of properties that limit the ability of a substance to conduct electricity. Salt in water decreases the resistance, which results in a lower reading on the scale. Therefore, the more saline the water, the lower the reading on the meter. Keep the two probes an equal distance apart when making comparative measurements and hold the probes still until the numbers on the scale stop moving. Inexpensive multimeters are available at electronics supply shops.

Figure 1.20 A multimeter, set on the ohm scale, measures electrical resistance. Salt water decreases resistance, so the multimeter can be used for indirect measurements of salinity.

Part 2—Creating currents
1. Fill the clear plastic container or aquarium about 2/3 full with salt water. The salinity should be the same as the salinity of the water you used in Part 1. A simple way to do this is to prepare enough salt water to fill both the soft drink containers *(for Part 1)* and the aquarium *(for Part 2)* at the same time.
2. Add 3–4 drops of food colouring to the brine that was left after you made the 'sea ice' in Part 1.
3. Pour this coloured water slowly and gently down the side at one end of the plastic container or aquarium and observe what happens.

Figures 1.21 and 1.22 Colouring the brine (left) and creating a coloured water current (right). Take care to pour the water slowly down the side of the container.

Note: If time is an issue (e.g., if you have rotating classes for short periods of time) you may need to prepare the 'sea ice' in advance so that the students can perform the salinity tests on it and do Part 2 during class time. Part 2 could also be done as a teacher-led observation lesson for the whole class.

Discussion

1. To represent the formation of sea ice, why did you need to insulate the container from the bottom and sides before you put it in the freezer? *(This is to keep the water in your container from freezing from the sides or the bottom—sea ice forms only on the top of the ocean.)*
2. Why did you have to have all your water samples at room temperature when you tested them? *(Temperature also affects density and you want to test only one variable at a time.)*
3. Which sample had the highest salinity? *(the water remaining in the container after you removed the 'sea ice')* Which had the lowest? *(the melted ice)* Why? *(When salt water freezes most of the salt is not included in the structure of the ice. This makes the remaining water saltier.)*

Extensions/Adaptations

1. Have students make their own hydrometers:
   a. Attach a small piece of modelling clay to one end of a drinking straw. Make sure the clay completely seals the straw so that no water can get in. Adjust the amount of clay so that the hydrometer floats upright with about 5 cm out of the water. If it sinks to the bottom, remove some clay. If it tilts to one side, add more clay.
   b. To calibrate your hydrometer, place it in a deep clear container (such as the bottom of a 2-litre soft drink bottle) of fresh water. There should be enough water so that the hydrometer floats without touching the bottom of the container. Grab the straw at the water line and pull it out of the water. Draw a line on the straw at this point with a permanent marker. This represents the density of fresh water. Use the same volume of liquid, at the same temperature, when you test your other samples.

Figure 1.23 Calibrating the hydrometer.

2. Investigate how salinity affects the freezing point of water. Fill several identical plastic containers with the same amount of water. Measure and add different amounts of salt to each one. Put them in a freezer and see how long it takes each one to freeze.
3. For younger students, try this simple experiment to show how temperature affects water density *(Figure 1.24)*:
   a. Prepare ice cubes from water coloured with blue food dye.
   b. Place one ice cube in a glass of fresh water and one in a glass of salt water.
   c. Let the ice cubes melt, observe what happens and discuss the results.
   (Cold water is denser than the warmer water, so the blue water sinks to the bottom in the freshwater glass. It gains heat energy as it moves through the warmer water, so as it moves along the bottom it begins to rise. By contrast, in the saltwater glass, the cold blue water melts and sits in a band on top of the warmer salt water, showing that even though it is much colder, it is less dense than the heavily saline water.)

Figure 1.24 The glass on the left is salt water; the one on the right is fresh water.

EXAMINING ICE CRYSTALS
(Thanks to Jane Dobson and Sandra Zicus, Australia)

Lesson at a glance
Students freeze thin layers of ice then examine the crystals using a light table and polarising filters.

Background
Ice crystal structure
All minerals, including ice, have a specific crystal structure that determines the shape of the individual crystals. The atoms and molecules within the crystal are arranged in an orderly and repetitive pattern called a *crystal lattice,* which is unique to that specific mineral. Each crystal type can be described by a set of three or four intersecting axes in a particular geometrical arrangement reflecting lattice symmetry.

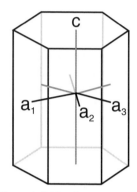

Figure 1.25 Ice has a hexagonal crystal structure with three equal length axes (a_1, a_2, and a_3) and a longer c axis perpendicular to the other three. This gives it a special optical property known as birefringence.

If the spacing and arrangement of the atoms are the same along all axes, such as in a cubic crystal like a grain of salt, the crystal structure is *isotropic* and its physical properties are the same in all directions. If the spacings and arrangements are different along different axes, then the crystal is called *anisotropic* and its physical properties vary in different directions.

Ice has a hexagonal (six-sided) anisotropic crystal structure *(Figure 1.25)*. Three of the axes (called a_1, a_2, and a_3) are of equal length within the same plane (at 120° to each other), while the fourth (the c axis) is longer and perpendicular to the plane of the other three.

Because of this crystal structure, ice crystals have a special optical property called *birefringence*, meaning 'double refraction'. The speed of a beam of light passing through the crystal depends on the direction of the light beam and the alignment of its *polarisation* in relation to the c axis and the a axes. This means that an ice crystal actually has two slightly different *refractive indices*. This causes a typical beam of light to split into two polarised beams (with polarisations perpendicular to each other), which travel through the ice at different speeds.

Scientists use this special property of ice crystals, along with polarised light, to examine ice specimens in more detail.

How it works
Light is made up of electromagnetic waves. To get a basic idea of polarisation, we need consider only the electric field part of the wave. The electric field is always pointing perpendicular to the direction that the wave is travelling. A polarising filter only allows light to pass through with the electric field in one linear orientation *(Figure 1.26)*.

To study the ice crystals, scientists place thin sections of ice between two polarising filters. After passing through the first filter, all the light waves hitting the ice are polarised in the same direction.

The second polarising filter is arranged with its polarisation direction at right angles to the first one. If there was no ice between the filters, and the filters were perfect, no light would emerge from the second filter.

Because the individual ice crystals in the sample have slightly different structures and orientations of crystal axes, the polarised light gets split into two beams that are refracted differently (doubly refracted) within each individual crystal. Accordingly, the pairs of beams of emerging light are polarised in different directions (at right angles to each other). They have also travelled through the ice at different speeds, depending on the particular

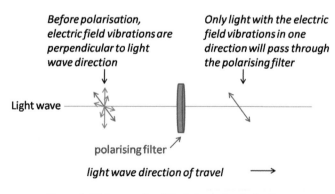

Before polarisation, electric field vibrations are perpendicular to light wave direction

Only light with the electric field vibrations in one direction will pass through the polarising filter

Light wave

polarising filter

light wave direction of travel ⟶

Figure 1.26 A very simplified view of polarisation.

characteristics of the crystal through which they passed. The differing speeds cause the wave crests of the initial wave (that was split into the two polarisations) to become progressively out of step. The distance between points on the two light waves that were originally in step is called the *retardation*.

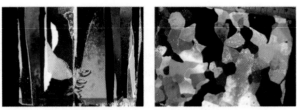

Figure 1.27 Interference colours seen in columnar ice crystals when examined under crossed polarising filters. The image on the left shows a vertical section; the right-hand image is a cross-sectional view.

Both light beams then pass through the second polariser. Here the pairs of differently polarised beams of light that were produced by the crystals are recombined into new polarised beams. The nature of each new beam depends on the alignment between the polarising filter and the polarisations of the pairs of beams from the ice crystals.

When they recombine, the two birefringent light waves can fully, or partially, cancel each other out. This is called *destructive interference*. The same thing can be seen when two stones are thrown into a pond and the resulting combined wave pattern has places where the waves add together *(constructive interference)* and flat spots where the waves cancel each other out *(destructive interference)*.

If we start with white light, which contains all the visible colours (i.e., a range of wavelengths), this interaction of the emerging rays results in the interference colours the scientists can see, since the retardation after travelling through the same thickness of ice under differing conditions leads to different wavelengths (colours) constructively and destructively interfering. The colours produced depend on a number of properties of the ice crystals being observed including thickness, shape, and crystal axis orientations *(Figure 1.27)*.

This technique allows scientists to see the individual ice crystals within the sample. The orientations, shapes and sizes of the crystals (which can range from sub-millimetre to tens of centimetres long) give scientists information about the environmental conditions in which the ice formed. The largest ice crystals, which may be up to one metre long, form in calm sea water close to the coast.

Time
Preparation: Several hours *(to freeze water samples)*
Class time: 45 minutes

Materials
(per group of 3–4 students)
• a light source such as a light table, light box, or overhead projector
• clear glass or plastic Petri dish
• 2 sheets of polarising film *(or camera polarising filters)*
• magnifying hand lens
• small flat-bottomed plastic containers
• water samples

Activity Directions
1. The day before doing the activity, freeze several different water samples (e.g., tap water, salt water, distilled water) in the plastic containers. Use about 1 cm water in each container.
2. Place one sheet of polarising film on top of a light source such as a light table or light box.
3. Gently pop the layer of ice out of one of the containers and place it in the Petri dish, then set it on the light table on top of the polarising film.
4. Examine the ice sample with the hand lens and describe what you see.
5. Hold the second piece of polarising film over the sample and slowly rotate it. Examine the sample through the hand lens as you rotate the film. Describe what you see. Are there any differences?
6. Repeat with the other ice samples and see if you can notice any differences in the appearance of the samples.

Figure 1.28 A sea ice scientist is using polarising filters to examine an ice sample.

Discussion

1. Why are scientists interested in the structure of ice crystals? *(They can tell a lot about the environmental conditions under which the ice formed, and it can help them distinguish ice of different origins in the same location, such as sea ice, ice from melted refrozen snow, pieces of icebergs that got frozen into the sea ice, etc. Climatologist and meteorologists also study how ice crystals form in clouds. Astrophysicists are interested in the possibility of ice on other planets.)*

2. In what other ways is the technique of crossed polarisers used? *(Engineers can use it to identify areas subject to stress failure in buildings. They build a model out of plastic and subject it to different stresses. By examining it through two polarising filters, they can see interference colours at the points of greatest stress. Students can explore this easily by examining and stretching or twisting [i.e., applying stresses] clear plastic items like rulers, protractors or cling-film between their polarising filters. Gem cutters may also use polarising filters to examine crystals such as diamonds before cutting them.)*

Extensions/Adaptations

The natural ice samples that glaciologists study are usually aggregates of many ice crystals, just as many rocks are. They try to use thin layers of ice just one crystal thick. Scientists usually examine the crystals in a piece of ice approximately 2 mm thick. When you look at a 1 cm thick piece of ice, you are actually looking at layers of crystals, rather than a single crystal. Use the polarised filters to examine your 1cm thick piece of ice, and then devise a way to make it thinner and study it again. (You can make the sample thinner by placing it on a hot plate or a light table.) Keep checking it between the polarised filters as you make it thinner and thinner. What changes do you notice?

PENGUIN REUNION
(Thanks to Nancy Pearson and Louise Huffman, USA)

Lesson at a glance

Participants play a group game to demonstrate how penguin parents and chicks are able to find their families in large, loud rookeries.

Background

A female emperor penguin feeds in the ocean for many months while her mate remains on the ice to incubate a lone egg and then care for the newly hatched chick. When the adult female returns to the crowded penguin colony, the only way she can find her family is by recognising the vocal sounds of her mate. Later, when the chick is older, he and his mother must recognise one another's calls in order to reunite. The survival of the offspring depends on the family's ability to recognise each other by sound.

Adélie penguins incubate their eggs in rocky nests on subantarctic islands, and the coasts and islands of the Antarctic continent.

Figure 1.29 Emperor penguins in Antarctica.

Both males and females share the feeding and incubation duties. Adélies also use vocal sounds to recognise each other in their large rookeries, which may contain up to a million individuals.

Time

Preparation time: 20–30 minutes *(to prepare cards, depending on group size)*
Class time: 15–20 minutes *(depending on group size and level of discussion)*

Materials

(per participant)
• 1 rhythm card

Advance Preparation

Prepare sets of rhythm cards using printed dashes and diagonal lines (one card per participant). Each dash represents a clap, and each diagonal line represents a pause. Each of the penguin pairs or family groups you want to end up with should have a different rhythm. *(Example of a rhythm card: __ __ / __ / __ __ / __)*

Activity Directions

1. Show the students a sample rhythm card and explain what the symbols mean. Have the whole class practice the rhythm shown on the card.
2. Give each student a card and explain that they must use the rhythm on their cards to search for their family members. Tell them not to show their cards to others until they are reasonably sure that they have found their 'mate' or 'offspring'.
3. Tell the students to begin. Each student should then clap out the rhythm on his or her card. The game is finished when all students have found their partners.
4. If some parents and chicks have not found each other after a reasonable time, ask everyone to stop making their family sound because there is a 'poor lost chick'. Have the 'lost chick' clap its rhythm while the rest of the class listens carefully. The other 'family members' should answer with the same rhythm and the chick joins its family.

Note: This activity is rather noisy, but so are penguin rookeries. The active nature of this game will engage students and help increase their interest in learning more about polar animal adaptations or life in the polar regions.

Discussion

1. What did you find difficult about this game?
2. Why is this behaviour important to penguins? What happens if a penguin is not very good at locating her chick, or a chick is poor at finding a parent?
3. Would you have survived as a penguin? Would most of your classmates?

Extensions/Adaptations

1. For younger students: Divide the class into two groups of equal size. (If there are an odd number of students, you may need to participate.) Tell one group they are the chicks and instruct them to remain stationary. The second group represents the parents returning from the sea. The parents must move around the room. Both parents and chicks clap their rhythm as the parents move around and try to find their chicks. When they find each other, they stop clapping and stand together until all family groups have reunited.
2. For older students: To increase the difficulty, make the rhythm by clicking the tongue instead of clapping. This removes the visual clue of watching the clapping.
3. Vary the environmental conditions: Shut off the light in the room to simulate the bad visibility that often is significant in Antarctica due to blizzards, or do the activity outside on a really windy day with a lot of ambient noise.
4. Some people say that a human mother can distinguish the sound of her baby crying from among many different babies crying. How is this similar to penguins? What advantage would this adaptation have? Take it a step further and look into pheromone communication between mothers and their babies, see http://www.ncbi.nlm.nih.gov/pmc/articles/PMC2717541/.

OCEANS

The meridional overturning circulation and the global carbon cycle are key concepts needed for understanding the role of the ocean in polar science.

Vertical mixing of ocean water is an important aspect of global ocean circulation. While surface currents are mostly wind-driven, vertical currents are caused primarily by the rising and sinking of water masses at high latitudes in both the Arctic and the Antarctic. Together, the two processes form a global ocean current system known as the *meridional overturning circulation*. This circulation is critical because it distributes heat, gases and nutrients needed by marine ecosystems, as well as other life, around the Earth. It also affects the climate over timescales ranging from years to decades.

Water density is affected by both temperature and salinity. Warm surface currents transport heat towards the poles where it is released to the extremely cold polar atmosphere, leading to an increase in water density that causes the water to sink.

In addition, the seasonal formation and melt of sea ice in the polar regions affects the density of surface ocean waters. As sea ice forms, salt is discharged into the water and heat is given off to the air. The addition of salt to the water underlying the ice also increases its density.

These cold, salty dense waters form the bottom currents of the ocean. Oceanographers sometimes call the resulting large-scale circulation *thermohaline*, from 'thermo' for temperature, and 'haline' for salinity. Any changes to the densification processes could have an impact on this circulation and, thus, on global climate.

In the present Arctic Ocean, incoming surface waters have relatively high salinities largely due to the influence of water from the Gulf of Mexico that is transported north by the Gulf Stream and the North Atlantic Drift. These salty waters lose heat as they travel north, becoming even denser. The sinking water in this area drives the northern branch of the global thermohaline circulation.

Freshwater run-off from land also affects water density in the Arctic Ocean, and demonstrates how local changes can have global impacts. Changes from snow to rain at certain times of year, earlier thawing of lakes and rivers due to warmer air temperatures, permafrost degradation, and increased melting and erosion from Greenland can all change the timing and amount of fresh water coming from land into the Arctic Ocean.

Sufficient fresh water from land, mixing with other Arctic Ocean waters at a certain time of year or in certain regions, could decrease the salinity of outgoing Arctic water, and again impact the global circulation. An understanding of future climate, and of future global ocean productivity, requires a better understanding of this complex and integrated Arctic land-ice-ocean system.

The ocean, especially in the polar regions, also plays a key role in the *global carbon cycle*. The ocean contains approximately 50 times more carbon dioxide than the atmosphere, and strongly controls atmospheric carbon dioxide levels. Carbon dioxide enters the surface ocean by exchange across the sea surface and is then redistributed by biological and physical processes. As atmospheric carbon dioxide levels increase, more is

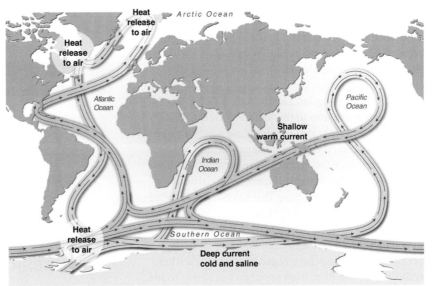

Figure 1.30 Simplified diagram of global ocean circulation.

absorbed by the ocean. This is part of an extremely complex interaction that is being closely studied by climate scientists. The solubility of carbon dioxide decreases as ocean temperatures increase. This lowers the ability of physical processes, known as the *physical pump,* to remove carbon dioxide from the atmosphere.

There is also a biological aspect to the ocean's role in the carbon cycle. Phytoplankton form the base of marine food webs. Carbon dioxide fixed by these organisms during photosynthesis transfers through the food chain to zooplankton and higher organisms. Some of this fixed carbon sinks into the ocean, acting as a *biological pump* of carbon into the deep water and ocean sediments.

Figure 1.31 Big waves in the Southern Ocean.

This is important for the global carbon cycle. In the polar regions, the effectiveness of the biological pump depends on complicated interactions of physical, chemical and biological processes. Mixing in the polar ocean brings up important major nutrients such as nitrogen or phosphorous from below, but vigorous mixing can also carry phytoplankton, the base of the ocean food web, out of optimal sunlit waters. Too little mixing *(stratification)* caused by surface warming or by the increased input of fresh water from run-off or ice melting can also isolate the phytoplankton from the underlying nutrients.

The carbon cycle is not only being affected by processes within the ocean, but also by interactions between the air and the ocean. Winds carry dust with iron and other trace elements that are biologically essential to phytoplankton production in polar oceans. Increased desertification and increased global wind could bring more iron to the Southern Ocean, or increased westerly winds surrounding Antarctica could tend to isolate parts of the Southern Ocean.

More seriously, the gradual increase of atmospheric carbon dioxide has caused an increase in carbon dioxide in the surface ocean. This has caused a slight but detectable change in ocean pH, making it more acidic.

Many oceanic microorganisms make carbonate shells. As they grow, they remove carbon from the ocean. The enzymes these organisms use to facilitate and control shell formation are highly sensitive to pH. Increased ocean acidification raises the disturbing possibility of a decrease in the ability of the ocean to process carbon. In this and many other ways, the remarkable productivity of the polar oceans depends on interconnected global factors.

The following teaching resources give you ideas how these multiple factors can be illustrated in the classroom, on a variety of scales ranging from global to local.

Oceans Activities

SURFACE CURRENTS

DEEP WATER CIRCULATION

SEA ICE POROSITY AND OCEAN ECOSYSTEMS

POLAR FEASTS!

BLUBBER INSULATION

 **SURFACE CURRENTS**
(Thanks to Turtle Haste, USA)

Lesson at a glance

Students investigate how surface ocean currents interact and how each one can be characterised.

Background

Surface currents, found in the top 400 metres of the water column, involve about 10% of all ocean water. They are generated primarily by wind blowing long distances over the ocean. On a global scale, circular rotations of water, called *gyres*, develop from a combination of prevailing wind patterns, the *Coriolis effect,* and the shape of the ocean basins. Surface currents also shift seasonally, which is most apparent in the equatorial currents.

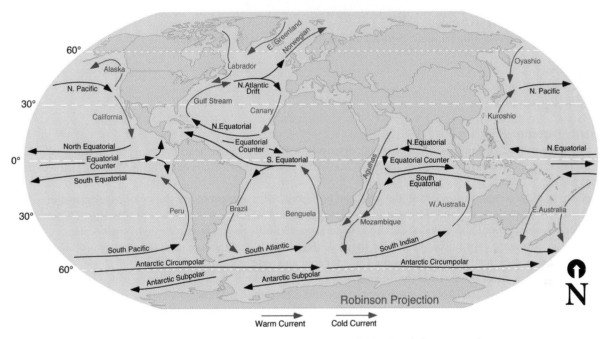

Figure 1.32 Major global surface currents are principally wind-generated. Circular patterns called gyres develop as a result of the Earth's rotation, prevailing wind patterns and the shape of the ocean basins.

Wind-driven surface currents in the open ocean move at approximately 1/100th of the speed of the wind at ten metres above the ocean surface. A phenomenon known as the *Ekman spiral* causes a current to flow at an angle to the prevailing winds. This angle changes with depth resulting in a spiral motion, until the water at about 100 metres depth is moving in the opposite direction to that of the wind. The result is a net transport of water at 90° to the wind direction. The velocity of the current also decreases with depth.

Major ocean currents transport huge volumes of water. For example, the *Antarctic Circumpolar Current* (ACC), which is the only ocean current that completely circles the globe without being obstructed by land, moves about 130 million cubic metres of water per second—the largest volume of water of any current in the world.

Many organisations study the surface movement of the oceans using a variety of methods. The US National Oceanographic and Atmospheric Administration (NOAA)'s Ocean Surface Current Analyses Real Time (OSCAR) programme tracks surface currents with satellite altimeters. NOAA and the Atlantic Oceanographic and Meteorological Laboratory launch drifter buoys that are transported around the oceans by currents. Items that have been transported by currents and washed up onto shore, called 'flotsam', are collected and analysed by other people and groups. Global armature networks look for flotsam and send out worldwide alerts when new materials appear. Scientists interested in the movement of polar sea ice also use buoys and ships in the ice to observe how the currents move the ice over time.

SURFACE CURRENTS continued

Time
Preparation: 20 minutes
Class time: 1–2 class periods *(~45 minutes each)*

 Table of Surface Currents Handout
World Map Handout

Materials
(for demonstration)
- clear flat-bottomed glass container with water, such as a mixing bowl or large beaker
- drinking straw
- several very small pieces of paper *(dried herbs also work well)*
- overhead projector
- *Table of Surface Currents* handout
- transparency of *World Map* handout *(without currents shown)*, or large world map

(per student)
- red and blue coloured pencils
- *World Map* handout

Activity Directions
1. Using the world map (and a globe if possible), discuss how the atmosphere heats unevenly *(see activity 'Why is it cold in the polar regions?' in the Atmosphere section)*. Discuss how the Coriolis effect helps form the shape of the gyres.
2. Place the glass container of water on the overhead projector. Ask a student to put the small paper pieces or dried herbs into the water and use the straw to blow gently and steadily on the surface of the water. Discuss the students' observations and explain that this is what happens in the ocean, but on a much larger scale.
3. Give each student a copy of the *World Map* handout *(Figure 1.33)*. Ask them to label the equator and the major ocean basins, and then make a map legend (blue for cold and red for warm water currents).
4. Read one of the descriptions from the *Table of Surface Currents* aloud. As a group, decide where to place the current on their maps and how to represent the size and direction of the flow.
5. Label the current on the map, and repeat the exercise with the other currents in the table.

Discussion
1. What patterns do the currents make? *(circular patterns called gyres)* How does water at the Poles moving towards the equator differ in each hemisphere? *(Northern Hemisphere gyres move clockwise; Southern Hemisphere gyres move anticlockwise.)*
2. What would happen if you were to drop a whole truck of toy ducks into the water near the coast of Peru? Where would they eventually go? What currents would they travel through?
3. Predict what might occur in northern India if colder polar water does not enter that part of the ocean. *(This is one reason that this part of the world experiences powerful monsoons.)*
4. Find and identify the largest volume current. *(the Antarctic Circumpolar Current)* How does the geography of the land affect the direction of the wind and water? Why is the flow different between currents? *(E.g., currents flow faster when a large volume of water is forced to flow through a narrow gap.)*

Extensions/Adaptations
1. Track a drifter buoy through NOAA's Adopt a Drifter Program (http://www.adp.noaa.gov/).
2. Look up the Arctic and Antarctic currents and place them on the map. Who might depend on the seasonal ice movement?
3. Look up and add smaller local currents and research their names.
4. Research the rate of transport for each current.
5. Look up the Great Sneaker spills. Join *Beachcombers Alert* (www.beachcombers.org).

TABLE OF SURFACE CURRENTS

Ocean and Name	Hemisphere	Location	Flow	Temperature	Characteristics
Atlantic (North Atlantic Drift)	Northern	Northern edge of Atlantic basin	From Canada to Europe	Cooling	Slow, shallow and wide
Atlantic (Canary)	Northern	Eastern edge of Atlantic basin	From Pole towards the equator	Cold	Slow, shallow and wide
Atlantic (Gulf Stream)	Northern	Western edge of Atlantic basin	From equator towards the Pole	Warm	Fast, deep and narrow
Atlantic (North Equatorial)	Northern	North of equator	From Africa to South America	Warming	Slow, shallow and wide
Atlantic (Benguela)	Southern	Eastern edge of Atlantic basin	From Pole towards the equator	Cold	Slow, shallow and wide
Atlantic (Antarctic Circumpolar)	Southern	Southern edge of Atlantic basin	West to east around Antarctica	Cooling	Slow; largest volume current
Atlantic (South Equatorial)	Southern	South of equator	From Africa to South America	Warming	Slow, shallow and wide
Atlantic (Brazil)	Southern	Western edge of Atlantic basin	From equator towards the Pole	Warm	Fast, deep and narrow
Pacific (Kuroshio)	Northern	Western edge of Pacific basin	From equator towards the Pole	Warm	Fast, deep and narrow
Pacific (North Pacific)	Northern	Northern edge of Pacific basin	From Asia to North America	Cooling	Slow, shallow and wide
Pacific (North Equatorial)	Northern	North of equator	From Central America to Southeast Asia	Warming	Slow, shallow and wide
Pacific (California)	Northern	Eastern edge of Pacific basin	From Pole towards the equator	Cold	Slow, shallow and wide
Pacific (Peru)	Southern	Eastern edge of Pacific basin	From Pole towards the equator	Cold	Slow, shallow and wide
Pacific (East Australian)	Southern	Western edge of Pacific basin	From equator towards the Pole	Warm	Fast, deep and narrow
Pacific (Antarctic Circumpolar)	Southern	Southern edge of Pacific basin	West to east around Antarctica	Cooling	Slow; largest volume current
Pacific (South Equatorial)	Southern	South of equator	From South America towards Australia	Warming	Slow, shallow and wide

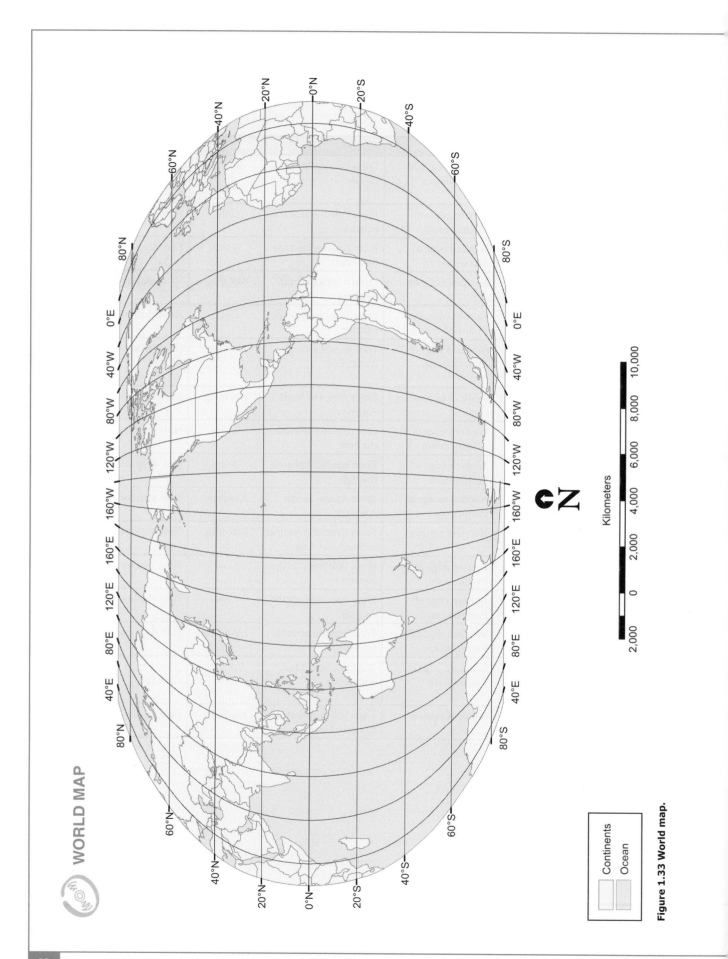

N

Kilometers

2,000   0   2,000   4,000   6,000   8,000   10,000

Continents

Ocean

Figure 1.33 World map.

DEEP WATER CIRCULATION
(Thanks to Turtle Haste, USA)

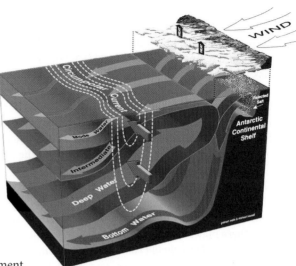

Lesson at a glance
Students use data tables and graphs to explore the role of salinity and temperature in deep ocean circulation.

Background
Circulation in the ocean is unified through a global conveyor belt that connects ocean surface and deep-water circulation. Deep ocean circulation is driven primarily by slight differences in water density that are caused by variations in temperature and salinity, and is sometimes referred to as *thermohaline circulation.*

Thermohaline circulation involves the creation and movement of unique *water masses*. These are large homogeneous volumes of water that possess a characteristic range of temperature and salinity. Most deep water masses form at high latitudes at the ocean surface where they acquire their unique low temperature and high salinity.

Figure 1.34 Distinct water masses in the Southern Ocean near Antarctica play an important role in global ocean circulation.

In the North Atlantic, the main driver producing the *North Atlantic Deep Water* (NADW) is the strong heat loss to the atmosphere. In the Southern Ocean, precipitation patterns and sea ice formation in the Weddell and Ross Sea regions around Antarctica drive the formation of *Antarctic Bottom Water* (AABW), which is some of the densest water on Earth.

These extremely dense waters sink until they reach an area where the surrounding water has the same density. There they begin to flow 'horizontally', channelled by submarine features. These deep waters move slowly in comparison to the well defined gyres of surface currents; in fact, water at the bottom of the Pacific can be as much as 800 years old.

The water masses gradually warm and mix with overlying waters as they flow towards lower latitudes, rising slowly at the rate of only a few metres per year. This upward mixing is also important in sustaining the global overturning circulation. If there was no upward mixing, the ocean would fill up with cold water and the overturning circulation would be suppressed. The upward mixing balances the formation of deep waters near the Poles.

The identification of different water masses allows scientists to monitor the transport of water on a global scale.

Time
Preparation: 30 minutes
Class time: 1–2 class periods *(~45 minutes each)*

Materials
(per student)
• graph paper and pencils
• *Water Mass Exercise* worksheet
• colour copy of *Pine Island Glacier Data Reports*

(per class)
• overhead of *Water Mass Exercise* worksheet

Water Mass Exercise Worksheet

Pine Island Data Reports

Activity Directions
1. Show the students the North Central Atlantic Ocean Sample Data Table on the *Water Mass Exercise* worksheet *(Table 1)*. Explain that a water sample was taken from a stationary research vessel in the central North Atlantic Ocean. Researchers lowered a CTD (Conductivity, Temperature, and Depth device) down to the bottom of the ocean. (Show a picture of the CTD, *Figure 1.35.*) The CTD took salinity and temperature measurements as it was lowered; as it was raised, it collected water samples at specific depths. These water samples were then analysed for different chemical and biological properties.

2. Have the students graph the temperature and salinity data from *Table 1*. Place salinity (33.5 to 36.5 psu) on the x-axis and temperature (–0.2 to 20.0 °C) on the y-axis.

3. Ask the students why water collected from one location might have such different properties. Discuss their ideas.

4. Tell them to use the Water Mass Table *(Table 2)* to identify the water masses listed in the North Central Atlantic Ocean Sample Data Table *(Table 1)*, and then write the water mass names by the appropriate description.

5. Ask them to label the water masses, in order by depth, at the sample site shown on the Central Atlantic Ocean Profile *(Figure 1.36)*. Note: Mediterranean Intermediate Water (MIW) will be identified through the process of elimination for the 1,000 m depth, as all of the other properties also fit within the range for North Atlantic Central Surface Water (NACSW).

6. Use a world map to discuss where the water masses might be formed based on their names.

7. Show students the *Pine Island Glacier Data Reports (Figure 1.37 and 1.38)*. Ask them to use the temperature and salinity data to identify where the different deep water masses might be located on the CTD graphs. Discuss why there may be more of one type of water mass present than others. *(This sample was taken during an austral summer. Students should consider the influence of melting fresh water from sea ice and the glacier as well as the proximity to AABW in the Ross and Weddell Seas.)*

Note: Units for salinity were traditionally given as parts per thousand. However, the current convention is to use *practical salinity units* (psu) because salinity measurements are now generally based on electrical conductivity rather than an analysis of dissolved salts.

Discussion

1. What environmental or atmospheric factors cause the formation of the different water masses? *(Temperature differences and density differences resulting from the addition or removal of salts from ocean water through evaporation, sea ice formation and melting, melting of land-based ice, precipitation, etc.)*

2. Why are some water masses formed in the polar and others in the equatorial regions? *(Both the formation of sea ice in higher latitudes and evaporation in the tropics remove fresh water from sea water leaving denser water.)*

3. What might be at the bottom of the northern Atlantic Ocean that would channel the newly formed North Atlantic Deep Water as it moves along the bottom? *(Use an ocean floor map and discuss how submarine features may direct the flow of water.)*

Extensions/Adaptations

1. For kinesthetic learners, illustrate the water column by physically arranging the students in a line corresponding to different depths.

2. Research the geographic locations where the Atlantic Ocean water masses form.

3. Investigate why the Arctic Ocean does or does not contribute to the formation of high latitude water masses.

Figure 1.35 CTD rosette.

A Conductivity, Temperature and Depth (CTD) device measures water salinity and temperature at different depths in the ocean. Ocean water is also collected using a set of bottles (called Nisken bottles) arranged around the CTD in a rosette.

The CTD rosette is winched out from the side of the ship and lowered to within 10 metres of the ocean floor, measuring temperature and salinity as it goes down. All of the Nisken bottles are open as it is lowered. As the instrument is being raised to the surface, each bottle is closed by remote control at a different depth, providing a water sample from that depth.

As well as getting data about salinity and temperature at different depths, scientists conduct a range of tests on the water samples to learn more about dissolved oxygen, phosphate, nitrite, ammonia, silicon, organic carbon, alkalinity, and even bacteria and viruses.

Table 1: North Central Atlantic Ocean Sample Data Table

Depth Collected (metres)	Temperature (°C)	Salinity (psu)	Density (g/mL)	Water Mass Name
100	15.0	36.0	1.0267	
500	4.0	34.2	1.0273	
1,000	10.0	35.8	1.0276	
2,000	4.0	34.9	1.0283	
4,000	0.0	34.7	1.0281	

Table 2: Water Mass Table

Water Mass Name	Temperature Range (°C)	Salinity Range (psu)	Density (g/mL)
Antarctic Bottom Water (AABW)	0.0	34.6–34.8	1.0270–1.0265
Antarctic Intermediate Water (AAIW)	3.0–6.0	34.1–34.3	1.0275–1.0280
North Atlantic Central Surface Water (NACSW)	9.0–17.0	35.1–36.3	1.0270–1.0280
Mediterranean Intermediate Water (MIW)	9.0–14.0	35.6–36.5	1.0270–1.0280
North Atlantic Deep Water (NADW)	3.0–6.0	34.1–34.4	1.0270–1.0280

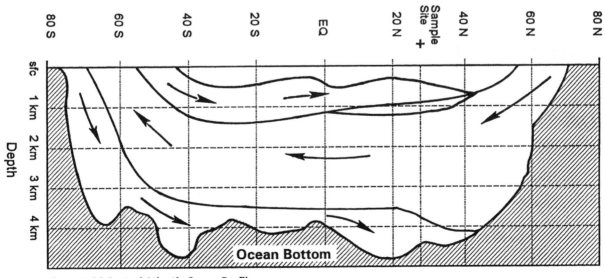

Figure 1.36 Central Atlantic Ocean Profile.

CTD data from Pine Island Glacier in the Amundsen Sea, Antarctica collected during the Nathan B. Palmer Cruise (NBP0901).

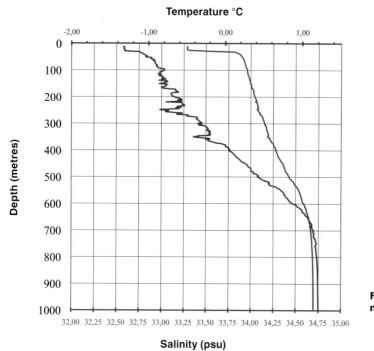

Figure 1.37 Pine Island Bay near Pine Island Ice Shelf.

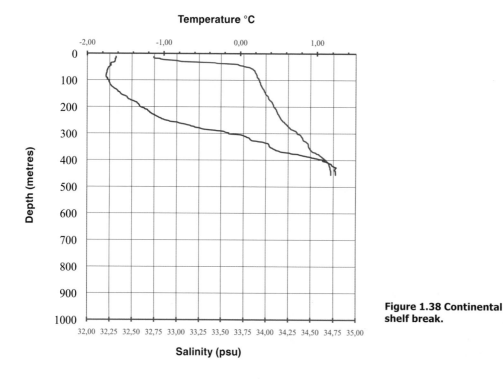

Figure 1.38 Continental shelf break.

✳ SEA ICE POROSITY AND OCEAN ECOSYSTEMS

(Thanks to Josep Marlés Tortosa, Spain)

Lesson at a glance

Students use ice samples and a coloured dye to investigate differences in the structure of sea ice and freshwater ice.

Background

The structure of sea ice is critical to the stability of polar marine ecosystems. Sea ice is made up of a combination of solid ice, air and liquid brine. The existence of brine channels in the sea ice is a major difference between sea ice and freshwater ice. During spring and summer, the brine channels extend through thousands of square kilometres of sea ice, and host entire microbial ecosystems. These ecosystems are an important food source for other marine organisms, especially after ice break up when the material trapped and accumulated within the brines over the winter is released into the open ocean.

Brine channels form when sea water freezes. The salts in the water cannot be incorporated into ice crystals, so they are expelled as the crystals grow. As a consequence, the salt concentration in the interior remaining water increases, and this highly concentrated brine becomes trapped in inclusions between the pure ice platelets. Larger connected brine channels also form, which help facilitate fluid flow through the ice. This makes sea ice much more porous than freshwater ice.

The main organisms living in the brine inclusions are microscopic algae and bacteria. The algae are the primary producers and provide the initial food source for *heterotrophic* organisms such as bacteria, protists, and eventually crustaceans and larger organisms.

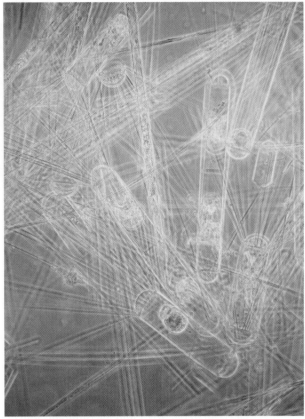

Figure 1.39 Diatoms, common algae found in sea ice brine channels.

Heterotrophic bacteria in all ecosystems, including those that occur in the sea ice, grow by consuming dissolved organic matter. The dissolved organic matter comes from the excretions of organisms living in the ice and cells of dead organisms. The bacterial transformation of organic molecules into inorganic matter *(remineralisation)* is an essential mechanism for the life of the algae, because the algae require the inorganic molecules as nutrients.

Algae constitute the primary producers in the marine ecosystem, since they are the base of the food web. The trapping and growth of these algae in the brine pores and channels of the pack ice, and their release during the months of melting are fundamental to the existence of all organisms that are part of the polar ecosystems.

Time

Preparation: Several hours *(to freeze ice cubes)*
Class time: 45 minutes

Materials

(per group of 3–4 students)
- 1 saltwater ice cube and 1 freshwater ice cube
- dropper bottle of dye in alcohol solution *(e.g., food colouring dissolved in rubbing alcohol)*
- shallow plastic dishes *(to place the ice cubes)*

Activity Directions

1. The day before doing the activity, prepare two different types of ice cubes—freshwater and saltwater. To prepare the saltwater ice, dissolve 3.5 grams of kitchen salt in 100 millilitres of demineralised or distilled water.
2. Give each group of students one saltwater ice cube, one freshwater ice cube and a dropper bottle of dye. Instruct them to place a drop of dye on each of the ice cubes and observe what happens.
3. Discuss their observations and the significance of the differences.

Figure 1.40 The ice fragment on the left is saltwater ice; the fragment on the right is freshwater ice.

Figure 1.41 This photo shows the colour difference a few minutes after the dye was placed on the samples.

Discussion

1. What differences did you observe between the two ice samples? *(The dye has run off the freshwater ice, which remains mostly white in colour. The saltwater ice has soaked up the dye and turned blue.)* What caused the differences? *(The dye moved directly into the brine channels in the saltwater ice. The freshwater ice is not porous enough to absorb the dye solution.)*
2. Why is it important for the ocean ecosystem that sea ice is porous? *(Many organisms live in the brine inclusions and channels, forming an important part of the marine food web—see background information for more detail.)*
3. Can sea ice have differing salinities? *(Yes)* What could cause this? *(The salinity is influenced to some extent by the salinity of the water from which the sea ice formed. Ice that formed in brackish areas where sea water and fresh water are mixed, such as in the Baltic Sea in northern Europe, has a lower salinity. However, most sea ice forms in the open ocean in the Arctic and the Antarctic, and here the age of the sea ice determines the salinity. Cold, highly saline brines are very dense and can drain out of the sea ice over time. The rate of ice formation can have also a small influence on the salinity—rapid ice growth can trap more brine, so that ice gains a higher salinity.)*
4. What is happening to multi-year sea ice in the Arctic (ice that lasts for more than one season and does not melt during the summer), and why is it important to the ocean ecosystem? *(Multi-year sea ice is decreasing in the Arctic. This is detrimental to the ecosystem because there are many ice-associated organisms that survive better at the underside of sea ice than in the water column. These organisms need the sea ice for protection over the summer. Multi-year sea ice is also thicker and stronger, and better able to support the weight of large marine mammals such as polar bears.)*
5. What is the benefit of dissolving the colouring in alcohol before doing this experiment? *(Adding alcohol lowers the freezing temperature of the dye. If the ice is very cold, without alcohol [or salt, which also depresses the freezing point], the dye may freeze before it has time to percolate down into the brine channels.)*

Real Science: Sea Ice Porosity Research in Antarctica

Although it may look like a bizarre art project, Dr Ken Golden, a theoretical mathematician from the University of Utah, was studying sea ice porosity during the IPY SIPEX voyage in the Antarctic.

He and his assistants cut rectangular blocks of sea ice with a chainsaw and hauled them out of the water. They turned one block so that it was right-side up and another so that the underside of the ice was facing up. After cutting a couple of grooves in the tops of the blocks, they poured salt water tinted with orange food dye into the grooves and watched what happened.

The purpose of the experiment was to improve their understanding of how fluids such as brine or seawater move up and down through sea ice—an important factor in both biological and physical studies. The speed with which the coloured water percolated down through the ice showed how porous the ice was. The coloured water also highlighted the structure of the brine channels.

Sea ice porosity depends on temperature and salinity, with warmer ice being much more porous. The underside of the ice block, which had been in contact with the ocean water, was much warmer than the surface, which had been in contact with the colder air. When the coloured water was poured on the upside down block, it spread downward through the ice much more rapidly than it did on the block that was right-side up.

The data from these experiments will be used to test the ability of mathematical models to predict the fluid transport properties of sea ice. The data will also be used to test models of electrical conductivity.

Figures 1.42, 1.43, 1.44 (top to bottom): Pouring the dye, timing the percolation in the two blocks; brine channels highlighted by the dye.

POLAR FEASTS!

(Thanks to Claudia V. Garcia, Anne Giangiulio, Vanessa Lougheed, Bill Robertson and Craig Tweedie, USA)

Lesson at a glance

Students discover how different organisms that live in the polar regions depend on each other and what might happen to the food web if one or more organisms disappears from it.

Background

All animals must eat other organisms to obtain energy for processes such as cell growth, reproduction, movement and respiration. This can be represented by a simple *food chain* with arrows connecting the organisms. The arrows show the direction of energy transfer, starting from the Sun, and then going from one living thing to another.

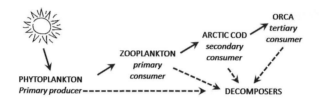

Figure 1.45 Simple marine food chain.

- *Primary producers* are at the bottom of the food chain. They use energy from the sun, water and carbon dioxide to grow. Most primary producers on land are plants; most primary producers in the ocean are phytoplankton, commonly known as algae.
- Primary consumers (*herbivores*) are animals that get their energy from eating primary producers.
- Secondary consumers (*carnivores*) get their energy from eating mainly meat from other animals.
- Tertiary consumers (*top predators*) are carnivores at the top of the food chain. Generally, when they are adults, no other animals eat them.
- *Decomposers* such as bacteria and fungi are also an important part of all ecosystems. When an organism that is not eaten by something else dies, its body is broken down by decomposers; the resulting nutrients, such as carbon, nitrogen and other elements, are recycled in the ecosystem.

Most animals do not eat just one thing, nor are they eaten by only one thing. This results in a *food web*—a complex feeding relationship among organisms that interconnects all organisms in a community. By understanding how a food web is organised, it is easier to make sense of which organisms have stronger interactions within the community.

Time

Preparation: 20 minutes *(to photocopy and cut out food web)*
Class time: 50–60 minutes

Materials

(per group of 3–4 students)
- *Antarctic* or *Arctic Food Web Cards*
- small poster board or space on a whiteboard or chalkboard
- tape
- markers or chalk *(depending on board type)*

 Antarctic and Arctic Food Web Cards

Activity Directions

1. Review the concepts of food chains and food webs with the students.
2. Divide them into groups and give each group a set of food web cards. (If you want to compare the two polar regions; give some groups Antarctic and others Arctic cards.)

3. Tell them to build a food web, using the information on the cards. They should start with producers and work up to the top consumer. Remind them to study the relationship between each organism carefully.
4. When they are satisfied with the placement of the organisms, they should secure their food web onto the poster board with tape and draw the arrows showing the direction of energy flow.
5. Let them play a food web game with another team to see how well they understand the feeding relationships of the community. Give the following instructions:
   a. The purpose of the game is to crash your opponents' food web by removing as many cards as possible from their food web in three turns.
   b. In this game, you cannot eliminate the primary producer—only consumers.
   c. Start the game by removing an organism from your opponents' food web. Your group will keep the card and discuss what happened to the food web when you eliminated that organism. If there are any animals that feed *only* on the organism you took out (i.e., they have no other food source), you may take those cards too.
   d. The other team then removes one or more cards from your food web.
   e. The winning team is the one who gets the most cards from their opponents in three turns.

Discussion
1. Which organism depicted in this food web is a primary producer? Where do producers obtain their energy? *(Algae are the primary producers in this food web and they obtain their energy from the sun by the process of photosynthesis.)*
2. Which organisms in this food web are primary consumers? Which one is the top consumer and why? *(Krill [in the Antarctic] and copepods [in the Arctic] are important primary consumers since they feed on the primary producers [algae]. The top consumers in the Antarctic web are the orca and leopard seals. The top consumer in the Arctic web is the polar bear. These animals are meat eaters or carnivores; they are considered top consumers because they have no natural predators other than humans.)*
3. How do you think tiny krill provide enough energy to sustain whales? *(Both krill and copepods occur in large swarms and are a fat-rich source of food. A single swarm of krill can weigh more than a ton!)*
4. What would happen if krill were to vanish from the ecosystem? *(Krill are key prey species for many animals like whales, penguins and crabeater seals. Other animals depend indirectly on them. For example, seals and penguins feed on fish that feed on krill. Without krill the population of many organisms would rapidly decline.)*
5. Which organisms have the most selective diets? Can this be an advantage or disadvantage? *(The Antarctic organisms with the most selective diets are the crabeater seals and fish; both feed mainly on krill. This can be a disadvantage. If they only feed on one organism they will be affected if their prey declines in numbers.)*

Extensions/Adaptations
1. Have the students write journal entries (using pictures and/or words) describing how the food web works. Have them label the producers and primary, secondary and tertiary consumers. Ask them to add humans to the web and describe their role.
2. Have students research other organisms that live in the Arctic or Antarctic and add them in the appropriate places to their food webs.
3. For younger students: Use the game board provided at http://ipyroam.utep.edu/education/polar-resource-book to learn about food chains.

Photo: Patti Virtue

Algae convert solar energy into chemical energy.

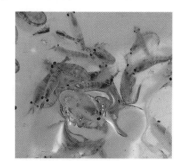

Photo: Simon Marsland

Krill feed on microscopic algae.

Photo: Adrian Boyle

Leopard seals eat a wide variety of prey: krill, fish, penguins and young crabeater seals.

Photo: Sandra Zicus

There are 8 species of **penguins** in or near Antarctica. Most penguins feed on krill and fish.

Photo: NOAA

Humpback whales feed on krill and small fish.

Photo: NOAA

Orcas (Killer whales) feed on penguins, fish, and some seals (e.g., crabeater seals). They may feed on other species of whales, including young humpbacks.

Photo: Paul Thomson

Many species of **fish** in Antarctica feed on krill.

Photo: Jerzy Strzelecki

Crabeater seals feed on krill (not crabs!).

Photo: Adrian Boyle

Antarctic petrels eat krill, squid and small fish.

Photo: Patti Virtue

Algae convert solar energy into chemical energy.

Photo: NOAA

Copepods and other invertebrates (animals without a backbone) feed on microscopic algae.

Photo: Sandra Zicus

Polar bears prefer to eat ringed and bearded seals, but will also eat arctic fox, walrus and beluga whales.

Photo: Merrick Peirce

Arctic fox eat ringed seal pups.

Photo: NOAA

Arctic cod eat krill and other aquatic invertebrates.

Photo: Sandra Zicus

Ringed seal eat arctic cod, as well as other fish.

Photo: Sandra Zicus

Walrus eat bottom-dwelling organisms such as clams.

Photo: NOAA

Beluga whales eat primarily fish, such as Arctic cod.

Photo: Fisheries and Oceans Canada

Clams eat algae.

BLUBBER INSULATION

(Thanks to Louise Huffman and Bill Grosser, USA)

Lesson at a glance

Students experiment with a 'blubber glove' to see how insulation affects heat transfer and how blubber helps polar animals survive in bitterly cold conditions.

Background

Many animals in the Arctic and Antarctic are fat . . . really, really fat. Whales, penguins, seals and walruses all have a thick layer of fatty tissue called *blubber* under their skins that helps insulate them from the cold climate. Blubber can make up as much as half of the body mass of some marine mammals. In some large whales, such as right whales and bowheads, the blubber layer can be up to 30 centimetres thick.

Blubber is an especially effective insulator for deep-diving animals because it does not compress under pressure. It also has extra blood vessels that constrict in very cold conditions, further limiting heat loss.

For some marine mammals this layer of insulation means that they have to develop behaviours to prevent themselves from overheating, especially when on land or when very active. Seals, for example, may fan their flippers out to increase their surface area for cooling when resting on land, or they may rest in shallow water to keep cool.

Blubber has other important functions in addition to thermoregulation. It contains special fat-like substances called *lipids*. Arctic and Antarctic animals go without food for long periods and then gorge on plentiful food for brief periods. Lipids serve as a key storage medium to help them survive the fasting periods.

Blubber also helps give animals a streamlined shape for swimming, which makes them more energy efficient when moving through water.

Time

Preparation: 60 minutes
Class time: 60 minutes

Materials

(per group blubber glove)
• 2 hand-sized (~4 litre) food storage bags with zip strips
• ~ 4 cups vegetable shortening
• duct tape

Fat Bird, Skinny Bird Worksheet

(per group of 3–4 students)
• 1 large plastic bin, ¾ full of water and ice *(to serve as the cold polar 'ocean')*
• 1 blubber glove *(see directions for construction)*
• 2 large zipper lock plastic food storage bags *(zipped together to make a double layer)*
• 1 paper *(to draw a data table and graph, see 'Fat Bird, Skinny Bird' worksheet.)*
• 2 thermometers
• 2 small jars *(each full of room temperature water)*

Advance Preparation

To make the gloves:
1. Place the vegetable shortening inside one of the zip food bags.
2. Turn the other zip bag inside out and put your hand in it. Put the hand protected by the clean bag into the bag with shortening and knead the shortening all around your hand until it is completely insulated.
3. Remove your hand and zip the two bags together, match the zip sides of the bag on your hand to the opposite colour zip strip on the bag with the shortening in it.
4. Reinforce around the zippers with tape to avoid accidents when children handle the glove.

Activity Directions

Part 1—Testing the gloves

1. Have the students place the blubber glove on one hand and the empty zipped-together bags on the other hand, then predict how long they will be able to keep each hand in the ice water.
2. Have them test their predictions by placing both hands in the cold 'ocean' being careful not to let water enter either bag. A partner might need to help hold the tops up out of the 'ocean'.

Part 2—Quantifying the results

1. Discuss the students' experience with the blubber glove. Which hand felt warmer? Explain that they are now going to validate their claims by gathering some evidence with a quantitative experiment. The blubber glove will represent a 'fat' penguin, and the empty bags will represent a 'skinny' bird like a stork or egret that lives in a warm climate.
2. Give the following instructions:
    a. Put a thermometer in each of the small jars of room temperature water and let them stand for at least 1 minute. They should both be the same temperature.
    b. Draw 2 identical blank graphs, with time on the x-axis (from 0–10 minutes) and temperature on the y-axis (with 25°C at the top and 0° at the bottom). Label one graph 'Prediction' and the second graph 'Experimental Results'. *(See 'Fat Bird, Skinny Bird Example Graph' worksheet.)*
    c. Make a key on each graph, using different colours to represent the two birds.
    d. On one graph, draw your prediction for each bird. How do you think the temperature will change during 10 minutes in the cold 'ocean'?
    e. Place one of the small jars of water inside the blubber glove and the other jar in the empty plastic bags.
    f. Take a temperature reading of the jars of water and record this as the starting temperature on the 'Experimental Results' graph.
    g. Place each bag in the ice water, being careful not to let any water from the 'ocean' leak into the bags.
    h. Take readings every 30 seconds for 10 minutes and record them on the experimental graph.
    i. Compare your predicted results with your experimental results. Write a reflection paragraph about your observations. What did this activity demonstrate about animals with blubber?

Discussion

1. How does blubber help animals survive in cold environments? *(It serves as insulation to stop heat transfer to the cold and provides an energy reserve to generate heat and provide nutrition when food resources are scarce in the winter.)*
2. Does blubber keep the heat in or the cold out? *(Heat energy flows from areas of more energy to areas of less energy, so blubber insulates by keeping the warmth of the animals' bodies from going into the cold ocean.)*
3. What are some other body adaptations that allow animals to live in very cold places? *(Some animals have an antifreeze protein that keeps ice crystals from forming in their blood. Penguins have a layer of air trapped under their feathers, which also helps insulate them. They also have extra blood vessels in their feet to increase the surface supply of blood. This keeps their feet from freezing when they touch the cold ice. In addition to blubber, polar bears have a dense coat of underfur with an outer layer of hollow-shafted hairs.)*

Extensions/Adaptations

Discuss other ways animals are insulated against the cold. Penguins have about 10–12 feathers per square centimetre, which trap air against the bird's skin. Is air an effective insulator? Try this activity to answer the question:

1. Put a flat, empty plastic food bag on your hand and place an ice cube in the palm of your hand. Do you feel the cold?
2. Now blow up the bag and zip it closed, trapping air inside. Place it in the palm of your hand with an ice cube on top. Describe your sensations.

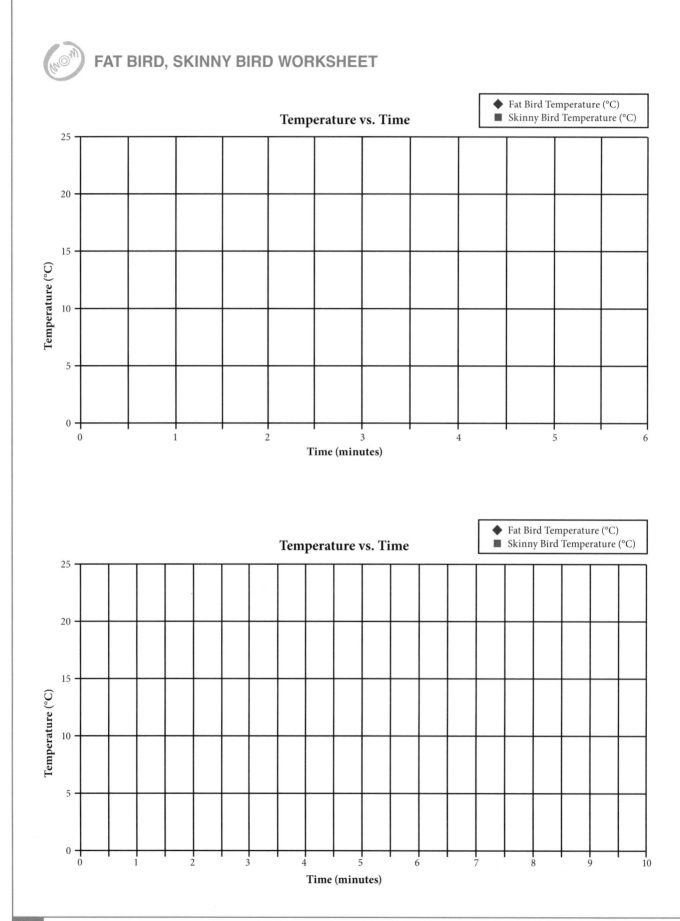

LAND

Studying Arctic and Antarctic land masses provides us with numerous examples of how soil and fresh water interact to form complex ecological systems and how these fragile systems react to dramatic environmental changes.

Snow and ice cover are declining in the polar regions, exposing the underlying soil to the forces of wind, rain and solar radiation. As a consequence, local warming and thawing cause a complex web of alterations in vegetation, water availability, the migration patterns of animals and the survival strategies of human populations in these extreme environments.

Expansion of shrubs due to climate change in the Arctic can alter the way wind flows over the surface, and affect the location and depth of snow accumulation. Snow accumulation may be increased in the shelter of shrubs. Nearby, the snow might be completely blown away, leaving the ground uncovered. Because snow is a good insulator, uncovered ground may freeze more quickly or deeply; however, it might also warm and thaw more rapidly in the sunlight. These alterations have implications for grazing animals and small animals that live in burrows under the snow. Changes in the habitat and migration of grazers and burrowers may induce further changes in vegetation. These changes also affect the availability of food resources for human populations in the Arctic.

Arctic warming is causing a decrease in sea ice, which is also affecting the landscape. Coastal regions are eroding by as much as 30 metres per year from a combination of sea level rise (due to warmer sea surface temperatures causing ocean thermal expansion) and larger waves reaching the coast (because there is less sea ice to damp the waves). Changes in sea ice conditions could also be influencing weather patterns in the Arctic and beyond by altering the heat exchange between the atmosphere and the ocean.

Arctic hydrology is also changing as a result of thawing *permafrost*, changes in weather patterns, and melting snow cover. The timing and amount of freshwater run-off from rivers has an impact on local ocean chemistry, circulation, and sea ice cover. Changes in these systems influence erosion on land, and also affect ecosystems in the polar seas.

In Antarctica, mountain ranges with peaks towering more than 3,000 metres high are covered by enormous inland ice sheets. These regions hold clues to understanding how melted glacial ice affects

**Figure 1.46
A tenacious willow clings to the rocks in the Canadian Arctic.**

streambed ecology and hydrology. Why, for example, does the growth of green algae in perennial frozen lakes in Antarctica change from year to year? How can measurements of Antarctic streambed pebbles tell us something about streambed characteristics and their effect on vegetation?

Understanding this intricate web of soil, water, vegetation, animal and human interactions is one of the most interdisciplinary challenges in polar science. The activities in this section give you a chance to explore some of these complex questions.

Land Activities

THE EARTH THROUGH TIME

RECONSTRUCTING PAST CLIMATES AND ENVIRONMENTS

FORMATION OF GLACIAL VALLEYS

PERMAFROST AND TEMPERATURE CHANGES

OPTIMAL FORAGING

THE EARTH THROUGH TIME
(Thanks to Sandra Zicus, Australia; and Louise Huffman, USA)

Lesson at a glance

Students build a 'living timeline' to visualise how the Earth developed over the past 650 million years, and how this has affected the polar regions.

Background

The Earth's climate has alternated between 'hothouse' and 'icehouse' conditions for at least 2.5 billion years when progressive *protozoans* and the first simple multicellular organisms formed. During an icehouse period, temperatures in the polar regions are low enough for large areas to be covered by permanent ice, sea level is lower, and the overall global climate is cooler and drier. By contrast, there is no year-round ice on the surface of the Earth during a hothouse period, sea levels are higher, and global climate is warm and humid.

The geometry of Earth's orbit around the Sun, the proportion of carbon dioxide (CO_2) in the atmosphere, and the positions of the continents are some of the main long-term factors that determine whether hothouse or icehouse conditions predominate. Each of these factors creates its own feedback system, making it very difficult to unravel its exact role in the climate process.

According to the *theory of plate tectonics*, the Earth's rigid outermost layer is broken into several large and small plates that move relative to one another on top of a hotter, more mobile material. At certain times in the Earth's geologic history, there have been large continental masses over one of the poles. This, combined with low atmospheric CO_2 levels, has favoured the formation of glacial ice. More ice increases the Earth's albedo and leads to further cooling, resulting in an icehouse epoch that may last tens of millions of years.

The Earth has gone through several major glacial stages in the last 600 million years. The most recent ice age started about 35 million years ago and peaked in the last 700,000 years (the latter part of the Pleistocene). During an icehouse epoch, there are oscillations of colder and warmer times, where continental glaciers advance and retreat. The present arrangement of cold ice-covered regions at both poles only dates to around 3 million years ago. We are presently in a warm phase of the current icehouse epoch, known as an *interglacial period*.

Within this global icehouse condition, cycles of ocean-atmosphere interaction give rise to regional climate variations on scales of decades to centuries. Identifying and predicting the impacts of human-induced climate change requires a careful understanding of these natural forces of planetary change.

Time

Preparation: 30–45 minutes
Class time: 45 minutes or more *(depending on the level of discussion)*

Materials

(one set)
- 6.5 metres rope *(1 cm = 1 million years)*
- Earth history information and *Earth history cards*
- *palaeomaps*
- markers

**Earth History Cards
Palaeomaps**

Advance Preparations

Mark the rope every 10 cm into 65 equal sections. This will make it easier to find the right approximate positions on the rope when you make the timeline.

Activity Directions

1. Stretch the rope across the floor or along a wall. Explain to the students that the rope represents Earth's history from 650 million years ago, when the first *macroscopic* (i.e., large enough to be visible to the naked eye) multicellular organisms began to appear, to the present day. Discuss the concept of scale and tell them that each centimetre on the rope equals 1 million years of Earth history.

2. Post the palaeomaps near the line at the appropriate points and introduce or review the concept of plate tectonics.

3. Distribute the cards for the different time events to the students.
4. Instruct them take their cards and stand on or near the rope at the appropriate locations.
5. Take a tour of the timeline by having the students read their cards aloud, starting 650 million years ago and continuing up to the present.

Discussion
1. How did the position of the continents affect the global climate? *(The position of the continents controls the shape and connectedness of ocean basins, and affects the circulation of the ocean between the equator and the Poles. If there are no continents along the equator, the Equatorial Current can circle the Earth repeatedly, picking up a lot of heat. This will raise the temperature of the ocean and moderate the global climate. When continents are located along the equator, as at the present day, ocean water spends less time in the tropics and is deflected into higher latitudes to cool.)*
2. What other events impacted climate over geologic time? *(Changes in the composition of the atmosphere, especially the content of greenhouse gases, have large impacts. Higher levels of atmospheric CO_2 and methane correlate with higher global temperatures due to the absorption of heat in the atmosphere. Low levels of greenhouse gases generally correlate with periods of lower global temperatures. Changes in the greenhouse gas content of the atmosphere have been linked to large-scale volcanism, which can cause short-term cooling due the input of aerosols and longer-term warming due to increased CO_2. The rise of large mountain ranges can cause cooling by consuming CO_2 through weathering and erosion of rocks, as the rising of the Himalaya Mountains may have caused cooling over the past 20–30 million years. The burial of large amounts of carbon as coal or carbonate rock can decrease CO_2 in the atmosphere and result in cooling. It is suggested that large asteroid or comet impacts on Earth could result in climate change, but this has not been confirmed. Cooling also tends to trap methane on the seafloor as gas hydrates and in tundra at high latitudes, further limiting greenhouse gases. Warming may break down gas hydrates, and release large amounts of methane from the sea floor and from tundra.)*
3. What do you think will happen in the future and why?

Extensions/Adaptations
1. For younger students: Shorten the timeline to consider just the past 65 million years (more or less from the time of the dinosaurs to human beings).
2. For older students: Have them research other events in the geologic past to add to the timeline. They could also research how the Earth's tectonic plates are moving now and how the continents will be positioned at various times in the distant future. They could investigate what organisms have appeared and disappeared during Earth's history, and why certain organisms have gone extinct.
3. Experiment with concepts of scale by changing the scale on the timeline. How many metres of rope would you need to go back to the formation of the Earth 4.6 billion years ago if you were to use the same scale?

EARTH HISTORY INFORMATION

(Adapted from Chris R. Scotese Palaeomap Project at www.scotese.com)

650 Million: 'Ice House' world, more severe than present day. Development of the first macroscopic multi-cellular organisms.

600 Million: Present-day Antarctica is located near the equator, surrounded by India, Africa and South America.

530 Million: Sudden appearance and rapid expansion of marine animals with hard shells. Continents are flooded by warm, shallow seas. Supercontinent Gondwana is located near the South Pole.

458 Million: Oceans separate the barren continents and ice caps form across much of Gondwana. Marine mass extinction due to changing sea levels and ocean *anoxia* (lack of oxygen).

425 Million: Coral reefs expand as climate warms and land plants begin to colonise the previously barren continents.

364 Million: Glaciers cover parts of South America, located close to the South Pole. Major marine extinction event, possibly associated with volcanism in Eastern Europe.

356 Million: Assembly of supercontinent Pangaea begins as continents merge and move northward. Southern Hemisphere cools and an ice cap begins to grow at the South Pole.

325 Million: Rainforests cover the tropical regions of Pangaea, bounded to the north and south by deserts. Southern polar ice cap expands.

306 Million: Western half of Pangaea is complete with extensive coal swamps along the equator and glaciation across the Southern Hemisphere.

280 Million: Much of the Southern Hemisphere is covered by glaciers. Coal forms in both equatorial rainforests and in temperate forests during the warmer 'interglacial' periods.

250 Million: Assembly of Pangaea is complete. Equatorial rainforests disappear and deserts expand. Rapid global warming may have created a super 'Hot House' world.

250 Million: Global extinction of 90% of all species, possibly due to changing climate, sea levels and ocean circulation, and massive volcanism in Siberia.

237 Million: Life begins to recover and re-diversify after the great extinction. The interior of Pangaea is dry and the polar regions are warm, even during the winter.

206 Million: Major mass extinction event, possibly due to climate change from massive global volcanism and a large meteor impact.

180 Million: Strong monsoon climate in eastern Pangaea; interior is very arid and hot. Deserts cover present-day Amazon and Congo rainforests.

152 Million: Initial break-up of Pangaea with rifting between Laurasia and Gondwana. The interior of continents becomes less dry. Seasonal snow and ice in the polar regions.

150 Million: Africa and South America start to separate. Laurasia drifts northward.

140 Million: Mild 'Ice House' world. There is snow and ice during the winter seasons, and cool temperate forests cover the polar regions.

94 Million: Opening of the South Atlantic Ocean separates South America and Africa. India separates from Madagascar and moves rapidly north. North America is still connected to Europe, and Australia to Antarctica. 'Hot House' climate with no ice at the Poles.

90 Million: Australia and Antarctica begin to separate.

66 Million: Atlantic Ocean widens. India approaches the southern margin of Asia. Mass extinction of 60–80% of all living species, possibly due to major asteroid impact, extensive volcanic activity, and rapid changes in sea level and global temperatures.

55 Million: Opening of the North Atlantic Ocean. 'Hot House' climate with palm trees in Greenland and Patagonia, and mangrove swamps in southern Australia at 65° South. Alligators swim in swamps near the North Pole.

50.2 Million: India collides with Asia forming the Tibetan plateau and Himalayas. Australia separates from Antarctica and moves rapidly northward. Drake Passage begins to open, separating South America and Antarctica.

35 Million: Tasman Gateway opens between Australia and Antarctica, allowing formation of the Antarctic Circumpolar Current. Rapid cooling in Antarctica and formation of ice at the South Pole.

25 Million: Fram Strait begins to open between Greenland and Canada.

14 Million: Antarctica is covered by ice and northern continents are cooling rapidly. Global climate is similar to present, but warmer with palm trees and alligators in England and northern Europe.

12 Million: Persistent ice sheets cover Antarctica.

5 Million: Bering Strait opens, separating Asia and North America.

3 Million: Sea ice covers the Arctic Ocean. North and South America join together.

18,000: Last glacial maximum (Wisconsin Ice Age). Ice sheets and glaciers cover much of northern North America and Europe.

10,000: End of last glacial event. Global extinction of Pleistocene megafauna (except in Africa).

150: Burning of fossil fuels begins adding carbon dioxide to the atmosphere.

100: Warmest century in past 2,000 years.

100 years into the future: ???

RECONSTRUCTING PAST CLIMATES AND ENVIRONMENTS
(Thanks to Mieke Sterken and Anton Van de Putte, Belgium)

Lesson at a glance

Students learn the basic principles of palaeoclimatic and palaeo-environmental research by simulating the analysis of microfossils in a sediment core and reconstructing environmental conditions through time.

Background

During the last 50 years, the Antarctic Peninsula has been one of the most rapidly warming regions on Earth. Decrease of the Antarctic ice sheet stability and sea level changes have already caused dramatic ice shelf collapses and increased drainage of ice streams into the sea. Thus, it is very important to understand how the climate has changed throughout the geologic past in order to make predictions for the future.

Since it is impossible to travel back in time and gather first-hand data, researchers use proxies. Proxies may include things such as fossils, tree rings, or the chemical composition of trapped air bubbles in ice cores, which provide indirect evidence of past environmental conditions. In Antarctica, climate reconstructions are based mainly on analysis of ice cores, and on marine and lake sediment records.

Palaeolimnologists (people who study changes in lake environments through time) often use fossil diatoms as a proxy. Diatoms are unicellular algae that grow in all kinds of wet environments like oceans, lakes, rivers and wet soils. Their cell walls consist of a firm silica skeleton that, under the right conditions, can remain fossilised for millions of years. Each diatom species has a different skeleton. This can be used to identify species in fossil diatom assemblages found in sediment cores *(Figure 1.47)*.

By studying modern conditions, we learn about the relationships between different diatom species and the environmental conditions (temperature, pH, salinity, light and nutrient availability) in which they show optimal growth and competition. Changes in the fossil diatom species compositions over time indicate that the environment has probably changed. By comparing fossil diatom compositions, we can estimate how climate conditions have changed throughout the past. For example, when temperatures increase, diatom species compositions will be dominated by more warm-adapted species.

In Antarctic lakes, yearly diatom blooms occur, after which the dead diatoms sink to the lake bottom. In these lake sediments, the skeletons of the diatoms can remain preserved.

To analyse the diatom composition of samples at different depths, palaeolimnologists take a vertical profile (core) of the lake's sediments *(Figure 1.49)*, and analyse the diatom compositions of subsamples at several depths *(Figure 1.48)*. The sediments, being older towards the bottom of the core, are dated by carbon-14 (^{14}C) measurements. Finally, the relative abundances of all diatom species measured in percentage are plotted against depth and/or age. They can now be interpreted in terms of past environmental conditions, on the basis of what we know about the relationships between the species and the environment they live in today.

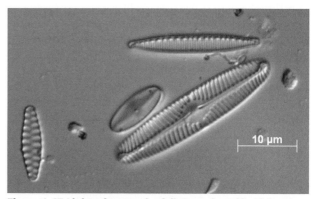

Figure 1.47 Light micrograph of diatoms found in Livingston Island lake sediments on the Antarctic Peninsula.

Figure 1.48 A lake sediment core is being subsampled for diatom analysis.

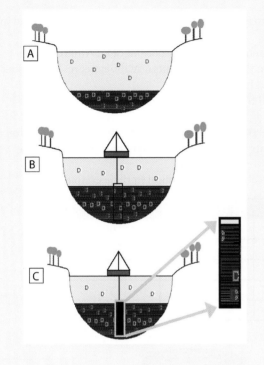

A. Diatoms and other microorganisms bloom and die, then settle to the lake bottom where they are buried in layers of sediments.

B. A coring mechanism with a hollow tube is lowered through the water into the sediments.

C. The corer is removed from the water and the core of sediment is taken out for analysis. It gives a picture through time because the layers at the bottom of the core are the oldest and the youngest sediments are on top.

Figure 1.49 The basic principle of palaeolimnology.

Time
Preparation: 1 hour or more *(depending on class size)*
Class time: 30 minutes or more *(depending on level)*

Materials
(per student or pair of students)
• 1 round flat container *(such as a cheese spread box or plastic Petri dish with cover)*
• 40 beads, coloured candies or other small objects *(4 or 5 colours)*
• paper
• felt-tip pens

Figure 1.50 Sample container.

Advance Preparation—Making a Mock Sediment Core
1. Develop a key for the different colours or other small objects that will represent fossil species in your mock 'sediment core'—e.g., red for a species that is adapted to extremely warm conditions, yellow for moderate conditions, green for cooler conditions, and blue for cold conditions. (For more advanced students, you can complicate it further by adding other colours for variables such as dry or humid conditions.)
2. Place about 40 beads or other objects in each of the round boxes, using a mixture of 4 or 5 colours. Each box will represent a specific depth in your 'sediment core'. You can use any distribution of colours (representing different environmental conditions) that you like, as long as you keep a rather smooth transition in the numbers of each colour from one depth to the next. Depending on the age of your students, you can use more beads, more colours, or even different shapes, objects, plants, etc.
3. Label each box with a sample number, the 'depth' it came from, and the 'age' *(Figure 1.50)*.

RECONSTRUCTING PAST CLIMATES AND ENVIRONMENTS continued

Activity Directions

1. Discuss with the students how climate scientists collect information about past climates by using clues found in lakes or ocean sediments. Introduce the concept of *proxies*.
2. Explain that they are going to simulate the analysis of a sediment core from the bottom of an Antarctic lake. Show them the bead-filled boxes, stacked by age, and tell them that this represents a sediment core. Each colour in the boxes represents a different fossil species that was found in the core.
3. Give each student or pair of students one of the boxes, and tell them to count and record how many beads of each colour their box contains.
4. Compose a summary diagram on the blackboard, with the vertical axis representing the depth and respective age of each box. Write the names of each colour (this represents the species) to the right of this axis. Post the colour-temperature key where the students can see it.
5. Have the students fill in the appropriate number of beads of each colour they found in their sample:

Age	Red	Yellow	Green	Blue
200	25	10	5	0
400	25	10	5	0
600	25	10	5	0
800	10	10	15	5
1,000	10	10	15	5

Note: To make this table more attractive and help visual learners, you can also draw circles next to each 'age', which the students have to colour in, so that it becomes a graph *(Figure 1.51)*. Now you will get a 'palaeoclimatic curve'—the more red you see, the warmer the lake water was during that period. The curve can be constructed on the board or on a personal piece of paper so the students can take it home or post it in their science notebooks.

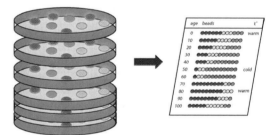

Figure 1.51 Constructing the palaeoclimatic curve.

Discussion

1. How did the climate fluctuate in your sequence? Has it been colder or warmer than today? *(To do this, compare the climate evolution through the 'core' from the oldest sample to the most recent.)*
2. Are there other types of palaeoclimate research that can build on the same basic principles? *(Yes, glaciologists drill ice cores from ice sheets and glaciers. The uppermost metres are the youngest layers of the ice. Scientists investigate the chemical and/or isotopic composition of trapped air bubbles in the ice, and sometimes they also find microfossils, volcanic ash or dust that were blown in by the wind or carried in precipitation).*

Extensions/Adaptations

1. Depending on the age of the students, you can focus on the counting exercise (e.g., for seven-year-olds), or explain about species and their environmental optima, and discuss the environmental consciousness of the students (10- to 12-year-olds). Older children can learn how to recognise several types of fossils, or can improve their writing skills through an essay about this topic.
2. Adapt the activity to marine sediment cores and ice cores, using different time scales if necessary.

✳ FORMATION OF GLACIAL VALLEYS

(Thanks to Alexandre Trindade Nieuwendam and José Xavier, Portugal)

Lesson at a glance

Students make 'mini-glaciers' and model the way glaciers help form the landscape through processes of erosion and deposition.

Background

Glaciers form on land in areas where snowfall exceeds snowmelt. As the snow piles up over time, the bottom layers are compacted and recrystallised, which allows the ice to flow under its own weight. In Greenland and Antarctica, the glaciers merge into large bodies of ice known as ice sheets or continental glaciers. In other regions, glaciers are found only in high mountain valleys. These are called mountain or alpine glaciers.

Figure 1.52 Glacier and glacial valley in Antarctica.

As glaciers flow, they shape the landscape through processes of both erosion and deposition. Glacial ice picks up pieces of rock and other debris as it flows, making the ice rough and abrasive. As the glacier moves, the rough ice acts like sandpaper and erodes the ground beneath it. If the glacier is flowing over bedrock, it may smooth the rock *(glacial polish)* while also leaving long scratches that are orientated in the direction of flow *(glacial striations)*.

In another erosional process known as *plucking,* the friction with the rock floor causes the base of the glacier to melt. The meltwater seeps into cracks in the bedrock and freezes. This bonds pieces of rock to the base of the glacier. As the glacier continues moving, it takes some of this rock with it. These erosional processes form the classic 'U' shape of a once-glaciated valley.

When the glacier reaches an area where it starts to melt, it deposits the rocky debris picked up in its journey down the valley, leaving glacial deposits called *moraines*. Moraines can be terminal (at the bottom end of the glacier), *lateral* (along the sides of the glacier) or *medial* (in the area between glaciers coming from two different valleys when they merge into one). Glaciers also deposit a great deal of unsorted smaller rocks and gravel known as *glacial till*.

Time

Preparation: Several hours *(to freeze mini-glaciers)*
Class time: 30 minutes

Materials

(per group of students)
- water
- soil and gravel
- flour
- oil
- plastic bag or cup
- aluminium foil
- ramp *(PVC or wood)*
- shallow rectangular pan

Advance Preparation
The day before the activity, make the mini-glaciers by placing a small amount of soil and gravel in the plastic bags. Add water (but do not fill) and mix it together. Seal the bags and freeze them overnight.

Figure 1.53 Setting up the glacial valley model.

Activity Directions
1. Place the ramp in the rectangular pan, propping one end up to make a slope.
2. Cover the ramp with a crumpled sheet of aluminium foil.
3. Spread cooking oil on the foil and cover it with a thin layer of flour. The flour represents the bedrock.
4. Remove the plastic bag from the freezer and remove the glacier from the bag.
5. Set the glacier on the top of the ramp and give it a little push.

Discussion
1. How does this activity differ from the way glaciers actually move? *(Here you are pushing the 'glacier' down the slope. Glaciers do not move as a block sliding down an inclined plane. Instead, they flow because of stresses deforming the ice crystals in the interior of the glacier. This internal flow is called 'creep'. See the activity 'Growth and flow of ice sheets' for more detail.)*
2. What would happen if you had a thin layer of water under the glacier? *(The glacier might flow faster because the water lubricates the surface under the glacier, resulting in less friction. This motion is called 'basal sliding'.)*
3. What kind of landforms do you see in your model? *(Depending on the amount of flour used and how the students pushed the glacier, they might be able to identify lateral and terminal moraines. If their glaciers contain a lot of sand and they push fairly hard, they may also leave scratches in the foil, like glacial striations.)*
4. How is the shape of a glacial valley different from one that was eroded only by a stream or river? *(Water-eroded valleys tend to have a deep 'V' shape, while glaciated valleys are broader and more 'U' shaped.)*

Extensions/Adaptations
Use photos of actual glaciated landscapes and have the students identify the glacial features.

PERMAFROST AND TEMPERATURE CHANGES

(Thanks to Jerry Brown and Louise Huffman, USA; Torsten Sachs, Germany; and Jenny Baeseman, Norway)

Lesson at a glance

The experiment investigates how permafrost in different types of soil reacts to temperature changes.

Background

Layers of perennially frozen ground known as *permafrost* exist under about 25% of the landmass of the Northern Hemisphere. Permafrost occurs on land in both the Arctic and Antarctic, as well as beneath the ocean around the Arctic coast and in many high mountain areas. Permafrost is any rock or soil that remains at or below 0°C for two or more years. Seasonal thawing and freezing of the soil forms a shallow *active layer* that overlies the permafrost. In contrast, deep permafrost, frozen to depths of 500 to 1,000 metres, may have existed in a frozen state for thousands of years.

When wet soils and sediments freeze, ice forms and the soils expand and heave upward. Winter cooling of the active layer and uppermost permafrost may also lead to the formation of *ice wedges*. As the frozen ground cools, it contracts and cracks appear (like cracks in drying mud). Water from melting snow runs into the cracks and freezes upon contact with the deeper, still frozen ground. This seasonal cycle may repeat year after year, further enlarging the ice wedges (like annual growth rings on trees).

Frozen soils have greater mechanical stability than unfrozen soils. However when the ice in the ground melts, permafrost degradation can damage roads, pipelines or buildings, and may even cause them to collapse.

Torsten Sachs, a young permafrost scientist at the Alfred Wegener Institute in Germany, observed incidents of permafrost degradation while on an expedition in Siberia: "Sometimes permafrost degradation can happen very quickly. The crack seen in the first picture (*left*) was at first 50 cm wide. A week later it was already five metres wide, and another week later the whole 10 x 20 x 5 m block of land had slipped into the Lena River. This happens when warm river water undercuts the land and cracks appear along the ice wedges. Sometimes, this process can be aided by ice wedges melting, which creates breaking points along which the blocks can fail."

Figure 1.54 The initial permafrost crack was 50 cm wide.

Figure 1.55 Within a week, the crack had widened to five metres.

Figure 1.56 Another week later, a large block of land had slipped into the Lena River.

Time
Preparation: 24 hours *(to freeze samples)*
Class time: 20–25 minutes *(experiment)*, 30 minutes *(discussion)*

Materials
(per group of students)
• 2 clear, wide-mouthed plastic containers *(~ 500 mL each)*
• 6–10 ice cubes
• sand and local soil *(enough to fill one container with each)*
• toothpicks and modelling clay
• water

Figure 1.57 Prepared 'permafrost' sample.

Activity Directions
Part 1—Preparing the permafrost
1. Put a layer of wet sand in one plastic container and wet soil in the other, filling each 1/3 full.
2. Place 3 to 5 ice cubes on top of the sand or soil to represent the ice wedges, filling the container to the 2/3 mark.
3. Cover the ice with a second layer of sand or soil.
4. Moisten the entire sample with water (like watering a potted plant). Make sure there is only enough water to dampen the sample and not so much that there is standing water at the base.
5. Freeze for at least 24 hours.

Part 2—Conducting the experiment
1. Construct two small structures from clay and toothpicks and place them on top of the frozen samples. Use the toothpicks to hold the structures in place.
2. Predict what you think will happen as the frozen soil and ice thaws? What will happen to the ice, the soil, and the structures?
3. Allow the samples to thaw and note what happens.

Figure 1.58 After the 'permafrost' thaws.

Discussion
1. How did the thawing of the permafrost affect your structures? Did the type of soil make a difference? *(Soil of clay or silt is less stable than sand when thawed, and the structures should have moved.)*
2. What happened to the surface of the ground when the permafrost thawed? How might this affect vegetation or animals in permafrost regions? *(The surface should subside [settle] and water should accumulate. This could disturb plant roots, disrupt underground burrows, and drown insects if they cannot move away.)*
3. Permafrost contains large quantities of stored organic carbon. How might the thawing of permafrost affect levels of atmospheric greenhouse gases such as carbon dioxide and methane? *(When organic matter decomposes, it gives off CO_2 and methane to the atmosphere.)*

Extensions/Adaptations
Have the students set up a controlled experiment to determine the effect of soil particle size on soil stability as permafrost thaws, then graph and explain their results.

OPTIMAL FORAGING
(Thanks to Isla Myers-Smith, Canada, adapted from University of Alberta Biology 208 lab manual)

Lesson at a glance

Students model the foraging activity of different species and discuss how changes in the polar regions might affect species survival and reproductive success.

Background

Optimal foraging theory states that organisms feed in the most efficient way considering both the energy in the food, and the time it takes to find, catch and eat it. When animal habitats are stable, each species is adapted to one unique *ecological niche* (a particular role or function within the ecosystem). As environmental conditions change, different species may compete for the same food sources, again triggering adaptation in these species over time to the changed environment. This competition between species and their adaptations to specific environmental conditions drives the evolution of new species.

Figure 1.59 A snowy owl bringing a lemming back to its nest on Bylot Island in the Eastern Canadian Arctic. This picture was taken with a motion sensor camera.

Specialists are organisms that focus on one type of food. *Generalists* eat a broad range of foods. In harsher, less productive ecosystems such as the Arctic and Antarctic, and during times of rapid change, generalist species seem to have a survival advantage. Specialists will thrive when competition is high between species for different food resources, and the specialist can adapt to feed more efficiently on a particular prey. Whether the specialist or the generalist feeding strategy is better for a given animal depends upon the habitat in which it lives.

A warming climate, and resulting changes such as decreases in lichens, loss of sea ice, or earlier hatching of birds, changes what food is available for different species throughout the year. This could mean that animals will have to change what they feed on to optimise their foraging strategy. Caribou may have to feed on different tundra vegetation; polar bears may have to learn to forage from land, and Arctic raptors may have to eat different prey. If these animals cannot adapt fast enough to cope with the pace of climate warming, then their populations will decline and eventually some species may go extinct.

Time

Preparation: 2 hours
Class time: 1 hour

Materials

(per class)
- 50 short pieces of drinking straws
- 50 small pieces of foam sponge
- 50 short pieces of yarn or string
- 50 small pieces of cork or similar objects
- 1 stopwatch, timer or watch

(per person for ¾ of the students)
- plastic fork, knife or spoon *(1 utensil each, divided evenly)*
- paper or plastic bags for 'stomachs' *(1 each for ¾ of the students)*

(per person for ¼ of the students)
- pencils and paper

Arctic Raptors Information Sheet

Activity Directions

1. Introduce the students to the idea of optimal foraging. Discuss how species can adapt over time to prey upon specific foods, using the example of snowy owls, rough-legged hawks, and peregrine falcons in the Canadian Arctic (*see 'Arctic Raptors Information Sheet'*).

2. Ask the students which strategy, being a generalist or specialist, might be better. What sort of conditions might change whether one strategy is better than the other? Discuss the 3 raptors.
3. Divide the students into 4 groups—one for each of 3 predator species—forks *(Forkus prongimus)*, spoons *(Spoona scoopima)*, knives *(Nifeinus sharpimus)*. The fourth group will serve as biologists who monitor feeding behaviour and record the number of surviving individuals after each feeding period.
4. Tell the students they are going to determine what foraging strategy works best for their species. Explain the rules:
   a. Each feeding period represents one summer. An energy unit consists of any one of the following: 3 straws, 1 foam, 2 yarn, or 3 corks. Resources are not interchangeable—e.g., 2 straws plus 1 cork does not comprise an energy unit.
   b. The 3 predator species will harvest the resources using only the utensil provided to pick up the food and place it in a 'stomach' bag. They are not allowed to pick up energy units by hand, or to use their fingers to hold energy units on the utensil while 'feeding'.
   c. The food will be considered eaten when an entire energy unit is placed in the bag.
   d. At 30-second intervals, the biologists will count and record the number of energy units eaten by each individual. Any individual who eats fewer than 5 energy units in an interval dies of starvation. Those who eat more than 5 energy units die of exploded gut syndrome. Only those who eat exactly 5 energy units will survive into the next time interval.
5. Distribute the energy units (~50 of each of the 4 resources) over a lawn or open area. Have the students spread out around the edge of the area, grouped by species (each corner of the area could be a habitat for a different species) and establish a field camp area for the biologists.
6. Begin the foraging cycle. After the first 30 seconds, have the students run back to their species' habitats. Ask the biologists to check the stomach contents, and count any mortalities. Continue to repeat the feeding cycle until 2 of the species are eliminated.

Note: Use caution because the plastic utensils may be sharp, especially if broken.

Discussion
1. Which species did the best and why? Which went extinct first? Which one survived?
2. How were the different utensils best suited to foraging for the different resources?
3. How would each student describe their own foraging behaviour? Did they focus on one type of energy unit? Did they go for the easiest ones to pick up or the ones with the highest energy value? Did they instead forage for whichever energy units were closest to them?
4. How would both these strategies (specialist and generalist) fit the optimal foraging theory? Were some students acting as generalists while others were specialists? What feeding strategy was the best?

Extensions/Adaptations
Rerun the activity with different biological variables:
- Shorten the feeding period from 30 to 15 seconds: Bad weather has shortened the growing season. This could simulate a future Arctic climate with more extreme weather events in the summer, such as snowfall that kills prey species.
- Have the biologists collect most of the sponges and corks: Climate change has altered the plant species in the tundra environment, causing some of the prey species' populations to decline.
- Break some tines off the plastic forks or blindfold students: An outbreak of disease due to warmer conditions has impacted the health of plant and animal populations.
- Have the biologists hide the sponges and corks in the grass, or around the room: Vegetation has grown higher and now it is more difficult to find the prey items.
- Come up with your own ideas on how to change the feeding conditions!

Have these variations on the original activity changed which species went extinct first and how fast? Did poor weather or disease influence the success of one species versus another? Have they changed each student's foraging behaviour?

ARCTIC RAPTORS INFORMATION SHEET

Snowy owls, rough-legged hawks and peregrine falcons all live in the tundra across the Canadian Arctic. Each of these species could be feeding on the same prey; however, they have different adaptations for hunting and feeding, such as different sized beaks, talons and flight feathers.

Figure 1.60 Baby snowy owls, eight days old from a nest on Herschel Island in the Western Canadian Arctic.

- **Snowy owls** have feathers that reduce the sound of flight and large talons for grabbing their prey. They perch on high points of ground looking for their prey. They preferentially feed on lemmings, although they can eat a variety of different species from sea birds to snowshoe hares. Snowy owls could be considered specialist predators in the summer months. They prefer lemmings when they are available, but lemming populations fluctuate. In years when lemmings are abundant, snowy owls are very successful, hatching lots of young. When there are few lemmings, the owls must switch to other prey. If they cannot find enough food, they do not breed.

- **Rough-legged hawks** are large birds with broad wings that are good for hovering, but they have relatively short toes for a bird of their size. Rough-legged hawks eat small mammals and small birds, and hunt from the air while hovering over the tundra or from a perch. They are a more generalist predators—able to hunt from the air, but not especially adapted to rapid or quiet flight. If the tundra vegetation grows taller and woody shrubs increase, they may no longer be able to see their prey. If they cannot see small mammals, they might have to switch to hunting songbirds and sea birds, which are the primary prey of the peregrine falcon.

- **Peregrine falcons** are smaller birds with bodies designed for rapid flight. They have specially adapted nostrils and eyelids to protect them from the hazards of flying really fast. Peregrines could be considered specialist predators. They feed mostly on birds, although they will also eat small mammals, including lemmings. They hunt like the rough-legged hawk and dive to catch their prey at speeds of up to 320 km per hour! If populations of sea birds are low they may have to forage for small mammals such as lemmings, and being a fast flyer may not be very useful when hunting animals on the ground.

All three raptors are dependent on finding adequate prey during the Arctic summers, not only to survive, but also so that they can breed and rear their young. Snowy owls in particular reproduce in much greater numbers when lemmings are abundant. In recent years lemmings have not been reaching peak densities—the population cycle seems to be dampening. This may be due to changing climate or some other yet to be determined factor. Fewer lemmings have meant lowered reproduction in snowy owls in some areas. If lemming numbers stay low over the long term, it could lead to a decline in snowy owl populations.

Researchers from the IPY ArcticWOLVES project are investigating interactions among snowy owls, lemmings and other components of the Arctic food web to try and understand the future of wildlife populations. Some of the questions they are researching are where snowy owls spend their winters and how far they move when picking a nest site between years. It appears that snowy owls are searching huge distances to find summer and winter habitat with the most available prey.

How does the behaviour of the snowy owl, travelling long distances to find food, fit with optimal foraging theory? *(It must be more advantageous for snowy owls to expend energy travelling to find an abundant food source, than it is to stay in one location and feed on local food resources.)*

PEOPLE

People living and working in the polar regions face special challenges involving physical, ecological and legal issues.

More than four million people live in the nations surrounding the Arctic. As access to the region and facilities improve, more people are moving to certain regions of the Arctic from other parts of the world. Mineral resource discoveries and a growing tourism industry are also contributing to a population increase in some regions.

Indigenous populations vary from more than 80% in Greenland to less than 5% in the Russian Arctic. Arctic indigenous people whose economies are largely based on subsistence activities such as hunting, fishing, gathering, reindeer herding and farming are especially vulnerable to environmental and social changes. For example, although the polar regions generally do not contain significant sources of industrial or commercial contaminants, wind and ocean circulation systems transport pollutants to the poles.

These contaminants show up in the ecosystems of both the Arctic and the Antarctic, often in dangerously high concentrations in animals at the top of polar food chains. These animals, which include bears, seals and fish, form a major part of the traditional diets of northern societies. Pollutants that are emitted into the atmosphere in industrial capitals have been affecting, and will continue to affect, the health of Arctic residents, especially breast-feeding mothers.

Migratory birds, fish and other animals also carry pollutants and diseases, and their seasonal migrations between temperate and polar regions can result in very rapid transmission of human health problems. As polar weather, polar climate and polar ecosystems change, the routes and fates of these pollutants may also change.

Studying trends of migration and mobility among local Arctic residents is another key area of polar social science. Understanding how communities reacted to past environmental changes allows us to draw conclusions about future developments. Based on current polar research, it is certain that accumulation of pollutants in the polar regions will continue. These trends remind us of inescapable global connections, and of the fact that local disposal actions always have distant and far-reaching consequences.

The Arctic has also become an attractive region for the exploitation of natural resources. Considering the complex connections among hydrology, ecology

and human populations, it will become increasingly important to discuss the use of natural resources such as reindeer and fish, as well as coal, oil and gas, and determine how, if at all, the exploitation of these resources can be legally regulated. This is complicated by questions of national claims to jurisdiction in the Arctic.

Antarctica, in contrast to the Arctic, has no permanent inhabitants, although there are currently 21 year-round and six summer-only research stations. Antarctic tourism is also a rapidly growing industry, bringing more and more visitors south every year.

Legal issues in the Antarctic differ from those in the Arctic. The Antarctic Treaty, which has been signed by 47 nations, set Antarctica aside as a special place for peace and science. The latter designation encourages international scientific collaboration and the sharing of knowledge and discoveries. The Treaty System also prohibits any military activity or mineral exploitation in this area, which includes about 10% of the world's land surface and a further 10% of the global ocean. Effective enforcement of the Antarctic Treaty System mechanisms is not always easy, however. For example, vessel-sourced pollution is often debated in terms of shortcomings of national regulations.

The following activities explore some of the various ways in which people affect and are affected by the polar regions.

People Activities

WHAT IS COMMUNITY?

UP THE FOOD CHAIN: POLLUTION IN THE ARCTIC

WHAT WILL BE THE FUTURE OF THE ARCTIC?

READY TO GO ON AN ANTARCTIC EXPEDITION?

KEEPING WARM ON POLAR EXPEDITIONS

WHAT IS COMMUNITY?
(Thanks to Kristi Skebo and Karen Edwards, Canada)

Lesson at a glance
Students will compare their community and their way of life with those of students living in a very different physical environment.

Background
The definition of 'community' has been widely debated across various disciplines for decades. In ecological terms, a community consists of populations of organisms of different species that interact with one another in a given geographical area. From a social science perspective, a human community is often described as a group of interacting people living in a common location or individuals who share cultural, ethnic and moral traditions who may live over a wide-ranging geographic area. The health and sustainability of any of these communities is highly dependent on the physical, social and economic environment in which it exists.

In today's digital age, even virtual 'communities' pop up every day on social web-based networks. Nowhere is the difference between 'traditional' and 'modern' human community more obvious than in the Arctic.

Figure 1.61 Aviaja 'chats' with her friends on a sunny day in July in Uummannaq, Greenland.

People have lived in the Arctic for thousands of years developing skills, strategies and community knowledge to survive harsh polar conditions. In recent centuries, resource exploitation and political activities imposed by non-Arctic communities have changed the livelihoods and well-being of Arctic residents in good and bad ways. Now, climate change is adding new challenges to the well-being of Arctic communities. The Arctic Human Development Report (AHDR) of 2004 outlines a number of challenges being faced by Arctic communities such as rapid changes in population, education, economy, industries, resources, culture, political structures and climate.

Arctic communities are often based on a long heritage of indigenous cultures. In the face of rapid change in both physical environments and the social demands of the modern age, maintaining a balance with traditional ways of living presents an increasing challenge.

Inuit Culture and Traditional Knowledge in Nunavut

Indigenous cultures, whether they are polar or non-polar, share common elements in their definition of 'community'. Many indigenous cultures emphasise the intrinsic connection between culture, language, place and land when they define 'who' they are as a people.

In Nunavut in the Canadian Arctic, Inuit *Qaujimajatuqangit* (IQ) refers to the Inuit way of doing things and encompasses eight fundamental principles of human conduct. According to the Nunavut Social Development Council, 'IQ embraces all aspects of traditional Inuit culture including values, worldview, language, social organization, knowledge, life skills, perceptions and expectations.' In common with the practice in many indigenous cultures, IQ stresses the importance of the community over that of the individual. *Piliriqatigiingniq*, one of the eight principles, is an Inuit term that describes the concept of developing a collaborative relationship or working together for a common purpose, rather than just to serve individual self-interest. You can find all eight principles at the end of Chapter 2.

Time
Preparation: 15 minutes
Class time: 2 class periods *(45–60 minutes each)*

Materials
(per class)
• *Defining my Community* worksheet
• large classroom map or globe
• Internet access *(for students to conduct further research)*

Oral Traditions Research Manual
Defining my Community Worksheet

Activity Directions
1. Discuss the concept of community with the students. What patterns, geography, activities, or environment define community for them (e.g., cultural traits, language, religion, family structure, land use, economic activity, transportation, communication, settlement patterns, etc.)?
2. Divide the students into small groups and give each group a copy of the *Defining my Community* worksheet. Give them time to discuss the topics and write down their ideas in relation to their community.
3. Bring the groups back together and have them share their responses with the whole class. Compare and contrast their ideas.
4. Discuss what a community is like on the opposite side of the globe. For example, if you live in a non-Arctic area such as Australia or the Midwestern United States, choose a community in an Arctic area such as Greenland or the Canadian Arctic, and discuss how a student there might answer these questions. If you live in an Arctic region such as northern Norway, pick a non-Arctic area like Brazil and imagine what peoples' lives are like there.

Note: With the rapid expansion of the Internet and instant messaging, chat rooms, social networking sites, etc., you may find that your students' concepts of community include (or maybe are even dominated by) the idea of these 'virtual' communities. This activity provides a good platform to explore the similarities and differences, as well as the strengths and limitations, of these alternate communities.

Discussion
1. Is any 'human community' independent of an associated 'ecological community'? Why or why not? *(This is a chance to explore how humans modify their physical environments to suit their cultural traditions, or as a result of new technologies or ideas, but ultimately remain dependent on the natural environment to support life.)*
2. What are the differences between your community and the community you chose to study from across the globe? What are the similarities?
3. How are the changes in your community different from those in your comparison community?
4. How might changes in your community affect other communities across the globe? *(This is a chance for students to explore the global impact of local changes they are experiencing. For example, according to the Intergovernmental Panel on Climate Change (IPCC) Fourth Assessment Report 2007 (AR4), Arctic temperatures increased at about twice the average global rate over the past 100 years. This is having a major impact on Arctic ecosystems and the health and livelihoods of Arctic residents. In other parts of the world, the major concerns may be changes in precipitation patterns— e.g., droughts and floods. In coastal areas, there are worries about damage from rising sea levels, as well as increasingly frequent and stronger extreme weather events.)*
5. How might communities mitigate or adapt to these changes? *(This would depend on the specific problems, as well as the social and financial resources available to the community or region.)*
6. What similarities did you notice in the challenges and the adaptation strategies between different communities and cultures?
7. What adaptations is your community making to changes that are happening now? How can you play a part in your community to address these changes?

Extensions/Adaptations

1. Ask a long-time community member or Elder to visit the class when you are discussing the concept of community and looking at changes that have taken place in your community.

2. One of the key cultural connections Inuit have with the land is the sharing of food from either hunting or farming. Have the students research and discuss where their food comes from, and relate this to their comparison community.

3. Have the students represent the similarities and differences in a variety of ways (e.g., visually or graphically). This can link the activity into other subjects such as mathematics if you record and graph quantitative data such as current population, population change over time, etc.

4. If resources are available, partner your class with a similar grade and class in a community on the opposite side of the globe so that students can share their finished projects, share questions or compare their experiences. This can be done through a pen-pal/e-pal exchange or blog site. To find sources for class exchanges, try searchable keywords such as 'connecting classrooms, collaborating, ePals, polar.'

5. Explore the concept of Traditional Knowledge in your community by using the *'Oral Traditions Research Manual'* and consult the activity *'Oral Traditions Research'* in the Going Further section of this chapter.

DEFINING MY COMMUNITY WORKSHEET

Name of Community	Facts and Sources	What changes am I noticing?
Population (total as well as age ranges if available)		
Location		
Climate		
Natural geography		
Biodiversity (flora and fauna)		
Kind of government (national and local)		
Economy and businesses		
Schools		
Land use		
Methods of transportation		
Language		
Culture(s)		
Religious beliefs		
Homes		
Recreation (sports, activities, clubs, etc.)		
Other		

WHAT WILL BE THE FUTURE OF THE ARCTIC?
(Thanks to Agathe Weber, IPF, Belgium; and Caroline Pellaton, Switzerland)

Lesson at a glance
Students participate in a role play exercise to begin to understand the complexity of Arctic land use and the conflicts of interest between economic, environmental and social issues.

Background
The Arctic Council is a high level intergovernmental group that was established in 1996 to promote cooperation, coordination and interaction among the Arctic states when dealing with common Arctic issues such as sustainable development and environmental protection. Decisions are made by consensus, so all parties have to agree. The Arctic Council has very limited political power, but it can provide advice and make recommendations.

The Arctic Council chairmanship rotates through the Member States every two years. Senior Arctic Officials meet every six months and a full Ministerial Meeting is held every two years in the host country. The organisation has several categories of participation:

Member States: These are countries that have land in the Arctic—Canada, Denmark (including Greenland and the Faroe Islands), Finland, Iceland, Norway, Sweden, the Russian Federation and the United States of America.

Permanent Participants: These are representatives from six different Arctic indigenous organisations. They are allowed to participate actively and have full consultation rights.

Observers: Representatives from non-Arctic states, global and regional intergovernmental and interparliamentary organisations, and nongovernmental organisations (NGOs) are allowed to be present at Arctic Council meetings as observers, and also have the right to participate actively in the Working Group meetings.

Working Groups: Six expert working groups carry out the programmes and projects mandated by the Arctic Council Ministers. Their focus is on scientific and social issues such as monitoring, assessing and preventing pollution in the Arctic, climate change, biodiversity conservation and sustainable use, emergency preparedness and prevention, and living conditions of Arctic residents. Observer states and organisations, as well as invited experts, often attend Working Group meetings and participate in specific projects.

Time
Preparation time: 20 minutes *(to cut out position cards and print additional information)*
Class time: 1–2 hours *(depending on level and amount of discussion)*

Materials
(per group of students)
• 1 position card
• Internet access *(for students to conduct further research)* OR
• print-outs of the web-based material for each position

Position Cards

Activity Directions
1. Divide the students into 4 groups, with an equal number in each group and tell them they are going to participate in a forum of a group called the Arctic Council. Set the background for the meeting by giving the students the following information:
   Imagine that a high-level intergovernmental forum that addresses issues faced by the Arctic governments and the indigenous people of the Arctic is at the point of making a crucial decision on the future of an Arctic region: either to give permission for the region's resources to be exploited by private enterprise, or to make it a natural reserve. To help them make this decision, the forum members have appointed a small interdisciplinary committee of experts (that's you!) to report to the forum promoting one alternative or the other. During the forum, you will present the issues from the perspective of the 'expert' role you have been assigned in order to help the forum members make a final decision on the future of the region.

Note: At present, the Arctic Council does not have the authority to make such decisions but the premise of the activity is to assume a time frame in the future when they hypothetically would have such authority.

It is also important to stress that during the discussion the students will have to adopt the positions they are assigned for the role play, even though the positions may not correspond to their personal opinions. In addition, you should discuss the fact that the roles they are given are simplified for the purpose of the discussion and that they do not represent the views of all members of any of the groups. If you want to find out more about the position of, for example, reindeer herding peoples on the question of resource exploitation of their herding territories, consult Chapter 4.

2. Give each group a position card that represents a particular role and ask the students to read and discuss the information on the card.
3. To prepare for the discussion, each group will also need to read documents containing information specific to their own 'field of expertise'. You can either choose the reading selections for each group (see possible web links below), or you may let the students search the Internet for information related to their roles. For student-directed research, ask each group to discuss what they would like to know in order to present their position, and to create a list of keywords and questions before starting their search.

   Possible websites for role research:
   - *Politicians:* http://www.thearctic.is/articles/overviews/changing/enska/kafli_0300.htm
   - *Researchers:* http://assets.panda.org/downloads/wwf_arctic_feedbacks_report_exesum.pdf
   - *NGO Representatives:* www.atkinsonfoundation.ca/files/Arctic_in_Peril.pdf (pages 10–23)
   - *Economists:* http://www.heritage.org/Research/EnergyandEnvironment/WM27.cfm and http://www. atkinsonfoundation.ca/files/Arctic_in_Peril.pdf (pages 9 to 10)

   Keywords examples:
   - *Politicians:* Arctic, economy, taxes, oil, riches, route / Arctic peoples
   - *Researchers:* Arctic, climate change
   - *Representatives of NGOs:* Arctic, peoples, climate change, industry / Arctic wildlife
   - *Economists:* Arctic, resources, taxes, oil, climate change

4. When the discussion takes place, moderate the negotiations among the groups.
5. After about 25 minutes of discussion, have each group make its closing arguments. The students then vote based on their own personal opinion as if they were forum members, rather than on the official position of the group they represented in the activity.
6. Summarise the main points brought up during the discussion and ask the students whether any compromises might have been possible (such as taxes for the benefit of NGOs, the establishment of wildlife or marine protected areas, etc.).

Adaptations/Extensions
Discuss the Arctic Council and its current roles in more detail. For more information about the Council, go to http://www.arcticportal.org/ and click on the 'Arctic Council' tab at the top of the page.

POSITION CARDS

You are a **politician**

You take a very serious view of the economic future of YOUR region, which borders the Arctic Ocean where your people depend on the land for food, economic support, and links to their traditional culture. New drilling and mining operations would create significant income that would be very lucrative for your country or region. The taxes paid by the oil companies alone would provide stable revenue for your country or region for at least 10 years. You are looking for ways to encourage sustainable development that would decrease the environmental impact of such development.

Your opinion: In principle, you support mining and drilling activities in the region that are sustainable and that would benefit your region for the long term.

You are a **researcher**

From your research, you know that the environment in the Arctic is suffering enormously from the effects of climate change and pollution, and that humans are the main culprits. In Alaska, for example, the permafrost (the upper part of the ground that stays frozen all year round) is the basis of the local ecosystem and it is thawing not only as the result of climate change, but also because of the infrastructure humans have built in the region.

Your opinion: You believe that making this region of the Arctic a natural reserve would be the only reasonable thing to do.

You are the **representative of an NGO**

Through your work in the field you have seen first-hand the impact that climate change and industrial pollution are having on both the life of local communities and the fauna. In addition, new human infrastructures (roads and pipelines) are harming the ecosystem and preventing local communities from continuing to live in their traditional ways (for example, keeping herds of migrant livestock or hunting). You feel that any new industrial operations are only going to make things more challenging for local communities and their environment.

Your opinion: In principle, you are very concerned with the negative consequences for the fauna and the local communities if this region is opened up to the major multinational corporations.

You are an **economist**

Through your job as a consultant in market economics, you have been able to see the initial effects of climate change in the country. For example, insurance companies have stopped providing coverage for houses in some areas where the permafrost is thawing. The costs of new infrastructures (roads, pipelines, etc.) have also greatly increased, as they need to be better built where the ground is no longer frozen solid. However, you can also see the positive side of these changes: the more the ice melts, the more oil and mining companies can explore to find new places to drill or mine. Ships may soon be able to travel north of Alaska, which means that there will be ports to build, having a very positive effect on the local economy.

Your opinion: For the most part, you are in favour of exploiting the Arctic's resources.

UP THE FOOD CHAIN: POLLUTION IN THE ARCTIC
(Thanks to Elizabeth Hodges Snyder and Nancy Nix, USA)

Lesson at a glance

 Students participate in a series of four interrelated activities that illustrate the concepts of bioaccumulation, biomagnification, bioconcentration, and global distillation of contaminants in the Arctic.

Background

Bioaccumulation and *bioconcentration* refer to the build up of substances such as pesticides, industrial and household chemicals, hormones, personal care products, or pharmaceuticals in an organism, to the point where the concentration in the organism is greater than the concentration in the environment. Uptake can occur through multiple pathways, including eating and drinking, breathing, or adsorption (the accumulation of liquids or gases on the surface of a solid) to the skin from soil, air and water.

Although the two terms are often used interchangeably, bioaccumulation refers to total uptake from any environmental source, such as contaminated food, water, aerosols or soil. Bioconcentration, on the other

Figure 1.62 Icelandic students who participated in the international Global POP programme prepare local fish samples for POP analysis.

hand, refers to uptake only from water. In the environment, as opposed to controlled laboratory conditions, it can be difficult to differentiate between bioaccumulation and bioconcentration.

Only substances that the body takes up faster than it *metabolises* (breaks down) and/or eliminates through defecation and/or urination will be bioaccumulated or bioconcentrated. In the case of *persistent organic pollutants* (POPs), which are of concern in the Arctic environment, the substance is stored in the fat of the organism that consumes it. Over time, if an organism is repeatedly exposed to small amounts (i.e., low concentrations) of these pollutants, they build up in the organism. Thus, bioaccumulation and bioconcentration are processes that occur in a single animal or *trophic level*—an organism's position in the food chain. *(See activity 'Polar feasts!' in the Ocean section and the 'Global POP' programme in Chapter 3 for more information.)*

Biomagnification, however, occurs across multiple trophic levels. As one moves up the food chain, from primary producers to herbivores to carnivores to top predators, the concentration of a substance that accumulates in a given organism can increase. Biomagnification can occur for multiple reasons, including *persistence* (resistance to breaking down in the environment), resistance to metabolism, and increased fatty tissue ratios in organisms higher up the food chain. Substances that are persistent and *lipophilic* (fat-loving) such as POPs are especially prone to bioaccumulation, bioconcentration, and biomagnification because they are stored in the fatty tissue. Humans and other mammals are at particular risk of harm because lipophilic pollutants can be passed to their offspring through breast milk.

Global distillation describes the process in which certain chemicals are transported from warmer to colder regions of the Earth. The process occurs through alternating events of *chemical vaporisation* at higher temperatures, and *condensation* at lower temperatures. It is through global distillation that some of these toxic substances can move towards the cold, remote Arctic from their sources in the south and become accumulated in the environment, animals, and human populations in the Arctic. This is an international problem, as the entire world is connected through the global commons of air and water.

Time

Preparation: 20 minutes per part *(to photocopy and organise materials)*
Class time: Part 1: 2–3 hours *(can be split over multiple days)*
   Part 2: 30 minutes
   Part 3: 30 minutes
   Part 4: 2–3 hours *(student preparation and activity; can be split over multiple days)*

Materials

Part 1
(per person)
- blank organism card
- pencil
- markers or coloured pencils
- research resources *(e.g., library books, encyclopaedias, Internet)*
- yarn or string

Part 2
(per class)
- 4 sheets poster board
- marker
- 4 easels or sticky tape

(per person)
- 4 colours of sticky notes

Part 3
(per class)
- 6 small jars with watertight lids
- 1 large jar with watertight lid
- water
- vegetable oil
- oil-based dye

Part 4
(per class)
- 30 pieces of yarn
  (~ ¼ the length of the space available to conduct the activity)
- 32 brown paper bags

(per person)
- completed organism card
- red and green sheets of construction paper
- scissors
- sticky tape

Activity Directions

Part 1—Creating a food chain
1. Assign students to one of five organisms: polar bear (1 student), ringed seal (2 students), cod (4 students), krill (8 students), or phytoplankton (16 students). If you have more than 31 students, assign some students partners as necessary. If you have fewer than 31 students, you can eliminate the phytoplankton from the food chain.
2. Have the students research their assigned organisms and fill out the blank organism cards. Punch holes and tie yarn onto each card so it can be worn around the neck.
3. Starting with the polar bear, have one person from each organism group come to the front of the class and share the information on the organism card. The student should conclude his or her presentation with what the organism eats, so as to introduce the next organism down the food chain.
4. Have the students save their organism cards for use in Part 4.

Part 2—Introducing key vocabulary and concepts
1. Before class begins, write one of the following on each poster board:
   a. Cod adsorb and retain Substance XYZ through their gills.
   b. Filter-feeding krill adsorb and retain Substance XYZ from the sea water and phytoplankton.

    c. The concentration of substance XYZ in the ringed seal is greater than the concentration in sea water and cod.

    d. The ringed seal that a polar bear eats is contaminated with substance XYZ, even though the substance was originally released in Florida.

2. Place each board in a different corner of the room, either on an easel or taped to the wall.

3. Review the definitions of the roots of the words *bioaccumulation, bioconcentration, biomagnification,* and *global distillation* (i.e., *bio, accumulate, concentrate, magnify, global,* and *distill*) with the class and discuss what the words mean.

4. Give each student four different colour sticky notes (one of each colour).

5. Assign each of the four words to a different colour sticky note. For example, the blue note represents bioaccumulation. You might find it helpful to write the assignment on the chalkboard or on a handout.

6. Instruct the students to read the sentences on the poster boards, and then attach each of their sticky notes to the board that illustrates the corresponding word. For added fun, you can give the students only 60 seconds to make their selections, and have all students go at one time.

7. Review the boards to see whether each board is covered with predominantly the same colour (and correct) notes.

8. Clarify the definitions as necessary in a class discussion. For global distillation, ask the students how else a substance might travel from Florida (or elsewhere) to the Arctic (e.g., biotransport, relocation of waste, etc.)

Part 3—Demonstrating the concepts

1. Before class begins, fill each small jar ¾ full with water. Half-fill the large jar with equal parts water and vegetable oil.

2. Explain to the class that the large jar represents an organism towards the top of the food chain (e.g., a polar bear). The water represents the water in the organism, and the oil represents the fat in the organism.

3. Explain that the contaminant of interest is *lipophilic* (i.e., it loves fat more than water). Ask the class, if you were to add a few drops of the dye (representing the contaminant) to the water and oil mixture, where would it end up? Would it colour the water? Would it colour the oil? Would it colour both?

4. Add one drop of dye to the large jar and shake. Allow the mixture to separate while sitting on the table (this may take several minutes). The students will see the dye 'partition' into the oil fraction, thus illustrating the accumulation of a lipophilic compound in fatty tissue. A bit of colour might remain in the water fraction, as well. This illustrates that some lipophilic chemicals do have a certain level of water solubility, which can contribute to partial elimination by the organism (water soluble chemicals are typically more easily eliminated by organisms).

5. While waiting for the water and oil in the large jar to separate, add 1 drop of dye into each small jar. Screw on the lid and shake well to distribute the dye.

6. Explain that each small jar represents an organism somewhere in the middle of the food chain (e.g., a ringed seal). The dye represents the substance that has bioaccumulated in the organism. It is the total contaminant in both the fat and water fractions of the organism.

7. One by one, pour the contents of 5 of the small jars into the large jar. The sixth small jar will serve as a control. Shake and allow to settle (this may take several minutes). Compare the colour intensity in the large jar to the colour intensity in the remaining small jar (which may need to be shaken again). The students will see that the colouring in the oil of the large jar will be darker. This represents the magnification of the substance up the food chain (e.g., the polar bear eats multiple seals and magnifies the substance).

Note: It is recommended that Part 3 be conducted by only the instructor, given the permanent nature of the dye. If you cannot find oil-based dye, you can make your own. Grate several carrots and cover them with water in a saucepan. Boil for 5–10 minutes, then cool and strain. This can also be used as an example of a fat-soluble vitamin (beta carotene—a provitamin A carotenoid that our bodies can use to manufacture vitamin A) if you are doing a unit on nutrition.

Part 4—Modelling bioaccumulation and biomagnification

1. Ask the students to make a total of 144 green rings and 16 red rings by cutting the construction paper into 3–5 cm strips and taping the ends together. (To determine how many rings each student should make, simply divide 144 and 16 by the number of students in your class. Some students will probably have to make more rings than others.) Also ask each student to clearly label the front and back of a brown paper bag with the name of their organism.
2. Ask the students to wear their organism cards from Part 1, with the organism picture facing outward.
3. Have the polar bear student distribute 9 green rings and 1 red ring to each phytoplankton student, and 1 piece of yarn to every student, except the polar bear.
4. While the students are receiving their rings, clear a large space in the room and place the open and labelled brown paper bags on the floor *(Figure 1.63)*. The distance between each 'trophic level' should be slightly less than the length of the yarn pieces. Ask the students to stand next to their bags with their rings and yarn.
5. Explain that the green rings represent food that is NOT contaminated with substance XYZ, and the red rings represent food that IS contaminated with substance XYZ. By sending the rings up the food chain via the yarn, they are illustrating the consumption of food.
6. Ask the phytoplankton and krill students to face one another. Each krill student will be facing two phytoplankton students.
7. Ask each krill student to grab the ends of yarn from the 2 side-by-side phytoplankton students in front of them.
8. Have each phytoplankton string his or her coloured rings onto the yarn being held by a krill student.
9. Have the phytoplankton students send the rings to the krill students by raising the end of the yarn. (Two phytoplankton students will send rings to a single krill student.) The krill students will then empty the rings into their paper bags.
10. Ask the krill students to count the number of green and red rings, and report it aloud. Record the ratio of green to red.
11. Ask the krill students to remove half of the GREEN rings. Collect these rings from the students and put them in the remaining paper bag. Explain that removing half of the green rings represents the conversion of food to energy. The remaining rings are converted to new body mass in the animal.
12. Ask the cod students to then grab the ends of yarn from two side-by-side krill students.
13. Have the krill students string their coloured rings onto the yarn being held by a cod student.
14. Repeat the process of sending the rings to the next trophic level, reporting the number of green and red rings, noting the ratio of green to red rings, and placing half the remaining green rings into the instructor's bag.
15. When the rings reach the polar bear, discuss the final ratio of green to red rings.

Discussion

1. What processes did Part 4 demonstrate? *(bioaccumulation and biomagnification)*
2. What did the green and red rings represent? *(uncontaminated and contaminated food)*
3. Why did we remove some of the green rings at each trophic level? *(to represent the use of food to supply energy)*
4. When might it be appropriate to remove some of the red rings at each trophic level? *(to illustrate that some of substance XYZ is metabolised, excreted, or environmentally degraded)*
5. What other activity did we do that demonstrated how a lipophilic substance accumulates? *(Part 3, the oil and water activity)*
6. Were you surprised at how the food colouring (i.e., substance XYZ) partitioned? Why or why not?
7. How might bioaccumulation, bioconcentration, biomagnification, and the process of global distillation affect animal and human health? *(Health could be affected only if substance XYZ has a toxic effect on the exposed organism and is present in high enough concentrations. Adverse health impacts might include weakened immune systems, growth problems, reproduction problems, disease, neurological [brain and nerve] effects, and death. Some of these impacts might take years to develop and be noticed. It is important to note that humans are at the top of most food chains, which means we could be exposed to the highest concentrations of substance XYZ.)*
8. How might we deal with the problem of bioaccumulation, bioconcentration, biomagnification, and global distillation of toxic substances?

Extensions/Adaptations

Adapt the activity to your own particular region or environment by focusing on local wildlife, plants, environment, and human health issues. This would make the topics more relevant to the students.

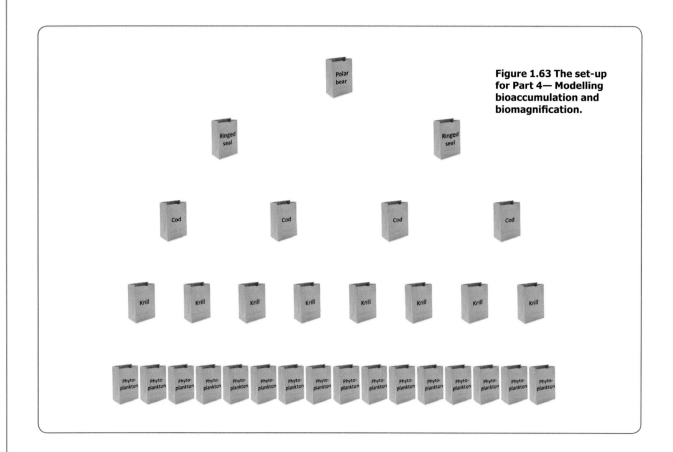

Figure 1.63 The set-up for Part 4— Modelling bioaccumulation and biomagnification.

ORGANISM CARD: FACTS

Organism name: _____

Latin name: _____

Habitat: _____

Ecological role: _____
_____
_____
_____

Physical description: _____
_____
_____

Diet: _____

Threatened or endangered? If so, why? _____
_____
_____

Geographic distribution: _____
_____
_____

Biology and behaviour: _____

Human uses? _____
_____
_____
_____

ORGANISM CARD: PICTURE

ORGANISM ILLUSTRATION

READY TO GO ON AN ANTARCTIC EXPEDITION?

(Thanks to Agathe Weber, IPF, Belgium)

Lesson at a glance

Students organise a mock Antarctic expedition, which helps them become more familiar with the Antarctic environment, learn how to work in groups, and develop their imagination and organisational skills.

Background

Antarctica is a frozen continent 14 million square kilometres in area surrounded by a vast ocean. At least 98% of the surface area of the continent is covered in ice, which is up to 4.7 kilometres thick in places. As much as 70% of the world's fresh water is stored as ice on the continent.

During the austral winter, no ships can reach the Antarctic coast because sea ice completely isolates the continent for a number of months, only breaking up during the austral summer (December to February).

Living conditions in Antarctica are harsh, with extremely low temperatures and frequently violent winds. Mean temperatures in winter range from about –40 to –70°C depending on location; while summer mean temperatures are between –15 and –35°C. The high inner plateau is much colder than the coastal regions. The climate is so extreme that there is virtually no life at all in the interior of the continent. The

Figure 1.64 During polar expeditions, the team members drag sledges holding all of their equipments behind them. This picture was taken during an expedition of Alain Hubert and Dixie Dansercoer in the Arctic.

largest animal found there is the wingless midge, an insect no more than 12 mm in length. Most life, such as seals, penguins and whales, is concentrated at or near the coast.

No human beings live in Antarctica on a permanent basis, but many adventurers undertake expeditions on the continent. Only the best prepared succeed. In the face of such harsh conditions, good preparation for the expedition is essential for success.

Time

Preparation: 10 minutes *(to copy or print the map and the material list)*
Class time: 1–2 class periods

Materials

(per group of students)
• *Partial List of Equipment for a Polar Expedition*
• *Antarctic Expedition Map*

Partial List of Equipment for a Polar Expedition

Antarctic Expedition Map

Activity Directions

1. After a short introduction discussing the conditions that expeditioners encounter in Antarctica, give each group of students a copy of the *Antarctic Expedition Map (Figure 1.65)*.
2. Tell the students to imagine that they are preparing for a polar expedition, with the goal of reaching the South Pole (elevation 2,850 m above sea level) with their team. They will travel on skis, each dragging a sledge holding all of their equipment. They will attempt the classic route leaving from sea level at Hercules Inlet. Remind them that before leaving, expeditioners would not only have to train to get into top physical condition, but also carefully select their route and prepare their equipment.

3. Instruct each group to do the following to the best of their ability:
   - Measure on the map the distance they will need to travel, and estimate the time they will need to reach the South Pole (assuming that they will cover about 18 km a day).
   - Decide the month of the year when they are going to leave from their departure point.
   - Make a list of personal equipment they need to take (clothes, skis, toothbrush, etc.) as well as equipment for the team (stove, pots, etc.). They should indicate the quantity of each item they need to take, depending on the number of people in the group.
   - Estimate the total weight of the equipment.
   - List the food items they need to take with them and estimate the total food weight.
   - Estimate the amount of water they need to take along.
   - Estimate the total weight of the equipment, food and water for the team, and determine how much weight each person in the team will have to pull.
   - Try to imagine what type of problems might hold the team up or prevent them from finishing the expedition, and how they could solve them (e.g., someone breaking an arm, running out of cooking fuel, etc.).
4. Compare the results of the different groups.
5. Give each group a copy of the equipment list handout.
6. Discuss this list and compare it to the lists prepared by the groups.

Discussion

1. What major technology innovations have made polar exploration easier and more secure? *(e.g., snowmobiles, planes and satellite radio transmission)*
2. Do you think it is a good thing that more and more people want to go on expeditions to the South Pole? What are some of the possible positive and negative impacts of these expeditions?

Extensions/Adaptations

1. After a short introduction to travel conditions at the beginning of the twentieth century, ask the students to imagine what the first expeditions to Antarctica might have been like around 1912. Remind them that polar explorers and their teams setting out from Europe would land in Antarctica after a sea voyage of seven months.
2. Have the students do some research on the expeditions of Amundsen and Scott, the first explorers to reach the South Pole.
3. Investigate the insulating properties of different materials in the next activity in this book, *'Keeping warm on polar expeditions.'*

PARTIAL LIST OF EQUIPMENT FOR A POLAR EXPEDITION
(Adapted from a list from the Belgian explorer, Alain Hubert)

DEPARTURE TIME

The austral summer runs from December to February. Anyone heading for the South Pole on skis departs at the end of November or beginning of December.

PERSONAL EQUIPMENT

- 1 pair bivouac foot-warmers
- 1 pair windproof over-mittens
- 2 pairs woollen or polar fleece mittens
- 2 pairs thin gloves made from polar fleece
- 1 windcheater jacket (anorak) with good hood to protect against the wind
- 1 pair windcheater trousers (shoulder straps and high waist recommended)
- 1 down jacket, preferably with a hood
- 1 polar fleece jacket (200 g) to be worn both in camp and while on the move during the day
- 2 pairs synthetic long johns (fleece or other)
- 1 pair vapour barrier liner socks (VBL): socks made from sturdy plastic
- 2 pairs thin socks, to be worn under the VBL (While they get wet each day, they dry very quickly inside the tent.)
- 2 pairs warm socks, to be worn over the VBL
- 1 warm beanie hat and windcheater, if possible
- 1 light beanie or cagoule for colder days
- 1 balaclava (Can also be worn as a scarf)
- 1 neoprene face mask for protection against headwinds
- 1 pair sunglasses, 1 tube sun block and 1 sun block lip salve
- 1 stiff brush for brushing clothes, and removing snow and ice from inside clothes, etc.
- 1 sturdy spoon (non-plastic), 1 eating bowl and 1 mug, insulated if possible
- 1 thermos: capacity 1.5 to 2 litres (for hot drinks, unbreakable)
- personal hygiene items: toothbrush, etc.
- small bags for personal gear and items for use during the day (must be easily accessible from the sledge)
- 1 penknife
- toilet paper
- 1 Nalgene night bottle (for urinating during the night)

TEAM EQUIPMENT

- tents, sleeping mats and sleeping bags
- snap hooks, rope and ice axes
- ice pitons, 3 per tent
- snow shovels, one for every two tents
- stove, fuel (Coleman white gas), lighter and cooking pots
- thermometer and anemometer
- map, GPS and compass
- repair kit for sledges and other spare parts
- basic medical supplies
- satellite phone, iPod, camcorder, camera, notebook and pencil, books, etc.
- universal distress beacon
- solar panel for recharging batteries for cameras, etc.

FOOD AND WATER

There are no animals on the Antarctic ice cap, so all food must be brought in from the outside. With the much lighter freeze-dried meals available these days, we calculate ~900 g of food per person per day. In addition to freeze-dried meals, we eat enriched supplements (cereals, energy bars, chocolate, cheese, etc.) and hot drinks. We do not carry water; we melt ice when needed.

APPROXIMATE WEIGHT OF A SLEDGE FOR 65 DAYS

- food: 900 g / day = 58.5 kg
- fuel (~16 litres): 14.5 kg
- sleeping bag: 3 kg
- sleeping mat: 1.5 kg
- down jacket: 2 kg
- various clothes: 6 kg
- 1/2 tent: 2.5 kg
- 1/2 cooking gear: 1 kg
- sledge: 6 kg
- part of shared equipment: 3 kg
- personal equipment: 2 kg

Total: ~100 kilos!!! This is why systems for providing fresh supplies of food and fuel are required. The sledges pulled by the members of an expedition led by a guide usually weigh between 35 and 60 kg.

However, for some professional expeditions, sledges can weigh up to 180 kg or more at departure. This extra weight is due to the rations required for long periods, communication and reporting gear or additional scientific equipment.

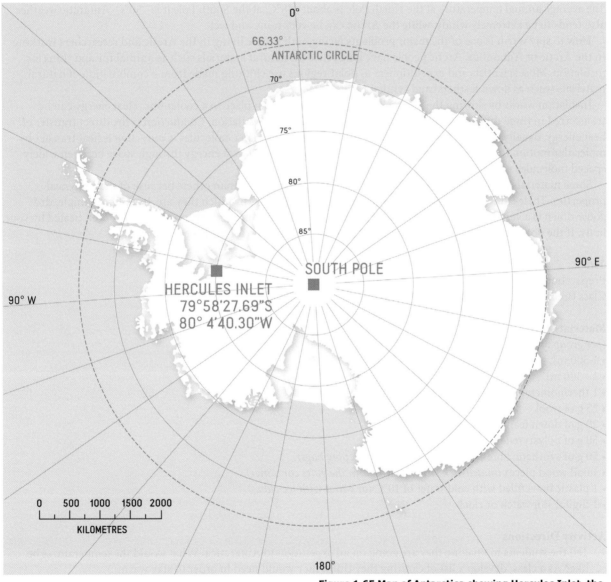

Figure 1.65 Map of Antarctica showing Hercules Inlet, the starting point for the 'classic route' to the South Pole.

KEEPING WARM ON POLAR EXPEDITIONS

(Thanks to Andrea Kaiser, Unilab of Humboldt University of Berlin, Germany)

Lesson at a glance

Students investigate different materials with respect to their ability to insulate a body against cold.

Background

The average annual temperature at the North Pole is about –18°C; at the South Pole it is –50°C. Antarctic weather also tends to be extremely windy, while the Arctic can be very rainy and wet.

How to stay warm is one of the major problems facing both people living in the Arctic and researchers working in the Arctic or Antarctica. Arctic people have long relied on natural materials such as animal fur and skins for insulation. Most scientists and expeditioners to polar regions use clothing made from a combination of natural materials (such as down feathers) and synthetic fibres.

Insulation works by slowing the flow of heat energy from a warm place to a cooler one. Heat energy can be transferred in three different ways: by conduction, convection and radiation. *Conduction* is the direct transfer of heat energy, usually in solids, by point to point contact of neighbouring molecules. *Convection* is heat transfer by molecular motion in liquids and gases. *Radiation* is the movement of heat energy through space between widely spaced molecules without the involvement of matter.

Some materials are more effective at slowing the flow of heat energy than others because of their physical properties. Their effectiveness may also be affected by the conditions in which they are used. For example, dry goose down is a very effective insulator because the feathers trap air between them; air that has been heated by your body. If the down gets wet, however, it loses this property and will no longer keep you warm.

Time

Preparation: ~30 minutes *(to collect materials, provide data tables, and heat water)*
Class time: 1 or more class periods *(~45 minutes each)*

Materials

(per group of 3–4 students)
- 1 500 mL wide-mouthed glass
- 1 ~300 mL small round tin container *(to be filled with 250 mL of 37°C water)*
- 1 thermometer
- 25 g of wool
- 20 g of down feathers
- 50 g of polystyrene *(in small pieces)*
- 50 g of synthetic fibres *(such as those used in sleeping bags)*
- small wood pieces *(matchstick size that will fit in the glass container)*
- 1 plastic bowl filled with cold water of 10°C *(or water with ice cubes)*
- 1 digital stopwatch or clock

Activity Directions

1. Tell the students to imagine they are going on an expedition to Antarctica. What would the temperatures be like? As a class, develop a list of clothing they think they would need in order to stay warm.
2. Discuss what materials would make the most suitable clothing. What would insulate them best and keep them warm? Make another list of possible materials.
3. Divide the students into groups of 3 to 4. Give each group a set of materials and the following instructions:
   a. Fill the small round tin container with 250 mL of warm water (37°C).
   b. Place this tin container into the glass.
   c. Put one type of insulation material (wool, feathers, polystyrene, synthetic fibres, or air) between the bottom and the sides of the two containers.

   Note: If you are using air as an insulator, put the small wooden pieces at the bottom of the glass before you put the tin container in the glass. This ensures there will be a layer of air as insulation at the bottom.

d. Measure the initial temperature of the water in the tin container and enter the result in the table.

e. Put the filled glass into the plastic bowl of cold water and start the clock.

f. Measure the temperature of the warm water inside the tin container after 10 minutes. Enter this result in the table.

g. Repeat the experiment again with a different type of insulation material.

4. In total, the students should complete 5 different rounds of measurements. After they are done, have them rank the materials in terms of insulating effectiveness and discuss their results.

Note: To save time, have each group investigate only one or two materials. For example, you could have group A test materials 1 and 2, group B test 2 and 3, group C test 3 and 4, etc. In this way, you would have at least two trials of each material. After the groups have finished the trials, compare the results from all of the groups.

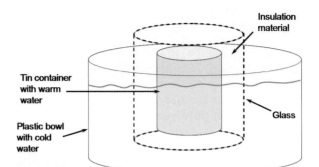

Figure 1.66 Set-up of the experiment.

Table for the results:		
	Initial Temperature in °C	Temperature after 10 minutes in °C
Air		
Wool		
Feathers		
Polystyrene		
Artificial fibres		

Figure 1.67 Example table to record the results.

Discussion

1. What variables did you have to control so you could compare the different materials? *(The thickness of the insulating material, the temperature of both the cold and hot water at the start of the experiment, the length of time between the first and second temperature measurements.)*

2. How does insulation work? *(By slowing the movement of heat energy from a warm place to a cooler one.)*

3. How does heat energy flow? *(By conduction, convection and radiation. You can illustrate this with the idea of a metal pot of water on a campfire. The pan heats by conduction, the water by convection, and the person near the fire is warmed by radiation.)*

4. Why were some materials more effective insulators than others? *(Because they have structures that are better at trapping air, which is warmed by the body as it emits heat, and isolate the body from the outside cold.)*

5. Would the results be the same if the insulating materials were wet? *(In most cases, no.)* Why or why not? *(When a material becomes wet, it is more thermally conductive because water molecules are a good conductor of heat.)*

Extensions/Adaptations

1. Investigate how well the same materials would insulate in wet conditions.

2. Investigate the effect of wind on insulating properties by using a cool stream of air from a hair dryer to cool the glass.

SPACE

By improving our knowledge about processes that connect the two hemispheres, we can dramatically improve our understanding of global geoelectric and geomagnetic systems.

The auroras, borealis (north) and australis (south), have forever fascinated and mystified observers. Carefully recorded observations by hundreds of volunteers across large regions during the previous Polar Years provided convincing evidence that auroral processes, at least in the North, occurred in a connected fashion across the Arctic. Spectacular imagery from humans in space and from satellites confirmed these hemispheric connections.

We now know that high energy particles from the Sun, guided by the Earth's magnetic field into convergence zones at the poles, collide with and excite atmospheric oxygen and nitrogen atoms and molecules. When the excited atoms and molecules relax, they release energy in the form of the light we see as the aurora. The energy emitted by nitrogen gives red and purple colours, while oxygen appears green. The changing and ephemeral nature of the aurora gives us clear hints of the dynamic processes of particle influx and magnetic field variations.

By conducting and comparing simultaneous measurements in both the Arctic and Antarctic, scientists have discovered correlations and interhemispheric coupling of geomagnetic processes and auroras in the Northern and Southern Hemispheres. Researchers have confirmed that an intersection of a magnetic field line with the Earth's surface at one pole has a conjugate, or paired, intersection in the polar region of the opposite hemisphere, causing auroral displays in a ring around both poles at the same time.

Observations from space also give us the opportunity to collect data about the polar regions on a global scale and across a wide range of scientific questions, giving us an unparalleled vision of past, present and future developments of polar ice, ocean and land masses. The Global Interagency International Polar Snapshot Year (GIIPSY) project, for example, is a global network of Earth observation satellites. These satellites have

Figure 1.68 A long exposure photograph taken in interior Alaska's boreal forest shows both the glow of Northern Lights activity and the trailing effect of the stars as the Earth rotates.

been providing polar photographs that will help us understand important environmental interconnections related to sea level rise, ocean circulation and polar air-sea interactions, as well as providing measurements of precipitation, hydrology and permafrost terrain.

In addition, the cold, stable conditions and the kilometres-deep clear ice of Antarctica also serve as an ideal platform for learning more about our universe through the study of subatomic particles called neutrinos.

The following activities suggest ways to bring some of these aspects of polar science into the classroom.

Space Activities

UNDERSTANDING AURORAS

VIEWS FROM SPACE

THE MISSING ENERGY MYSTERY: POPCORN AND NEUTRINOS

UNDERSTANDING AURORAS

(Thanks to Jane Dobson and Sandra Zicus, Australia)

Lesson at a glance

Students investigate the Earth's magnetic field using a map of the Earth, a bar magnet and iron filings, and relate it to the formation of auroras.

Background

People living or working in the polar regions are often treated to spectacular shows of shimmering coloured lights in the night sky. These light shows are caused by a series of interactions between the Earth and Sun.

The Earth behaves like a giant magnet. All magnets have two magnetic poles, called north and south. The space surrounding a magnet where the effects of the magnet can be felt is called the *magnetic field*. The rotation of Earth around its molten core generates electricity and causes a magnetic field that extends for several tens of kilometres into space. The magnetic force in the field is strongest at the poles of the magnet and weakest in the middle.

The Earth's magnetic poles are not located in the same place as the geographic poles (the axis around which the Earth rotates). The magnetic poles also move over

Figure 1.69 Aurora borealis seen in Greenland. The greenish colour is typical of auroras caused by the energy emitted by excited atoms and molecules of oxygen.

time by as much as 15 kilometres per year. The magnetic north and south poles are not directly opposite each other, and they move independently of each other. At present, the magnetic north pole is located near Ellesmere Island in northern Canada (approximately 83°N, 115°W).

The Sun is a ball of hydrogen gas powered by nuclear fusion that is taking place at its core. The Sun's outer layer is so hot that hydrogen atoms are split into protons and electrons, resulting in an electrically conductive gas known as *plasma*.

The plasma is continuously blown away from the Sun in a stream called the *solar wind*. Most of the solar wind does not reach the Earth's surface. The Earth's magnetic field causes it to blow around the Earth, creating a long cylindrical cavity called the *magnetosphere*. When electrons in the solar wind enter the Earth's magnetic field, these particles spiral down the polar magnetic field lines. When they reach the upper atmosphere they collide with atmospheric particles and their energy is released as a beautiful display of auroral light.

You can demonstrate the Earth's magnetic field by doing the activity below.

Time

Class time: 20 minutes *(more for discussion on auroras)*

Materials

(per group of 3–4 students)
• 1 large bar magnet
• picture of globe *(printed on a stiff sheet of paper or clear plastic)*
• iron filings

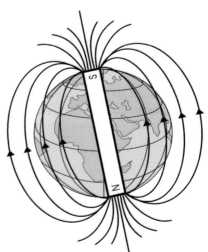

Figure 1.70 Earth's magnetic field.

Activity Directions
1. Place the picture of the globe on top of a large bar magnet, with the poles of the magnet tilted about 11° from the geographic poles on the globe. This represents the approximate location of the Earth's magnetic poles.
2. Sprinkle some iron filings on the plastic or paper and tap it gently. You should be able to see that the iron filings arrange themselves in pattern around the magnet forming closed lines that represent the magnetic field.

Discussion
1. What causes the Earth's magnetic field? (*This is still not clearly understood, although it appears linked to the Earth's rotation around the fluid metallic iron that makes up a large part of the inner core. This generates an electrical current, and we know that magnetic fields surround electrical currents.*)
2. Do other planets have auroras? (*Yes. The Hubble spacecraft photographed an aurora near one of Jupiter's poles. Images have also been taken of auroral activity around Saturn's poles.*)
3. Why is the Earth's north magnetic pole shown as the south pole of the bar magnet in *Figure 1.70*? (*This is just a matter of convention, based on the use of magnetic compasses to determine direction. On a bar magnet, the magnetic field lines are considered to exit from the north pole and enter at the south pole. A compass is simply a small magnet mounted so that it can move freely. The north arrow on the compass was originally called the 'north-seeking' pole of the magnet because it pointed towards geographic north. This term was later shortened to just 'north pole' for all magnets, including compass needles. Since opposite magnetic poles attract each other, the north pole of the compass magnet is attracted to a south magnetic pole—it just happens to be located in the Earth's geographic north!*)

Extensions/Adaptations
1. Here is an alternate way to demonstrate the Earth's magnetic fields without iron filings:
    a. Place the bar magnet on top of the picture of the Earth, with the poles of the magnet tilted at 11° from the geographic poles.
    b. Take a small magnetic compass and place it near the bar magnet. The compass needle will line up with the field lines around the magnet.
    c. Map out the field lines by using a pencil to mark the direction in which the compass is pointing at different places around the magnet:

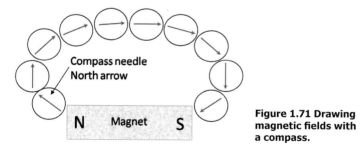

Figure 1.71 Drawing magnetic fields with a compass.

2. Have students experiment with different art techniques to draw pictures of an aurora. (*See the web links to this activity on the CD-ROM for access to good photographs.*)

VIEWS FROM SPACE

(Thanks to Matteo Cattadori, Uta Fritsch, Philipp Rastner, Christian Steurer and Francesca Taponecco, Italy)

Lesson at a glance

Students learn to extract information from satellite images and interpret their meaning using open source educational software.

Background

Satellite images provide an ideal data source for studying places such as the polar regions that are difficult to access. Due to the bird's eye perspective, they allow an analysis of the landscape and land cover on a broad scale. The use of information in visible and non-visible parts of the spectrum enables the user to determine the land cover in more detail and identify differences in an easy way. Multi-temporal imagery also allows analysis of long-term changes such as fluctuation of ice sheets or sea ice.

LEOworks is a free, open source, simplified version of image processing software that the European Space Agency (ESA) developed especially for educational purposes. With the software it is possible to analyse and process satellite images, in order to extract and interpret information. Satellite images include data from different parts of the electromagnetic spectrum such as visible light, near infrared and middle infrared. Each section of the spectrum is recorded

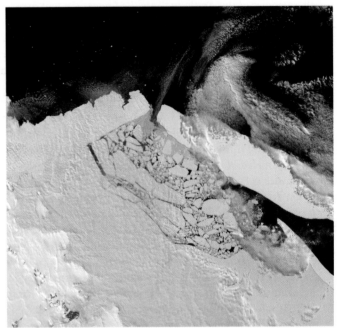

Figure 1.72 LandSat image of iceberg B-15A breaking off from the Drygalski ice tongue in 2005.

in a single *channel* as a black and white image. A coloured picture is then obtained using computer software by assigning and combining three channels to the colours blue, red and green. Different combinations of channels allow users to visualise different aspects of the land cover.

Time

Preparation: 30 minutes *(excluding software installation, data preparation)*
Class time: 30 minutes or more *(depending on the students' backgrounds and experience)*

Materials

(per person)
• *Analysing Satellite Images* student directions

(per group of students)
• computer workstations *(with installed LEOworks software)*
• satellite images

Analysing Satellite Images Student Directions

Advance Preparation

1. To access the software go to: http://www.eduspace.esa.int/eduspace/leoworks/leoworks.asp. Download and install the free LEOworks software and copy Landsat satellite images into a data folder on your school's computers. *(Note: The software version 3.0 is developed only for Windows operative systems; version 4.0 will be platform independent.)*
2. Print and photocopy the instructions and worksheet for the students.

Activity Directions

1. Ask the students to name different ways that scientific data can be collected. Make a list on the board and briefly discuss the advantages and limitations of the different methods. Why are some methods more useful than others for different types of research?

2. Tell the students that they are going to work as scientists, and look at and interpret some satellite imagery. Give them copies of the *Analysing Satellite Images* student directions handout and allow time for them to complete the activity.

3. Regroup the students and discuss their experiences. Refer back to the original list of research methods that they created at the beginning. Have their ideas changed after working with the satellite images? What did they learn from working with the images? What difficulties did they encounter?

Discussion

1. Why did the ice-free land cover appear in bright red in the colour infrared picture? *(In the colour infrared picture, red stands for a high reflection in the near infrared that gives a hint to active vegetation in the area.)*

2. What do you think satellite images could be used for? *(Remote sensing is used in many disciplines including geology, meteorology, hydrology, coastal management, forestry, agriculture, land use planning, and for military applications.)*

3. What are the advantages of the applied remote sensing? *(It allows for analysis without having to travel to a region; coverage of large areas; pictures are available for time series; allows analysis of regional and global phenomena like the fluctuation of the ozone layer; information that is not available with 'eyes only' opens new possibilities; easy interpretation and relatively cheap. Researchers can learn about Earth processes through broad-scale interpretation of pictures.)*

4. What are the disadvantages? *(Computer and software are necessary. It is difficult to know if the results are accurate as 'ground truthing' is expensive. There are limits to the scale and detail that can be analysed.)*

5. Why is satellite remote sensing especially important in polar research? *(It gives us the ability to analyse areas that are difficult to access, monitor surface dynamics caused by climate change, and observe dynamics of glaciers and ice sheets.)*

Note: Teachers or invited researchers who are supervising the activity play the role of tutors only when students need their help. The students learn by working in a self-directed way, but have the opportunity to have contact with scientists by approaching them directly.

Extensions/Adaptations

1. Repeat the exercise for a different geographical area of interest.

2. For more advanced students: Use the LEOWorks tool options to adjust other parameters and process the digital satellite image. For example, select and process a larger set of spectral bands within the electromagnetic spectrum to distinguish between snow and clouds. Analyse the sensitivity of the classification tool by varying different parameter values. Increase the number of classes and iterations, and compare the results.

THE MISSING ENERGY MYSTERY: POPCORN AND NEUTRINOS

(Thanks to Steve Stevenoski and Eric Muhs, USA)

Lesson at a glance

By measuring popcorn before and after popping, students will investigate the concepts behind neutrinos and then discuss the IceCube Project that is searching for neutrino sources in the universe.

Background

The first law of thermodynamics, also known as the law of conservation of energy, states that energy can neither be created nor destroyed. The following activity models a reaction in which there was an apparent loss of energy, which led to the discovery of a particle called a *neutrino*.

In the 1920s, study of nuclear reactions showed that when a neutron changed into a proton in a process called *beta decay,* it released an electron which became known as a *beta particle.* However, careful measurements showed that the proton and the beta particle together had slightly less energy than the original neutron.

This led Wolfgang Pauli, an Austrian theoretical physicist, to propose that another particle was released during beta decay, which carried the missing energy. Since the particle had to have a neutral charge and small mass, it was called a neutrino (which means 'little neutral one'). It was not until 1956 that scientists first experimentally detected a particle fitting these characteristics.

The IceCube Project in Antarctica is looking for high-energy neutrinos that originate from specific sources deep in space. Since neutrinos have no charge, they are not deflected by magnetic fields and travel in a straight line. Consequently, we can tell where a neutrino is coming from by its path and, in this way, learn about the sources that are producing these high-energy particles.

Neutrinos cannot be seen directly, but their paths can be detected by their interaction with other particles. When muon neutrinos (as opposed to the two other types—electron neutrinos and tau neutrinos) interact with *nucleons* (protons or neutrons), the incident neutrino is destroyed and a *muon* is produced. The muon is a charged particle which continues in the same direction as the incident neutrino. The muon lasts only 2.2 microseconds before it decays, but before it decays it has a polarising effect on atoms it passes. The muon tugs on the electrons inside atoms it passes via the electromagnetic force. After the muon passes, the electrons return to their prior state, releasing photons and resulting in a faint blue light known as *Cherenkov radiation.*

The IceCube experiment is set up at the South Pole because the ice is transparent enough for the faint blue light to be seen by special instruments called photodetectors, which amplify the signal so it can be recorded in digital form by

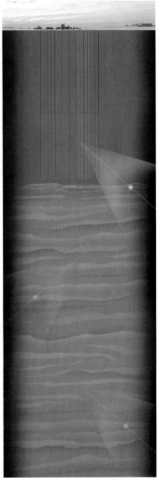

Figure 1.73 An artist's conception of a muon producing light as it travels through the ice at the South Pole.

computers. Holes are drilled deep in the ice by a hot water drill and a series of photomultiplier tubes are carefully lowered into the ice between depths of 1.5 and 2.5 kilometres. The deep ice is essentially bubble free and very clean, so the light can travel up to a couple hundred metres before being absorbed and has an effective scattering length up to 50 metres.

The big challenge is to make sure the muon is produced by a neutrino rather than from the much more numerous cosmic rays. Muons from the Northern Hemisphere get absorbed before they reach the detector at the South Pole. Neutrinos, however, can travel all the way through the Earth because they rarely react with other particles. So, the path of the muon must be reconstructed using the time when light was detected at each module. If it came from within

Figure 1.74 An IceCube light sensor that is being readied for deployment at the South Pole.

the Earth (from the Northern Hemisphere), we know it must be from a neutrino. If it came from the atmosphere and was heading towards the Earth's interior, it was most likely from a cosmic ray. At the depth of IceCube, there are about one million cosmic ray muons for each neutrino muon!

Time
Preparation: ~1 hour
Class time: 2 class periods *(~50 minutes each)*

Materials
(per class)
- 2 kinds of popcorn *(such as two different brands)*

(per group of students)
- popcorn popper *(Air poppers are easiest because they do not need oil.)*
- ~40–100 g popcorn *(depending upon the popcorn popper)*
- container for kernels and container for popped corn
- data recording sheet, student notebook, or computers with spreadsheet software
- balance *(sensitive enough to measure to at least 0.1 g and preferably to 0.01 g)*

Advance Preparation
Before the lab, get the popcorn, the popcorn poppers (poppers may be either purchased—e.g., at thrift stores—or brought into class by the students) and the balances. Try the experiment in advance to become familiar with it, and test the circuits in your classroom or laboratory to make sure there is enough wattage for all popcorn poppers to be used simultaneously.

Activity Directions
1. Ask the students if they think popcorn weighs the same, more, or less after it is popped. Have them make a prediction and explain their reasoning.
2. Ask them how they could test their predictions. What equipment will they need? How will they control the variables?
3. Remind them of the safety precautions and discuss the importance of accurate data collection and recording.
4. Review the proper use of the balances and the popcorn poppers, and then divide the students into teams. Give each team 40–100 g of popcorn (depending on the type of popper being used) and a balance. Give half of the teams one kind of popcorn, and half the other kind.
5. While the students are doing the experiment, circulate among the teams and ask them guiding questions such as:
    - Why not pop just one kernel?
    - According to the data, is your hypothesis correct? Did the mass of the kernels increase, decrease, or stay the same?
    - What variables are there in this experiment?
    - What difficulties did you encounter? How were you able to overcome them?
6. After all the groups are finished, bring the whole class together and discuss the results.
7. Tell the students about the discovery of neutrinos and ask them how the experiment they just conducted relates to this discovery.
8. Discuss how neutrinos are being used to 'map' part of the universe and why Antarctica is the ideal place for this kind of study. (See http://www.youtube.com/watch?v=nx5wphtHBZQ for a short video about neutrinos and the detector.)

Caution: If you are going to allow the students to eat the popcorn, take special precautions to wash lab tables, have clean containers, wash hands. Stress that students not eat the popcorn until after all the measurements are taken!

Discussion

1. How many teams found a gain in mass? A loss? The same mass?
2. Why might teams get different results? *(Get beyond 'bad measurements'—some possibilities are: Variation in popcorn? Variation in popcorn popper temperature or speed of popping? Variation in what group decided to count—e.g., what to do in terms of data and calculations with unpopped or partially popped corn?)*
3. What variables affected the results of this experiment? Would it matter if new or old corn was used? Why?
4. According to the Law of Conservation of Mass, can mass be lost? If mass was lost, where did it go? *(The students should figure out that the 'lost' mass is due to the water contained in the kernel escaping as steam.)*
5. How is this experiment an analogy for the beta decay process?
6. It took scientists a long time between proposing the neutrino as a hypothetical particle and collecting evidence that demonstrated its existence. Are there other questions in physics or science where a theoretical answer is in place, but actual evidence needed is lacking?

Extensions/Adaptations

1. Use a video camera to record individual kernels popping (easiest from a flat pan, but beware of spattering oil). Use a motion analysis software to make quantitative measurements of energy. Many individual energy estimates can be combined to produce an energy spectrum for the popped corn. This work should produce a data set suitable for statistical analysis.
2. Calculate the initial pressure inside the kernel, based on available quantitative measurements and reasonable quantitative assumptions.
3. Develop a method to collect, condense and weigh the water vapour released by the popping corn. Re-examine the earlier conclusions about conservation of mass vs. mass loss with this new information.
4. Prepare popcorn kernels at different states of dehydration (using different times in a drying chamber or low oven) and compare popping energy spectra.
5. Invent a way to damage the seed coats of the popcorn, and examine the effect of this damage on popping. Challenges include being able to quantify both the extent of the damage and its effect on popping.
6. Use an infrared camera to collect pictures of the popped kernels. What new kinds of analysis are possible with this new way to look at this phenomenon?

Figure 1.75 Gambell on St. Lawrence Island in the Bering Sea. The Alaskan island is closer to Russia than to mainland Alaska. The image looks towards the west with Russia 40 miles in the distance.

Going Further

We hope that the activities in the previous sections have given you some ideas of how to incorporate polar research and polar learning in your classroom or other venue. Here we introduce a few different techniques that IPY researchers and educators have used successfully. Teaching and learning about the polar regions is limited only by your imagination and creativity!

Oral History Research

Oral history research involves the systematic collecting of people's experiences and memories through interviews, stories and conversation. In recent years, it has been recognised as an important aspect of social research that gathers data that would otherwise be lost, and gives us a more personal understanding of the relationship of humans with their environments.

In many indigenous societies, oral history and storytelling are still important ways of transmitting knowledge from generation to generation. For example, indigenous Arctic communities have a knowledge system that is essential to survival in the Arctic, and to the continuation of strong indigenous cultures. Traditionally, Elders and other knowledgeable community members pass this information to the younger generations, who learn through watching and listening. Modern tools to aid in the transmission of traditional knowledge include computers, cameras and voice recorders.

Giving students the opportunity to act as oral historians helps them develop an appreciation for their culture, their environment and their links to the past, as well as gain a better perspective on the possibilities for their future. It is a technique that can be used in almost any cultural setting—not just in indigenous communities.

Developing Critical Thinking Skills

Every day we encounter information related to science in the media. However, it is often hard to tell what information is trustworthy and what information is not. An ability to analyse what we read, hear and see in a critical manner and to make reasonable judgements about its credibility is an extremely important life skill. It is an essential skill if we want to make responsible choices and environmentally sound decisions. With a few tips and a bit of practice, students can learn and maintain good critical thinking skills that they can use when they watch the news or read newspapers.

Going Further Activities

ORAL TRADITIONS RESEARCH

CRITICAL THINKING

ORAL TRADITIONS RESEARCH: USING THE SCHOOLS ON BOARD TRADITIONAL KNOWLEDGE COLLECTION KIT

(Thanks to Robin Gislason, Mark Heyck, Jessica Kotierk and Lucette Barber, Canada)

Lesson at a glance

Students take part in field-based research by conducting community interviews to explore local Traditional Knowledge related to climate change.

Background

Indigenous Arctic communities have a knowledge system that has been passed down through the generations. This knowledge system is essential to survival in the Arctic, and to the continuation of strong indigenous cultures. Indigenous peoples in the Arctic have an intrinsic relationship to the land and their environment. This connection to the land is passed onto new generations through the culture's Traditional Knowledge (TK).

In 2008, Schools on Board developed a Traditional Knowledge Collection Kit to be used during and after its IPY Circumpolar Inuit Field Program. *(See Chapter 3 for more information on the IPY-CIFP, IPY-CFL and SonB programmes.)* The kit provided the tools necessary for students to collect Traditional Knowledge related to issues of Arctic climate change, and to share this knowledge with other participants, Elders, and scientists involved in the IPY-Circumpolar Flaw Lead system study.

The project and kit were designed to be consistent with the underlying 'two-ways of knowing' philosophy of the scientific research study. This philosophy recognises that there are two knowledge systems in the Arctic— one that is based on indigenous knowledge built up over generations of interconnections between humans and their environment, and one that is based on scientific knowledge built up over years of research in the Arctic. It recognises the importance of integrating these two knowledge systems in order to gain a better understanding of the entire Arctic ecosystem. *(See Chapter 4 for more information on Traditional and scientific knowledge and the creation of new knowledge in polar research.)*

Time

Preparation: Time to review manuals and research guidelines so that they can be incorporated or adapted to appropriate grade level

Class time: 5–7 classes spread out over 2–3 weeks to include time for completing interviews

Materials

(per pair of students)
- digital voice recorder
- notebook and pencil
- digital camera
- *Getting started in Oral Traditions Research Manual*
- *Negotiating Research Relationships with Inuit Communities*
- ethical research guidelines *(found in both documents listed above)*
- consent form *(prepared by teacher or by students)*
- map of the local area *(optional, but useful for stimulating discussion and identifying important places and events)*
- small tokens of appreciation for interviewees *(e.g., tea, chocolates, cookies, etc.)*

Oral Traditions Research Manual

Negotiating Research Relationships with Inuit Communities

Activity Directions

1. Introduce background information on TK and scientific research on climate change. Ask the students to search for any oral traditions research previously conducted in the community, region, or territory.
2. Use the *Getting started in Oral Traditions Research Manual* as a guide to introduce the research procedures including ethical principles (consent forms), interview techniques, digital equipment, project timeline and expectations for final results.
3. Working in pairs, have the students develop a research plan that includes:
   - the *issue* or *problem* related to climate change that they are researching
   - *who* they plan to interview

- *what* questions they plan to ask
- *where* and *when* they will conduct interviews
- *how* they will process their data and share results with the class (*e.g., report, community presentation, poster*)

4. Have the students generate a list of interview questions that includes both general and specific questions. Encourage them to use open-ended questions that lead to more elaborate answers and discussions. Remind them that the questions might have to be translated for Elders. Questions might focus on students' own non-Arctic community but they might also aim at interviewees in Arctic communities. Questions might include things such as:

General questions:
- When and where were you born?
- What environmental changes have you experienced or observed?
- How have these changes impacted your way of life?
- Have you changed what you do because of changes to your environment? If so, in what ways?
- How did your parents/grandparents/Elders teach you about the land and the environment?

More specific questions that will depend on the topic students are researching:
- What are the most common uses of sea ice? Has this use of sea ice changed?
- Are there any polynyas around our community? What happens at these polynyas?
- Do you have place names that refer to ice features like a polynya or pressure ridge? Can you show me where these are located on a map?
- What do you think scientists should be looking at?
- Is there anything else that you would like to add that we did not discuss?
- What advice can you give young people like me, about caring for the environment?

5. Help the students identify possible interview partners. These people should be the most knowledgeable people in the community and/or individuals with close connections to the land—e.g., Elders, experienced hunters, and those experienced in traditional practices.

6. Give the students information about how to set up and conduct interviews while following manual instructions:
- Use both recorders and notebooks.
- Take photos that will enrich the presentations of results.
- Take notes of your first impressions after the completed interview.
- Organise your information and transcribe the recordings into text.
- Double-check the transcripts with the interviewees and get their approval.
- Interpret your findings and share the results.

7. Facilitate a group discussion for the students to share their thoughts on the process of collecting TK, the importance of TK to their understanding of climate change, the value of sharing this knowledge between generations, the similarities and differences between scientific and Traditional Knowledge, and the importance of TK to the scientific understanding of climate change.

8. Before starting the actual interview process, have the students work in groups to practise interviews through role play.

Note: The consent form can be created by searching the Internet for examples. This can be a separate activity for students or done in advance by the teacher. If interviews are being conducted outside of school hours, you need to ensure that interviewees are well known to the students, and that the students conduct interviews in pairs, or are accompanied by an adult.

Discussion
1. How has technology helped and/or hindered the process of learning from Traditional Knowledge?
2. Is Traditional Knowledge still important in the modern era? Why or why not?

Extensions/Adaptations
1. Invite a researcher who uses these methods to come to your classroom.
2. If possible, invite an Elder to visit your classroom.
3. Combine this activity with the activity '*What is Community?*' in the People section.

CRITICAL THINKING: SHOULD WE BELIEVE EVERYTHING WE ARE TOLD?
(Thanks to Agathe Weber and Laurent Dubois, IPF, Belgium and Switzerland; and Sandra Zicus, Australia)

Lesson at a glance
Students analyse the uses of language in the media by reading articles from opposing viewpoints and analysing them for credibility.

Background
Every day we encounter information related to science in the media. However, it is often hard to tell what information is trustworthy and what information is not. An ability to analyse what we read in a critical manner and make reasonable judgements about its credibility is an extremely important life skill. Without too much difficulty, students can learn and maintain good critical thinking skills.

These skills should help them:
- differentiate between scientific data, interpretations and opinions;
- identify possible sources of bias;
- make an educated assessment of the validity of the information.

The term *data* refers to quantitative or qualitative information about a variable or set of variables, as a result of careful measurements. Air temperature, wind speeds, precipitation, and sea surface temperatures are all examples of data related to weather and climate. An *interpretation* of this and related data might yield a long-term weather *forecast* or a climate change *prediction*.

A *personal opinion* may or may not carry scientific weight, depending on the person's knowledge of the subject and their purpose in expressing the opinion.

Language is also not value-neutral. There is no such thing as a completely objective report or a completely objective reader. The meaning that we give to words is based, in part, on a perception of the world that has been filtered through our history, our culture (global, local, family, etc.), and our personal experiences. Words can also have variable meanings depending on their context. They can be, and often are, used to promote specific agendas.

We often assume that what we read is true without examining our unconscious assumptions, or considering the underlying meanings of commonly accepted terms and concepts, the source of the information, or the particular interests of the author.

There are many ways to manipulate language (and images) to persuade. These include (but are not limited to):
- selection of words to use and information to report;
- emphasis on particular words;
- context of the material;
- use of specialised jargon;
- appeals to emotions;
- use of innuendo or implications;
- repetition of key words and/or phrases;
- use of 'expert' opinion or statements taken out of context;
- illogical reasoning.

Time
Preparation: 30 minutes to find and copy 2 different media articles
Class time: 2 classroom sessions of about 45 minutes, or 1 session plus homework time

Materials
(per student)
- 2 media articles, expressing different viewpoints, about an aspect of change in the polar regions (all students should receive the same ones)
- 3 highlighters (yellow, blue and green)
- *'I read it, so it must be true'* worksheet

 'I read it, so it must be true' Worksheet

Activity Directions

Part 1—Defining the terms

1. Begin with a discussion of the difference between scientific data, data interpretation, and personal opinion. Try to get a consensus about the definitions.

2. Post the following statements at the front of the classroom:
    - Global warming is killing the polar bears and destroying their home.
    - Claims that carbon dioxide is a 'pollutant' are fraudulent because carbon dioxide is a benign gas which is also a fertiliser and necessary for the growth of plants.
    - The year 2007 had the lowest summer Arctic sea ice extent since satellite measurements began.
    - More than four million people live in the nations surrounding the Arctic. Indigenous populations vary from more than 80% in Greenland to less than 5% in the Russian Arctic.
    - Warmer sea surface temperatures cause sea level rise, threatening millions of people who live in coastal communities.

3. Ask the students which of the statements (or parts of the statements) show scientific data, which are interpretations of data, and which are opinions. Discuss their reasoning.

Part 2—Identifying data, interpretation, and opinion

1. Copy and hand out the following sentences to each student, or write them on the board:
    - In 2100, climate change will have caused temperatures to rise by 7°C. The sea level will have risen by 50 cm, displacing 600 million people.
    - According to the Intergovernmental Panel on Climate Change (IPCC)'s AR4 in 2007, the average temperatures on Earth could increase by 1.1 to 6.4°C by 2100, which could produce a sea level rise between 18 and 59 cm. Also by the end of the century the number of people affected by flooding each year could reach as many as 420 million.

2. Ask the students to decide which of these texts seems more trustworthy to them and why. Discuss. *(The second statement is more precise. It cites its sources and emphasises that the figures mentioned are only estimates. Scientists are not psychics who can predict the future; they only evaluate probable events, basing their evaluations on observable phenomena and empirical data. Therefore they generally speak about a range of possible future situations.)*

3. Give the students a media article about some aspect of change in the polar regions. Ask them to read the article and highlight the scientific data in yellow, the data interpretation in blue and the personal opinions in green.

4. Review the article with the entire class and discuss their observations and ideas. Are they in agreement about the categories? Why or why not? What criteria did they use in their decisions?

5. Give them a second article that presents an opposing viewpoint and have them repeat the exercise.

6. Ask the students to make a judgement about the credibility of the articles. What are the sources? Do they come from a person, organisation, or agency with a particular special interest? What are the credentials of the author? Is his or her argument supported by evidence? Are the sources of information credited?

Part 3—Assessing bias

1. Go back to the original statements that were posted. Discuss the different ways that written language can be used to persuade the reader to accept a particular point of view. Can the students find particular words, phrases, or other devices in the examples that are being used to persuade or confuse the issue? For example:
    - Global warming is killing the polar bears and destroying their home. *(Appeals to emotions through negative connotations of the words 'killing' and 'destroying', and the poignant concept of 'home'.)*
    - Claims that carbon dioxide is a 'pollutant' are fraudulent because carbon dioxide is a benign gas which is also a fertiliser and necessary for the growth of plants. *(Selection of 'fact' to present – i.e., that carbon dioxide is necessary for plant growth; incomplete information. What is the context? Also, use of the word 'fraudulent', which indicates dishonesty.)*

- The year 2007 had the lowest summer Arctic sea ice extent since satellite measurements began. *(Can this be supported by evidence?)*
- Warmer sea surface temperatures cause sea level rise, threatening millions of people who live in coastal communities. *(According to whom? What is the source? What is meant by the word 'threat'?)*

2. Give them a copy of the *I read it, so it must be true* worksheet. Ask them to re-read both articles and make a list of the ways in which the authors try to persuade the reader of their points of view. Are there appeals to emotions or values such as fear, greed, or hatred? Are statements being used in the proper context? Does the language used imply things that are not stated directly? Are certain words or phrases emphasised more than others?

Discussion
1. How do your own preconceptions affect the way you interpret something you read or hear?
2. How do you judge the credibility of an 'expert' opinion?

Extensions/Adaptations
1. Ask the students (individually or in small groups) to find an article that presents scientific information that seems clearly untrustworthy to them and make a short presentation to the class explaining the content of the article and why it seems unreliable.
2. Extend the activity to look at personal values and discuss how values affect our interpretation of what we see or hear. You can use the following technique to begin a values discussion:
   a. Post two opposing statements on opposite sides of the room (e.g., 'Carbon emissions trading is essential to minimise future climate change.' 'Carbon emissions trading is worthless as a technique to minimise future climate change.)
   b. Put a piece of string or tape along the floor between the two statements and label it at equal intervals from 1 to 10.
   c. Ask the students to think about the statements and decide where they stand on the issue, then ask them to take a place along the line near the number that best represents what they believe. Emphasise that there is not a 'right' or 'wrong' answer and that everyone's opinion should be respected. Try to discourage the students from allowing themselves to be influenced by peer pressure.
   Ask the students why they chose the positions they did and give them an opportunity to discuss their reasoning.
3. Have the students work in teams to research an ecological topic of their choice and write a deliberately biased article, then discuss it with the rest of the class.
4. Do a science experiment with the students and have them present their results in written reports. As a class, discuss and analyse the reports for bias.

'I READ IT, SO IT MUST BE TRUE' WORKSHEET

Resource type (book, magazine, newspaper, web article, etc.): _____

Title: _____

Author: _____ Date: _____

Organisation, agency, or special interest group(s) represented: _____

Techniques of persuasion (list examples of any you find):

Appeal to emotions _____

_____

Emphasis of certain words, facts, or opinions _____

_____

Repeated words, phrases, or information _____

_____

Implications or insinuations _____

_____

Incomplete or inappropriate context _____

_____

Statements with unidentified sources _____

_____

Quotes or statements from 'experts' _____

_____

Personal character attacks _____

_____

Use of images (maps, charts, graphs, photographs) _____

_____

Logical fallacies _____

_____

Inclusion of irrelevant information _____

_____

Improper use of statistics _____

_____

Other _____

_____

Rate the article for credibility and give your reasons: _____

_____

_____

_____

Serious problems call for serious measures in Spitsbergen. This anemometer mast was originally solidly placed in the ice. It is now completely twisted by the movement of the glacier and needs to be straightened.

Authors: Jenny Baeseman, Louise Huffman, Kristin Timm and Janet Warburton
Contributors: Mary Albert, Miriam Hebling Almeida, Patricia Azinhaga, Robert Bindschadler, Paula Dionísio, Robin Frisch-Gleason, Cathleen Geiger, Cheri Hamilton, Turtle Haste, Joanna Hubbard, Martin Jeffries, Shelley MacDonell, Liz Murphy, Maria Manuel Passas, Maggie Prevenas, Samuel P. S. Rastrick, Mélianie Raymond, Rhian A. Salmon, Paul F. Schuster, Filipa Silva, Lucia Simion, Cristina Teixeira, Karl Tolstein, Betty Trummel, José Xavier and Sandra Zicus

Introduction

Current research during and beyond IPY points to large-scale changes at the Poles with urgent consequences which impact on the global climate, environment, society and economy, and which current generations must face and future generations will inherit. The advances made in bridging the divide between scientific knowledge and outreach were some of the greatest achievements of IPY, and have resulted in polar outreach activities on many issues of global concern. Part of this success can be attributed to the increasing need for scientists to share their understanding with non-technical audiences, and to a growing acceptance of connecting educators to scientists to fulfil this need, often resulting in greater student interest in science and science careers.

> "A (polar) scientist, when talking to kids about global warming or climate change, should make students understand that even though polar bears live in the North Pole and penguins in the South, they actually live in the same place: Earth—just like we and all the other creatures do."
>
> Miriam Hebling Almeida,
> teacher, Brazil

During IPY, educators globally found many ways in which to connect their learning environments and local communities to research being conducted in the polar regions. A large network of educators interested in polar research developed, was nurtured, and members found many ways to connect scientists' lab and field experiences to their classrooms. In addition, many young researchers were looking for ways to share their work with schoolchildren. The connection of these two groups was very powerful. During IPY, for example, virtual and 'snail mail' postcards gave short anecdotes or answered specific student questions from the field. Some teachers accompanying scientists carried school flags and t-shirts and took pictures with them in the polar environment to show students back home the geography of the research locations. Mascots like Geo-bears, Flat Stanleys, and other 'critters' travelled to field camps. Blogs in their voices and pictures of these characters were posted on the Web to share the adventure. Phone calls and videoconferences connected classrooms directly to the researchers and allowed students to see the science as it happened and ask questions in real time. Some of the most successful experiences involved classes that had a personal interaction with teachers and scientists, before they left, during the field experience, and when they returned. These interactions increased the classrooms' ownership of, interest and involvement in the expeditions.

It is obvious that teachers and their students benefit from working with scientists by increasing their scientific knowledge. What is less recognised is that scientists often learn communication skills and teaching 'tips' from working with professional educators. The partnerships that were developed between educators and scientists during IPY had a broad and long-lasting impact on scientists, teachers and their students—constituting one significant legacy of the International Polar Year.

Built on the experiences of educators and scientists and the lessons learned from these partnerships, this chapter is designed to help scientists effectively communicate their research to students and the general public. Here we summarise some of the specific tips and tricks for making science presentations to a wide variety of non-technical audiences. We also offer advice to educators working with scientists, and at the end of the chapter you can find summaries of four different aspects of successful science presentations.

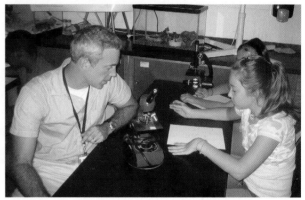

Figure 2.1 Polar scientist works with students in a classroom.

Paving the Way: Preparing for your Presentation

FINDING YOUR AUDIENCE

It is often challenging for scientists to know where to start with outreach. The first step is finding someone

"When scientists and teachers work together, so much valuable learning takes place, and it helps both sides do their job better, increases the number of students and teachers affected, and can generate a huge amount of excitement for science and learning!"

Betty Trummel,
teacher, USA

"Following eight expeditions to Antarctica and after the publication of a book, I decided I wanted to share my knowledge and my passion for the Antarctic with young children, teenagers and adults. . . . In primary schools I gave talks on Antarctica and asked students to write stories set there. The white continent is a very strong and positive example of international collaboration for young children and teenagers."

Lucia Simion, science journalist and
photographer, France and Italy

to talk to. For many it begins with a request from a personal contact like a son or daughter, spouse or other relative. It may also be a friend, colleague, neighbour, school teacher, or an organiser of a public event. The networks that were established during IPY make it easier for scientists and educators to find each other and to develop meaningful working relationships. *(For contact information, see 'Contributing Polar Institutions' and Chapter 3.)*

In some countries, scientists looking for schools and classrooms to visit can contact their Ministry of Education or local school districts and ask to be put on a Speakers' List. Teachers, who are looking for scientists, can contact professors at nearby universities, other research institutions, or check if their city has a Speakers' Bureau with a list of available presenters. Scientists looking for communities to visit should contact local government offices like the Mayor's office, the local Tribal Council, First Nations office, Métis office or cultural centre. You might also want to check if there is a local, state, or federal environmental agency office in the village or town of interest. Teaching and learning centres may also assist you.

TALK TO THE ORGANISER OF THE EVENT BEFORE YOU GO

It is imperative that you talk directly to the teacher, event organiser, or community representative before your classroom or community visit. In other words, know your audience! Always ask lots of questions before you give your presentation! These can help get you started:

- How many students/attendees?
- What age(s)?
- How much time will there be to present? Does that include time for questions?
- What date? What are the start and end times? Be aware that schools often work on exact schedules—you may be asked to begin at 8.23 a.m. Ask if there will be other activities at the beginning or the end of the period, or if you will have the entire time.
- What are the sign-in procedures? Should you check in at the office or is there a greeter or security? How will you find the room? Where can you park?
- What is the preferred form of media equipment? Do you need them to provide an LCD projector, screen, speakers, microphone or table?
- How will the room be arranged? Is it a big lecture hall or a small conference room?
- Will you be introduced, or should you introduce yourself?
- What related topics will the group have studied before the presentation?

- Are there certain things that the organiser would like you to talk about?
- Is the presentation part of a larger project or occasion, or a one-time event?
- What is the contact and emergency information in case anything changes before the presentation (e.g., you are running late or cannot make it)?

PREPARE YOUR PRESENTATION

> **"Presentations should be one part information and three parts inspiration."**
>
> Robert Bindschadler,
> polar scientist, USA

After you find out from the organiser what they would like you to discuss, you will need to prepare and focus your presentation. Remember, the presentation you use for a scientific meeting was designed for an audience of scientists that understand the jargon and like graphs. You will probably need to take time to develop a different presentation for your new audience. Here are some points that you should remember:

- Practice an education strategy called 'backward design'. Decide what you want the participants to know at the end of your presentation before you begin to plan it. Then make all of your points relate to those objectives. *(See Wiggins and McTighe (2005) for more details.)*
- Give your audience the conclusions or take-home messages at the beginning of your presentation and then again at the end!
- Practice your presentation before you go. Deliver it in front of a friend or family member and get feedback.

Along the Road: Key Aspects of Successful Presentations

THE HOOK!

It is important to realise that what seems commonplace to you, is probably very new to your audience. Although you may have been doing polar science for years, think about how you felt preparing for your first field season. Do not take for granted the novelty, excitement and 'coolness' of what you do.

The Icebreaker

Begin with an icebreaker or open your presentation in a way that will hook the audience's interest. An icebreaker could be a short game that you create to introduce the students to your research. It could be simply asking the students questions and engaging them in a conversation. It could be pulling out tools or equipment you use in the field that they have never seen. Interactive icebreakers help you assess the background knowledge of your audience. Activating prior knowledge is essential for providing a framework on which to add new knowledge. Be creative, but make sure to check out the details with the organiser before arriving.

> "With problematic audiences (noisy, not interested students, the teacher did not prepare the students), I start with a brief review of my career. Saying that you are a scientist who has been to Antarctica is more than enough to get their attention!
> An example for engaging audiences: In schools on the coast, I always introduce marine food webs with the role of them as humans in it. By asking them what types of fish they eat, they become engaged in understanding the concept I want to teach them."
>
> José Xavier,
> polar scientist, Portugal

The Story

Tell your science story and add your own favourite experiences appropriate to the age level of your audience. Tell them about living and working in the harshest environments on Earth; your field experiences are a great hook for engaging people in your science. A main goal of your visit is to inspire students and community members with your enthusiasm for science and to convey that scientists are 'real' people. You are the key to your presentation, not your data or your funding. How you say what you say, and how you present yourself are as important as what you say. People like to hear and want to relate to personal stories about the unique aspects of your job, why it matters, and how you got there.

> "Keep tabs on your audience; if they are not engaged, how can you get them more involved? Give students a chance to talk to each other or write about their thoughts on information you have shared. Every 10 minutes offer them some way to process the information."
>
> Joanna Hubbard,
> teacher, USA

ENGAGE YOUR AUDIENCE

Ask the audience questions, involve them in your presentation, and try to relate the science to their lives. If you are doing all the talking, you are doing most of the thinking. Give the audience a chance to think critically and personally; the experience will be more meaningful. About every 10 minutes, try to do something to engage the audience, for example, ask questions, poll the students, or find out how they might approach a similar problem or situation. Watch for the 'wiggles' and 'nodding off' signs of an uninterested group, and be sure to increase your interaction when this begins to happen. Below are a few tips and tools to help make sure your audience stays connected to you and your presentation—from start to end!

- Ask participants to turn to the person next to them and quickly tell them one thing they learned in the last five minutes. Before you tell an entire audience to talk, though, give them a signal for ending the discussion!

Figure 2.2 Young scientist and students team up to teach visitors at a museum event.

- Ask participants to give thumbs up if they agree with a statement, thumbs down if not.
- When younger students need to get up and move, have them stand. Ask questions and have them respond by raising hands overhead or touching toes to answer them. (This is particularly good when asking comparison questions on the Arctic and Antarctic: "Where do polar bears live?" Hands overhead for Arctic, hands on toes for Antarctic, hands on waist for both.) This is also a great way to assess what information they are retaining from your presentation, and if there are any misconceptions you need to clear up.
- Ensure that your activities, language and questions are age appropriate. Leave your acronyms at home unless they are truly vital to understanding the science.

> "Most kids do not travel and many are hooked into the research focus by vicariously sharing every step of the journey there. They love knowing about the preparation and planning, and the travel to the starting point. If they can 'join' in the pre-trip events, they feel as if they are taking a virtual journey. The way to accomplish this is through personal visits to classes, suggested reading material for teachers, and anticipatory questions. I made paper chains for many classes, with each link in the paper chains a question for the students to think about. The classes read and discussed a link each day that I was gone so they could stay connected to me and to my research. Questions were cross-disciplinary. They included math questions (story problems about Antarctica or temperatures), vocabulary questions, questions about the social aspects of the expedition, science and geography."
>
> Robin Frisch-Gleason,
> teacher, USA

> "For me, the most rewarding part of the experience was the conversation after my presentation with a quiet eight-year-old who wanted to become an Antarctic scientist—it made it all worthwhile!"
>
> Shelley MacDonell,
> polar scientist, New Zealand and Chile

- Show pictures of you and your teammates in the field and verbally describe in simple terms the way you gather the data. Show pictures to illustrate what your results may mean to your audience.
- Praise good and thoughtful questions—whether you answer them or not.
- If possible, give students a chance to think and wrestle with a problem related to your field of study. For example: Should scientists drill into a subglacial lake if the process of drilling will contaminate it? How is polar research relevant to their community?
- Leave time at the end for questions. Learn to validate attempts to ask questions and provide answers even when they are completely wrong. Here is an example. Your question: "Where do penguins live?" Student's answer: "The Arctic." Your response: "That would have been correct if I had asked where polar bears live, but penguins actually only live in the Antarctic."
- Provide closure before leaving by reiterating your important points.
- Invite them to stay connected by visiting your website, becoming 'friends' on an online social network, following your blog, emailing questions, etc.
- Make sure the organiser knows how to contact you with additional questions from participants.

USE PRESENTATION SOFTWARE PROGRAMS EFFECTIVELY

All too often we think of presentations as something that you do with a computer and a screen, using common presentation software. Computer presentations can be effective because you can use pictures, videos and sounds, but do not let slides become a crutch. Let them aid your words. Technology is often welcomed and encouraged in classrooms, but always be prepared with a back-up plan if the equipment fails. Occasionally, presentation software and technical equipment are not integral part of teaching methods at schools. In some indigenous communities, for example, it is requested

"The most memorable aspects of my talks are the ones that I gave to the littlest ones. My four-year-old daughter was in day care at the start of my biggest IPY project. With a one-month absence of her mom on the horizon, I had to carefully make plans to slowly prepare her for my time away. So, in addition to the interaction with a high school teacher, I developed some talks for my daughter's class. It was an amazing learning experience for me, as I had to draw out the essence of the climate and sea ice issues in a form that a small child would understand. This exercise helped me to cook my research thoughts into fundamental concepts without trivializing them. The little ones actually do understand a great deal of what is going on provided that it is conveyed in a form that they can relate to. The issues surrounding climate change and the changes in sea ice, when conveyed at a level for pre-kindergarten (below age five), cover many of the most fundamental elements that we, as human beings, need to understand. It was a wonderful and creative exercise for me to develop simple animated slides on this topic. As a scientist, I was able to tap within myself deep and latent levels of wonder by giving talks at this level. It also helped enormously with my family life as my daughter now understands why I need to go away sometimes for long periods to help understand how the planet works."

Cathleen Geiger,
polar scientist, USA

that the presentation reflect traditional ways by being only verbal and often given while sitting in a circle. For scientists intending to present in the Inuit communities of Nunavut, we provide you with the core principles of Nunavut's Department of Education at the end of the chapter. There, you also find useful information on how your computer presentation can be geared towards audiences with disabilities that can affect learning.

While it is important to be aware of these issues, it is equally important to understand what will make a good computer presentation in the first place. Here are some tips for using computer-generated presentations:

- Keep slides to a minimum! There is no magic number for the total slides you need, but a good rule is two to three minutes of talking per slide. If you have 30 minutes to give a presentation, 30 slides will be too many.
- Keep text to a minimum! If you show a lot of text, people will read the text and not listen to you. Use only short phrases.
- Make sure the fonts and colours you use can be seen from the back of the room! Minimise red and green for those in the audience who are colour-blind. Make sure there is enough contrast so that people can read the text.
- Use plain black slides or the black screen capabilities in software programs if you want the audience to focus on you. Learn which key will turn the screen black. In some programs, press the 'B' key to black the screen during your presentation; then press it again to go back to your slides.
- Use photos that show action or tell a story—showing the landscape, science, and life in polar regions, if possible.
- Embed short videos in your presentation, especially if they help explain abstract ideas (e.g., landscape changes or how scientific instruments work).
- Use sounds! For example, use a buzzer sound in your presentation for correct answers to let students know, which response to a question is correct— similar to a quiz show. They will love the buzzer sound!
- At the same time, do not get carried away with sounds and transitions. They can become distracting.
- Use graphs sparingly, if at all! If used, be sure to take the time to explain each axis and the meaning of the graph. Include a title that makes sense in case the reader misses your introduction to the slide. Too many data points can be confusing, so use animations to point out trends or show short videos of the changes in modelling scenarios.
- Keep in mind that many schools and communities do not have a wireless Internet connection or may have strict firewalls that will not allow Internet

access. Do not rely on visiting websites or accessing online illustrations unless you know that you can be connected. If you want to show a website, use a screen shot of it within your presentation instead of planning on actually connecting to it.

- Print out a few copies of your presentation or give a copy of your presentation on a CD or DVD to the organiser for later use.

BODY LANGUAGE

Body language is an important component of your presentation. Your audience will not only hear you but also watch you give your presentation. So here are a few tips for what you should and should not do.

- Make eye contact with your audience. Force yourself to look at different sections of the audience.
- If you call on people, choose them from different sections of the room and try to call on an equal number of males and females.
- Be aware of habits and work on appearing relaxed! Where are your hands? Do you rock back and forth? Do you roam? Do you grip the lectern? Do you nervously clear your throat?

USE PRESENTATION AIDES

There are so many interesting things that scientists use in polar research; share them with your audience. Use a multi-sensory approach—challenge yourself to

Figure 2.3 A teacher is showing the balloon used to collect stratospheric ozone at the South Pole. A student next to her is demonstrating the extreme cold weather gear used while working in Antarctica.

provide an object or experience that participants can touch, hear, smell and see. Give participants a sense of place by locating your field research on a map. Bring along a rock, tool or clothing from your field site. Play a sound recording or a short video. Think about how your audience will interact with the artefact. You might want to show it to them during the presentation, but let them have a closer look at the end so as not to break the pace. Be aware that props may provide a distraction and competition for the students' attention, so ask the teacher for suggestions. Whatever props or artefacts you bring, expect that all participants in the audience will want to interact with them. Select items that can withstand handling and are not too fragile.

A Turning Point: Refining your Presentation for Classroom Visits

Most students of whatever age are very well behaved when a guest speaker comes in to talk. However, do not be afraid to ask the teacher for assistance with behavioural problems if any arise during your presentation. If you have engaged the audience, this type of problem is extremely rare. Regardless of age considerations, remember to leave a flyer, worksheet, or your business card with the facilitator or teacher when you leave. This way the audience can take something home to share with their families, and they have a way to contact you for further questions.

Scientists who are nervous about how to present to a certain age group should rely on suggestions from the teacher. It is another possibility to imagine how you would explain your science to your own child, niece or nephew. It also helps to remember what you liked about science when you were a pupil. When working with high school students, you could ask yourself what you would discuss or do with undergraduate students at university during the first week of class. Here we provide some basic tips for giving presentations to students depending on their age group.

FOR YOUNGER STUDENTS (AGES 5–9)

- Limit your talking to 20–30 minutes—the more interactive the presentation, the longer their attention span will be.
- Physically get down to their level if possible.
- This age especially likes visuals, sounds and objects.
- Make the presentation very interactive.
- Remember that maps are great visuals, but may be somewhat abstract to some students at a young age.

Accompany maps with discussions of how you got from one place to another and how long it took you.

- No Graphs!
- Remember that this age child thinks concretely and will need concrete examples from their experience to understand any abstract concepts. Here are two examples: three metres equal the distance from here to the door; an emperor penguin is about the same height as a six-year-old.
- Be aware that young children often want to touch or hug you.
- Let them ask questions, but be prepared for stories and unrelated comments. If someone starts to tell you what they had for dinner last night, simply say: "That's really great, what do you think we eat in the field?" Bring the conversation back to the topic of your presentation. Be prepared not to follow a structured order for this group.

Figure 2.4 An educator with students in New Zealand. It is important with young students to literally get down to their level.

- Give them something to take home and share with their family. Puzzles, colouring sheets with facts and bookmarks are good for this age.

FOR MIDDLE GRADES (AGES 10–14)

- Limit your talking to 40–60 minutes, including time for questions.
- This age student likes 'flashy' things. They want to know who you are and how you got to where you are.
- The 'You can do this too!' career message is a good one at this age.
- Students at this age are beginning to think abstractly, but they still need models and examples.
- If you use graphs, make them very simple and explain them well.
- They appreciate interactions at an adult level. Do not talk down to them, but be sure to define terms.
- Prepare a list of websites or other resources related to your topic that you could leave with the students, in case they want to learn more!

FOR UPPER GRADES (AGES 15 AND UP)

- Talks will probably be limited by class periods, but if there is no limit, keep your presentation to 50–60 minutes or less, including time for questions.
- Be sure to define scientific terms and use the terms they have learned.
- Graphs are okay with this group because they are likely to have used them for lab assignments, but make them simple and clear.
- Use references to popular culture—a reference to the current popular band or film is a great way to keep their attention.
- This is the age where people can really be turned on by science as a career, so be a role model for them. Tell them your personal story. Where did you go to high school? What twists and turns did you confront in your path to becoming a scientist? Give them some advice on pursuing science as a career. Explain why you love your job, and why it is worth the trade-off for things you may like less (e.g., low salary, long hours, etc.).
- Because they are closer in age to the students, there is great value in young scientists visiting classrooms with this age students.
- Prepare something that you can leave behind such as business cards and brochures from your organisation or institution about careers in science.

Maintaining Momentum: Guidelines for Educators who Work with Scientists

Collaborations between scientists, educators and concerned community members can take many different forms. During IPY, these relationships ranged from short-term interactions to long-term associations, many of which will extend the entire career of both the educator and scientist.

Here are some simple things that educators can do to make sure these types of experiences are valuable to the scientist and the audience, and to maintain these valuable professional relationships.

- Establish a relationship with a scientist before the presentation. This will help both of you feel more at ease during the days leading up to the visit.
- If possible, prepare the audience before the presentation. Make sure they have the level of background knowledge the scientist is expecting. Have students read and research the topic that will be presented before meeting the expert. Encourage them to discuss the topic at home with family members. Familiarity with the topic will help students to avoid lower level questions like, "Could you tell me everything about…?" or "Have you seen any penguins?". It will encourage thoughtful, higher-level questions involving synthesis, analysis and evaluation. *(See Bloom and Krathwohl (1975), Anderson et al. (2000), Marzano and Kendall (2007) for more information.)*
- For a community audience, provide a short bio, website or information in the announcement, so participants can learn about the scientist's research prior to the presentation.
- Remember that the scientist needs time to prepare for the presentation and to get their slides and talking points tailored to the specific audience.
- Beforehand, tell the scientist what topics are currently being discussed in the classroom and the level of background knowledge the audience will have.
- Beforehand, also share your objectives of the visit or provide the guest speaker with a list of specific topics or concepts you would like the audience to learn.
- If the scientist will be presenting new material to the audience, make sure to follow up on some of the new concepts and terminology that were used. The follow-up from a presentation is just as important to understanding a scientific topic as the visit itself.
- Encourage the scientist to leave materials about the presentation with you for later use. Things they might leave are fact sheets, maps, photos, organisational brochures, reports, or a copy of their presentation.

"What strikes me most is that the more I bring in professionals it becomes easier to prepare both the visitor and students. Perhaps teachers are nervous that there will be judgments about their classroom, or they may worry about how students may behave; depending on my population, this can be a problem. The more collaboration, whether it is with small presentations, tours or collaborative projects, the easier it is to do. I have discovered for myself that it is easier to take more risks, with more practice. Heck, last year I walked up to a prominent Antarctic volcanologist and asked for his help with a student project. From there I stuck my nose out and contacted the Antarctic Sun folks for other contacts. Personally, I have decided that it is easier to ask those who are the content professionals for help in presenting what they do and involving them in what students are doing than to master the materials myself. After the first time or two, I have actually begun to look for those who are in the areas of our content and make an effort to include speakers as often as possible."

Turtle Haste,
teacher, USA

Summary: 'To Go' Principles for Science Presentations

TIPS AND TRICKS 'TO GO' FOR SUCCESSFUL PRESENTATIONS

- Learn all you can from the event organizer ahead of time.

- Know your audience. How many students? What are their ages? How much do they already know?

- Plan using 'backward design.' Decide what you want them to know at the end of your presentation before you plan it.

- Before your go, tell the organizer if you need technical equipment!

- Computer-generated presentations are a nice aide, but do not use too many words or graphs. Remember not to use red and green!

- Hook 'em with a good story, a strange or startling fact or a tool or artefact for them to touch.

- Use props!

- Engage them with activities and questions.

- Leave while there is still high interest! Do not overstay.

- Stay in touch. Tell them to follow your blog or send additional questions.

TIPS AND TRICKS FOR PRESENTING INCLUSIVELY TO ALL AUDIENCE MEMBERS

It is a misconception that presenting information to audiences which include people with disabilities that can affect learning (such as dyslexia, dyspraxia, auditory and visual processing impairments, or attention difficulties) involves giving less information at a reduced pace. Simply reducing the pace of your presentation will not help most people with learning difficulties. These tips show how to present information more inclusively, enhancing your presentations for students and community members with learning difficulties, as well as for the rest of the audience.

Make Text Clear

It is estimated that one in 10 individuals has some degree of dyslexic difficulty. When using text in a presentation, use larger fonts with greater space between words and lines. It is better to use short key phrases as bullet points instead of single words because many people with reading difficulties need words in context to decipher their meaning.

Use Appropriate Colours and Backgrounds

The total number of people in your audience that experience some degree of colour-blindness approximates up to five to eight per cent. Keep in mind that it can be difficult for people with colour-blindness to distinguish between red, orange, yellow, yellow-green and green, and between blue and violet. Also avoid dark red, magenta or thin lines on a dark blue or black background.

Reading words or phrases with high contrasts, such as white on black, can also be difficult. Reduced contrasts can improve reading comprehension and reading speed. A good choice is to use black text on light pastel shades of blue, yellow or green.

Provide Guide Notes

The provision of guide notes or handouts is often criticised for a number of reasons from being paper heavy on the environment to lowering attendance figures, but for some populations, they are essential. Bring along a few paper copies of your presentation for those who may want them.

Use a Multi-sensory Style to Break up your Presentation

Lapses of concentration and difficulty in maintaining focus are not only a problem for people with attention difficulties such as ADHD; they are also common to other learning disabilities such as dyslexia. Attention span may decrease due to the increased effort required to follow and read slides. Use props, video clips and sounds to add a multi-sensory dimension to your presentation. It will enhance learning in all groups, particularly those with dyslexia and other specific learning difficulties.

Watch your Words

Speak clearly and make the effort to face your audience—this aids communication for everyone, not only those who may need to lip-read. Providing clear signposts, targets and summaries as you proceed through your presentation, will reinforce understanding of your main points. A glossary of key words to be referred to as you speak will be a great help to those who have reading or spelling difficulties.

Samuel P. S. Rastrick,
research student with dyslexia, UK

TIPS AND TRICKS FOR PRESENTING TO COMMUNITIES

Personal Communication

Community-based outreach is often most successful when personal contact is the first line of communication. To the community, personal contact, such as a face-to-face meeting or a phone call, is an expression of commitment and dedication to the cause. Once a relationship is established, other follow-up forms like emails and blogs can also be very effective in maintaining momentum.

Choose an Open Forum

For community presentations, an open forum usually keeps the audience engaged. Encourage questions at any time during the presentation. You can also use humour, for example in featuring a community leader who most would know. But make sure you ask them first.

Show the Relevance of your Research

You can also show them how important your work is by putting a monetary figure on the science. For example, if the climate continues to warm, the salmon may not run in the same way; or if forest fires continue to increase, lumber and firewood availability may decrease as well as other ecosystem services.

GUIDING PRINCIPLES OF LEARNING IN NUNAVUT / INUIT QAUJIMAJATUQANGIT

These principles reflect crucial Inuit societal values and are not only used by governmental agencies but were also adopted by the Nunavut Department of Education. Scientists visiting Inuit communities should be familiar with them, and they may also be of interest to teachers worldwide looking for new ways to communicate science.

Inuuqatigiitsianiq: Respecting others, relationships and caring for people.

Tunnganarniq: Fostering good spirit by being open, welcoming and inclusive.

Pijitsirarniq: Serving and providing for family and community.
- Leadership role assumes responsibility to serve community;
- Knowledge and ability based leadership;
- Authoritative vs. Authoritarian;
- Serving in the interest of community as opposed to pure self-interest.

Aajiqatigiingniq: Decision-making through discussion and consensus.
- Inclusive decision-making;

- Ensures that all parties understand each other;
- Doing different tasks for a common purpose.

Pilimmaksarniq: Development of skills through practice, effort and action.
- Skill development to ensure success and survival;
- To ensure that all members are able to contribute to the community;
- Knowledge gained through observation and experience.

Piliriqatigiingniq: Working together for a common cause.

Qanuqtnurungnarniq: Being innovative and resourceful in seeking solutions.
- Improving when and where necessary;
- Maximum utilization of limited resources and budget.

Avatimik kamattiarniq: Respect and care for the land, animals and the environment.

Northern Bering Sea: Collecting measurements of snow depths overlying sea ice onboard a research vessel.

Author: Lucette Barber

Contributors: Jenny Baeseman, David J. Carlson, Karen Edwards, Bettina Kaiser, Lars Poort, Khadijah Adbul Rahman-Sinclair, Mélianie Raymond, Rhian A. Salmon, Elena Bautista Sparrow and Tim Straka

Introduction: A Rationale for Education, Outreach and Communication

Outreach is, as the name suggests, the process of reaching out and building connections between one person or group to another. The emphasis on education, outreach and communication (EOC) of polar research demonstrated during this most recent IPY reflects the growing recognition that scientists and researchers play an important role in raising awareness, providing valuable information to decision-makers, inspiring the next generation of researchers, resource managers, and policy makers, and engaging the general public in global issues such as climate change. This position is supported by many research funding agencies around the world, who share the goal of increasing scientific dialogue in society and who recognise the civic responsibility of scientists to share their knowledge and expertise.

During IPY, polar researchers worked with educators, musicians, artists, community leaders, policy makers and the media to bring IPY science and research closer to the global citizen. These partnerships resulted in new and exciting classroom materials, actual and virtual polar experiences, art, music, film, journalism, travelling exhibits, science training events and many more initiatives aimed at engaging audiences from around the world in polar research and polar education. Outreach has taken many forms and occurred at various levels of participation, from basic information sharing to collaborative outreach, as well as research partnerships that will be sustained well beyond IPY.

This chapter showcases—through a collection of successful initiatives submitted by educators, scientists, graduate students and other outreach professionals— the breadth of activities and programmes inspired by IPY. Moreover, it encourages readers to participate in polar education, scientific research and outreach, and appreciate the importance of the polar regions to the rest of the world.

The following list of 'Outreach at a Glance,' organised alphabetically, gives you an overview of the wide variety of forms of education and outreach activities that can be considered by those individuals or organisations interested in communicating science.

Successful IPY examples of some of these approaches appear as 'Outreach in Detail' in the next section. To make it easier to find a specific initiative, we include an overview of all projects at the beginning of 'Outreach in Detail'. We group these initiatives according to the audience they target: school level (teachers, primary, secondary or high school students), university level (undergraduate or graduate students) and general public level. If you are a teacher and would like to learn more about expeditions to the Poles for teachers, then browse the 'school level' section. If you are a scientist and would like to know more about projects communicating polar science through exhibitions, then you should check the 'general public level;' if you would like to get involved in classroom presentations, check the 'school level' section; and if you want to find out about graduate field schools, browse the 'university level' part of this chapter. Enjoy the amazing range of opportunities that might inspire you to get involved in polar science outreach!

Outreach at a Glance: A List of Outreach Categories

Classroom visits
- Going to a school to implement an activity, give a presentation or do a demonstration related to your work
- Going to a university classroom, lab or field session to give a presentation or do a demonstration

Communicating science with the media
- Preparing for media interviews for radio, TV and print
- Arranging for interviews with the media prior to going into, or while in the field
- Competitions or invitations to the media to visit research sites
- Organising a press conference
- Sending press releases and science or outreach stories to your institution's media office
- Working with the media on documentaries and other programmes related to polar research
- Publishing education, outreach and communication material

Conferences
- Planning an education, outreach and communication session at a science and education conference
- Hosting a networking session at a related conference for individuals interested in scientific outreach to network and share ideas
- Including your outreach and education activities in your scientific presentations and conference posters

Contests and competitions
- Using competitions and contests to generate interest in polar sciences e.g., poster or essay writing competitions

Correspondence from the field/lab
- Communicating regularly from the field using web-based, videoconferencing and video technology, e.g., dispatches or journals posted on personal, school, or project websites, blogs, podcasts, Skype calls, etc.
- Sending questions by email to scientists

Creating curriculum
- Working with educators and scientists to update existing curriculum or create new curriculum that links education in schools to polar research
- Offering your time and expertise in reviewing, editing, and writing curriculum content
- Creating new curriculum for university programmes and courses

Creating educational tools
- Using resources to create educational materials, lesson plans, educational kits, games, etc. that can be used by scientists and educators to teach a specific concept, skill or activity

Creative writing
- Using creative writing skills to communicate science outside the scientific community
- Writing an article for a related science or education magazine, school or other organisational newsletter or website
- Journal writing
- Writing fiction e.g., a children's book or novel based on scientific work or polar regions
- Storytelling
- Writing non-fiction
- Poetry and prose about polar issues such as climate change

Educational expeditions

- Providing your expertise by accompanying educational expeditions aimed at raising awareness of polar issues and the science behind polar research including methodology and findings
- Organising educational expeditions related to polar science and polar issues

Engaging audiences from Arctic communities

- Bringing data and results back to communities for active discussion and engagement
- Organising or participating in community feasts and celebrations
- Planning classroom visits while conducting research in the North
- Engaging Elders and community leaders in developing educational materials

Engaging audiences from mid-latitude countries

- Engaging audiences from mid-latitudes using unique methods to make global connections with the polar regions, e.g., using IPY data sharing systems for research in mid-latitude regions

Engaging students in doing outreach

- Working with students to prepare or review presentations to deliver in the community
- Accompanying students in their presentations and outreach activities
- Inviting youth leaders as speakers for events, forums and conferences

Events

- Organising a one- or two-day event focusing on polar education and polar research in collaboration with schools or public education agencies such as museums, science centres, or outdoor education facilities
- Linking polar activities to Polar Week, Earth Day celebrations or other international events

Exhibitions

- Using art to communicate science and polar issues such as art and photo exhibitions as well as dance
- Getting involved in and organising travelling exhibitions
- Creating local school exhibitions on the polar regions
- Creating exhibition displays for science centres, museums, etc.

Fairs and Festivals

- Participating in science festivals and university open days
- Engaging researchers from a wide range of disciplines and organisations to open their research to the public in a day or series of demonstrations, hands-on activities, movies, competitions and events
- Organising a scientific outreach event around a sport or music event
- Staffing information or activity booths in trade fairs, environmental festivals, local markets, etc.

Mentoring

- Internships
- Apprenticeships
- Arranging for students to receive credit while working with scientists in the lab or in the field
- Mentoring during field-based experiences
- Mentoring students at science fairs

Music

- Using new compositions to communicate science
- Taking musicians into the field to be inspired by their experiences
- Featuring the music from northern communities in science presentations and conferences e.g., Inuit throat singers or drum dancers
- Organising concerts with a polar theme

Posters

- Communicating with posters at science conferences
- Creating posters for the general public

Professional development for educators

- Bringing educators into the laboratory or the field
- Partnering with educators to learn scientific measurement, data collection and analysis techniques, and provide data sets that can be brought into the classroom
- Enabling educators to attend and participate in scientific conferences and workshops
- Organising summer schools and/or workshops for educators

Professional development for scientists

- Organising workshops on communicating science
- Creating opportunities for scientists to work with teachers and educators
- Creating outreach resources and tools for scientists
- Offering outreach, education, and communication sessions at science conferences
- Organising a workshop or session on communicating with the media
- Organising a mentor panel for early career scientists

Public presentations

- Speaking at specialised meetings like conferences or fundraisers
- Speaking at public venues like museums, science centres and other educational sites
- Speaking in communities

Research partnerships between educators and scientists

- Developing ongoing commitments between educators and scientists to provide authentic science and research experiences to students and teachers, either in the school or in the field
- Conducting science experiments in classrooms and laboratories, involving students in data collection and engaging students in ongoing scientific investigation

Science Fairs

- Providing ideas to students and teachers for science projects related to polar research
- Mentoring students throughout their science experiment
- Judging, presenting awards and donating prizes at science fairs
- Assisting with organising science fairs

Scientific expeditions

- Providing opportunities for students and/or teachers to join scientists during a scientific or research expedition, i.e., joining scientists in the field, in field camps, or on research vessels
- Scientists volunteering their time and expertise to interact with students and teachers while in the field

Video

- Using video or film to produce documentaries or feature films
- Creative use of web videos
- Creating two to three minute clips of science in the field that could be used in classrooms to link to curriculum, related activities, lesson plans, or classroom visits by scientists

Web-based

- Using websites to communicate science to the public by providing educational resources, virtual presentations, and by connecting scientists with schools, museums and the public
- Using social networking tools such as e-pals, web chats, and online conferencing software to connect to an interested public
- Blogging to bring polar science into the learning environment
- Creating remote classrooms
- Using the Web to create virtual expeditions or show life at remote field stations

Youth forums and student conferences

- Working with schools or other organisations to plan youth forums or student conferences related to polar research and climate change
- Volunteering to join an organising committee as a science advisor
- Recruiting scientists to participate in forums and conferences
- Becoming a speaker or group facilitator at a youth forum

Outreach in Detail: A Selection of Initiatives from around the World

School Level Initiatives

Student outreach programmes
SotaZero, Spain
Global POP, Norway
ALISON, USA
FortWhyte Alive, Canada
Polar Competition, India
GLOBE, Seasons and Biomes
    Program, USA
Keep Planting Trees, Malaysia
Danube Delta working group,
    Romania
Authentic proposal writing, USA
Art of Science exhibition, USA and
    Russia
Literacy and IPY, USA
Kiwis on Ice talks, New Zealand

Teaching resource projects
Class Zero Emission, Belgium
PoleS Project, Belgium and France
Ice, Ice, Baby resources, USA
Bamboozle jigsaw puzzle, Belgium
Discovering Antarctica, UK

Student expeditions and beyond
Students on Ice, Canada
Schools on Board (SonB), Canada
Schools on Board, Spain
IPY Northern Experience Program,
    Canada
Two Ways of Knowing, Canada
SonB Circumpolar Inuit Field
    Program, Canada

Teacher expeditions and beyond
ANDRILL programme ARISE, USA
Coole Klassen, Germany
US-Canadian expedition, Canada, USA
International Arctic expedition, USA
SIPEX field experience, Australia
SIMBA expedition, USA

Forums, Science Fairs, Internships
Arctic Climate Change Youth Forum,
    Canada
Alaska Native Science Fairs, USA
Polar Perspectives, Canada
Training Arctic youth, Canada
Circumpolar Young Leaders Program,
    Canada

University Level Initiatives

Field courses and expeditions
Polaris programme, USA
Antarctic expedition, India
IPY Summer Institute, USA and
    Russia
IPY international field school,
    Norway

Permafrost courses, Norway
IPY Arctic Observatory Network, USA
IPY-ROAM programme, USA

Professional development
APECS workshops, international
APECS mentoring, international
Researcher symposium, international

Other outreach ideas
Women's Narrative course, Canada
IPY data sharing methods, USA and
    Nicaragua
Sub-Zero soccer tournament, India

Public Level Initiatives

Multi-level initiatives
Cape Farewell, international
LATITUDE60!, Portugal
EALÁT-Network Study, international
Narwhal Tusk research, USA
Ways of Greenland, Romania
IPY, Sweden

Exhibitions
Ice Stories, USA
Science Express, Germany, India
CELEBRATE IPY exhibition, USA
ANDRILL photo exhibitions, France
DAMOCLES exhibition, Belgium
Ice Station Antarctica, UK
Active Earth Display, USA

Science Events
Urban international polar weekends,
    USA
Seattle polar science weekends, USA
Polar science weekend, Portugal
AGAP Project, USA
University of Delaware Seminars, USA

Music
Winnipeg Symphony Orchestra,
    Canada
Polar Synthesis for IPY, USA

Books
IPY Polar Books, international
White Heart of our Planet,
    international
The Arctic Fox, USA
Story of Antarctica, India
Two Windows on our Planet, Canada

Using other media
Promotion of Arctic Science, Canada
Ends of the Earth radio show, Canada
Arctic Station online, Netherlands
CHINARE 25 expedition, Belgium and
    China
Krill Game, Spain

School Level Initiatives

Student outreach programmes

SotaZero (BelowZero): educational research on life in extreme conditions

Submitted by Begoña Vendrell-Simón, ICM-CSIC, Spain

Categories: Correspondence from the field/lab, Research partnerships between educators and scientists

SotaZero was a collaboration between the Institut de Ciències del Mar (ICM-CSIC) and Frederic Mistral-Tècnic Eulàlia School, part of the general outreach project Welcome to the Antarctic. SotaZero's main aim was to promote the scientific spirit and interest in Antarctic science among students aged between five and 18 years old.

A group of scientists from ICM-CSIC, on board the German research vessel *Polarstern* during an Antarctic expedition (2003–04), communicated regularly via satellite with the students. The project had several objectives: to answer questions and stimulate kindergarten children to find out more about the characteristics of ice, the organisation of the ship and features about Antarctic animals; to answer questions and develop deductive skills among primary school students through building up charts on the different types of birds, and relating their occurrence to different water masses during the ship's passage towards the Antarctic. Finally, participants also carried out experiments proposed by a group of secondary school students related to the bacterial populations living in the Antarctic pack ice, and compared these with bacterial populations living in the ice-covered lakes of the Pyrenees.

The project won second prize in the 2004 eLearning Awards (Young Digital Poland Award for Best Use of ICT in Education).

Contact:

www.fundaciocollserola.cat/sotazero

Searchable Keywords: Antarctic, satellite communication, Polarstern, classroom, Spain

Global POP: International School Education—future scientists at work

Submitted by Eldbjørg Sofie Heimstad, Norwegian Institute of Air Research, Norway

Categories: Research partnerships between educators and scientists, Web-based

The main objective of Global POP was to engage and inspire young people in environmental issues and natural sciences through participation in an international education project. The project included hands-on school activities and scientific research on environmental contaminants in fish.

Key features

The schools sampled three fish of the same species (from sea or fresh water) that were among common food items in their local community. They gained an insight into how a researcher works by sampling fish using scientific methods, collecting and publishing metadata on the web, packing and correctly labelling the samples. The schools published each sample's metadata on the project website, as well as photographs of the fishing and sampling procedure.

NILU used a state-of-the art bioassay on the fish samples to measure concentrations of dioxins and dioxin-like compounds. The results were linked to the metadata on the website. Reports, presentations and videos from the schools were also made available on the website.

Keys to success

Key to the success of the project was the combination of novel research with the fact that students feel their work is appreciated by and valuable for the scientific community. Combining the fun of fishing trips with web publishing and data analysing is a good recipe for learning, and resembles how environmental scientists work. We found that collaboration between schools and research institutions benefits both partners.

Impacts

At present around 55 schools submitted fish for analysis and 41 of these schools have published their metadata on the project's website. We received and processed 200 samples, and results reveal that the majority of fish samples had concentrations of dioxins lower than safety limits set by European Commission.

Figure 3.1 Students preparing local fish samples for analysis.

To deal with today's environmental challenges, we must increase knowledge and awareness of environmental issues among people. A publicly available website is key to publishing results, guidelines of the project, and presentations from project leaders and schools. We are very happy to be able to present this large and important data set to national and international scientific communities. It would have been very difficult to acquire this data set without the efforts and skills of the schools involved, and we will encourage the scientific community to consider a more extensive collaboration with schools in order to establish similar cooperative projects.

> **Contact: http://sustain.no/projects/globalpop, post@sustain.no**
>
> **Searchable Keywords: pupils, education, research, dioxins, fish, data collection**

Alaska Lake Ice and Snow Observatory Network (ALISON)

Submitted by Kim Morris and Martin Jeffries, Geophysical Institute, UAF, USA
Categories: Creating educational tools, professional development for educators, Mentoring

ALISON gives teachers and students an opportunity to participate in genuine scientific research involving simple measurements of familiar materials—snow and ice. By practising science through hands-on, experiential learning with scientists, students and teachers enhance their knowledge and understanding about scientific inquiry and polar science.

Key features

ALISON's aim is to create a learning community of educators and students that increases knowledge of scientific inquiry and promotes polar science in school classrooms, reduces educators' physical and professional isolation, and improves links between schools and the post-secondary education sectors. This is achieved through a scientific research and science education partnership between the University of Alaska Fairbanks and Alaska's school education community. The science includes investigating spatial and temporal variability of lake ice thickness, depth, density and temperature of snow on the ice, and conductive heat flow from frozen lakes and ponds in Alaska. These data are available on the ALISON website and can be used to study inter-annual variability of lake ice thickness and snow properties, and to verify lake ice computer models.

Keys to success

Direct engagement of researchers with teachers and students ensures accuracy and adequate frequency of measurements to create a dataset on seasonality of ice and snow cover. Students develop science skills by using the same equipment and procedures as their scientist-collaborators. They learn the importance of collecting long-term data and the value of following procedures to arrive at reliable datasets. Researchers benefit from collaborating with school teachers and their students, acquiring greater appreciation for school science education issues, and developing communication skills to explain their science to younger audiences.

Figure 3.2 Measuring the snow depth and the snow-ice interface temperature with a temperature probe and digital reader.

A year in the life of a northern river: a geoscience education pilot project on the Nenana River, Alaska

This project provided students in the Denali Borough School District, Nenana River valley, central Alaska, with a chance to participate in hands-on scientifc learning. Fifty students at three rural schools studied seasonality of river ice. Using data sheets and a protocol specially designed for this project, they documented freeze-up and break-up processes on the Nenana River at a site near their schools. A smaller group of student volunteers measured the river's dissolved and suspended sediment loads during the open water season. Students created a unique, multi-year dataset, available on the project's website. Workshops were also held for the teachers to give them a background in climate change and the cryosphere, and training in the observation protocol.

Contact:
www.gi.alaska.edu, info@gi.alaska.edu

Searchable Keywords: science education outreach, Nenana River, Alaska, lake ice thickness, snow properties, river ice seasonality, dissolved and sediment loads in northern rivers

Arctic Sciences at FortWhyte Alive

Submitted by Jody Watson, FortWhyte Alive, Canada
Categories: Exhibitions, Events, Public presentations

FortWhyte Alive is one of Canada's leading privately operated, non-profit environmental education facilities that provides year-round programming to schools and the general public. During IPY, FortWhyte Alive collaborated with Schools on Board to offer a day of Arctic sciences and fieldwork to students and teachers.

Twenty Arctic scientists, researchers and graduate students from the University of Manitoba prepared exhibits and hands-on activities to introduce students to their fieldwork, research questions and methods.

Exhibits covered snow pits and sampling, ice coring, water sampling with plankton nets, water sampling with CTD and light profiles, sediment coring, weather observations, radiosondes and weather balloons, albedo and solar energy, people of the Arctic, beluga studies, and Inuit use of sea ice.

FortWhyte Alive's facilities provided an authentic setting for this event, and over 200 students and 20 teachers and aids participated in this outdoor event held in conjunction with the IPY Polar Week on Polar Oceans in October 2009.

Figure 3.3 Graduate student demonstrating water sampling at FortWhyte Alive event.

Contact:
www.fortwhyte.org, info@fortwhyte.org

Searchable Keywords: Schools on Board field programme,
experiential learning, Arctic Climate

Polar Competition with WWF-India

Submitted by Manish Tiwari and Rasik Ravindra, NCAOR, India
Categories: Contests and competitions, Posters, Events, Engaging audiences from mid-latitude countries

To involve school children throughout India, the National Centre for Antarctic & Ocean Research (NCAOR), in collaboration with WWF-India, held nation-wide competitions during 2007–08 for school children aged between 12 and 19. Almost 900 schoolchildren from across the country entered the competitions.

During the first year, students could either create posters or write slogans on the theme 'People and the Poles'. The following year, participants were asked to design stamps addressing the 25 years of Indian research in Antarctica.

The winning posters of 2007 were published as a calendar for 2008–09 and freely distributed across the country. Moreover, the three top winners of each competition received certificates, and were taken on a sightseeing and educational trip to Goa, where they visited NCAOR. There, students gained first-hand experience of polar science at NCOAR, the only Indian institute able to store and sample Antarctic ice cores in its special cold room facility maintained at –20°C.

Contact: www.ncaor.gov.in, info@ncaor.org

Searchable Keywords: Indian IPY activities, education
and outreach, school competition, WWF-India

Seasons and Biomes and The GLOBE Program: monitoring seasons through global learning communities

Submitted by Elena B. Sparrow, IARC and the School of Natural Resources and Agricultural Sciences at UAF; and Sheila Yule, The GLOBE Program, USA

Categories: Creative writing, Engaging audiences from Arctic communities, Engaging audiences from mid-latitude countries, Research partnerships between educators and scientists

GLOBE is an international environmental science and education school-based programme with primary and secondary students, educators and scientists working together. Seasons and Biomes is an inquiry- and project-based initiative that monitors seasons, specifically their interannual variability, to increase school students' understanding of the Earth system. It connects GLOBE students, teachers and communities with educators and scientists from three Earth system science programmes (the International Arctic Research Center [IARC], NASA LandSat Data Continuity, and Terra Satellite Missions) and other countries. It also provided opportunities for students anywhere to participate in IPY *(see boxes)*.

Key features

Seasons and Biomes engages school teachers and students in Earth system science investigations as a way of teaching and learning science. We provide professional development workshops on science content, scientific measurements and best teaching practices to educators and scientists in Alaska, other US states and internationally. Educators teach their students how to conduct Earth system science studies locally that also connect globally. Scientists and local experts, including indigenous Elders, mentor teachers and students. We provide equipment and follow-up support to teachers and students throughout the year.

The programme contributes to student understanding of the Earth system and, for example, how changes in polar regions affect other regions and vice versa. This project contributes environmental science data useful for climate studies and impact assessments, prevention and management of diseases, and validation of satellite data.

For IPY, we focused on the taiga/boreal forests and tundra biomes using protocols on the depth of soil freezing (frost tubes), ice seasonality freeze-up and break-up, in addition to GLOBE protocols on atmosphere and weather; plant phenology, hydrology, land cover, biology and soils.

Biome studies go beyond these areas and include temperate, tropical and subtropical forests as well as tropical and subtropical grasslands, savannas and shrublands. We partner with scientists and local experts in other countries to develop other protocols such as the mosquito, invasive plant species and flowering protocols for student investigations.

Figure 3.4 Students measuring depth of soil freezing using the frost tube protocol.

Impacts

Participants trained other educators and scientists on the Seasons and Biomes project, besides working with school students. Students in polar and non-polar regions conducted local Earth system/environmental science research. Some students participated in local, statewide or countrywide science symposia and fairs. Three native students from Shageluk, Alaska, as well as six students from two Model Secondary Schools for the Deaf in Washington, DC, and Indianapolis, presented their projects at the 2008 GLOBE Learning Expedition in South Africa, along with students from 23 other countries. Several Seasons and Biomes classrooms are participating in the GLOBE Student Research Campaign on Climate Change.

Figure 3.5 Thailand teachers practising the mosquito protocol.

IPY Pole to Pole videoconferences

As part of IPY Seasons and Biomes, Alaskan and Argentinean students from primary and secondary schools, as well as Arctic and Antarctic scientists from Colorado and Washington, DC took part in two IPY Pole to Pole videoconferences in 2007 and 2008. Participants discussed local environmental changes, seasonal indicators and climate change. The videoconferences, web chats and forums generated much interest and enthusiasm among students and scientists, and provided the impetus for student research projects and collaborations between schools.

Ice e-mystery polar e-books

In 2008, 12 Alaskan primary and secondary school classes partnered with 12 Australian secondary school classes in a collaborative project of the Australian Ice e-mystery polar e-books and Seasons and Biomes. Using online communication tools and software each pair developed a fictional book incorporating authentic polar science. Professional development workshops in the US and Australia brought together the educators and polar scientists for lessons on Arctic and Antarctic science and GLOBE Seasons and Biomes training. In June 2009, Alaskan teachers travelled to Tasmania to share their experiences, assess the project and discuss future collaborations. The books are freely available at http://.iem.tmag.tas.gov.au.

GLOBE IPY Ambassadors and GS-Pals—an online scientific discussion forum

IPY Ambassadors are GLOBE alumni, that is, students who graduated from GLOBE secondary schools and who are chosen as world regional representatives for the GLOBE Program. They are familiar with IPY, and the Seasons and Biomes investigations and teaching methodologies. They work with GLOBE country coordinators in their respective regions, and schools and communities in their countries to raise awareness of IPY, talk about how changes happening in polar regions are relevant to their own region, and engage school children in Earth system science research.

Their IPY outreach experience motivated GLOBE alumni and IPY Ambassadors to build GS-Pals, a web-based student-driven discussion forum and network for students' scientific inquiries on environmental issues such as climate change. GS-Pals is the result of successful education and outreach work and demonstrates the power of altruistically inspired and scientifically informed youth and can be accessed at http://gspal2.freehostia.com.

Contact: http://.iem.tmag.tas.gov.au, www.globe.gov, http://gspal2.freehostia.com, info@iarc.uaf.edu, www.iarc.uaf.edu

Searchable Keywords: Seasons and Biomes, GLOBE Earth System Science Projects, student networking, collaboration, mentoring

Keep Planting Trees initiative: an effort to create an understanding of the science behind climate change through tree planting in Malaysia

Submitted by Khadijah Abdul Rahman-Sinclair, YAWA, Malaysia

Categories: Educational expeditions, Engaging audiences from mid-latitude communities, Engaging students in doing outreach

Inspired by IPY, the Keep Planting Trees (KPT) initiative was launched in 2007 by YAWA, a youth action-based organisation committed to changing young lives. We believe, we can help raise awareness and reduce the impact of climate change on polar regions through tree planting.

With sponsorship from the corporate sector and national landscape departments, 12,000 trees were planted by 3,000 children in Malaysia between 2007 and 2009. This information was logged with the UNEP Billion Tree Campaign. Schools were approached through the Ministry of Education, and the tree-planting projects involved local and national landscape architects, NGOs and local authorities, as well as teachers and students. After the trees were planted, KPT monitored the trees for six months, after which local authorities took over their care. KPT visited the trees again a year after planting to measure their height, girth and condition.

Working with the State Forest Department, another NGO and corporate sponsors, KPT has replanted almost 10,000 mangroves. Seedlings are collected from wetlands and replanted in damaged mangroves. There are weekly and monthly visits organised by the NGO and the designated mangrove areas are cared for by the local authorities and the State Forest Department.

Contact: www.keep-planting-trees.com, www.yawa.org,
info@keep-planting-trees.com

Searchable Keywords: ecosystem, climate change, wetlands, rainforest, polar science, biodiversity

---

Polar zones and the Danube Delta: educational activities for schoolchildren and youth in the spirit of IPY Romania

Submitted by Teodor Gheorghe Negoita, Romanian Polar Research Institute, Romania

Categories: Creating educational tools

The working group 'The Danube Delta and the Law-Racovita Romanian Antarctic Station' was set up at the C.A. Rosetti School and its seven satellite schools in isolated areas of the Danube Delta Natural Reserve, a UNESCO Biosphere Reserve of 2,590 square kilometres.

Since its creation, the aim of this working group has been to equip and inspire students to take part in conservation work in the Danube Delta. Teachers, pupils, students and local authorities helped protect the delta through activities linked to environmental protection in Antarctica.

With public support, students and other members of the group removed piles of plastic bottles and other litter and waste from the Letea

Figure 3.6 Teodor Gheorghe Negoita with members of the working group at the C.A. Rosetti School in Tulcea, Romania.

Sandbanks Reserve, protected the unique flora from damage by the tourism industry, and tried to control poaching of wildlife and to discourage overfishing.

Pupils spoke about climate change at the Third International Symposium of Polar Scientific Research 2007–08, organised by the Romanian Polar Research Institute and the Romanian Academy. Articles were published in *Lotus* magazine and at conferences, information on the project was included in slide shows and DVDs, and teaching aids were produced.

Contact: www.polar-institute.ro

Searchable Keywords: environmental protection, education outreach, mentoring, workshop

Authentic proposal writing and research by high school students

Submitted by Matt Pruis, NWRA, USA

Category: Mentoring

In this project, secondary school students were asked to write their own research proposals. The two winning entries, which examined ice growth in sea-ice leads, were offered paid summer internships at NorthWest Research Associates (NWRA), and went on to successfully complete their research.

Aimed at letting high school students experience the excitement of new scientific discoveries, the project was designed to mimic as closely as possible a real-life 'request for proposal' (RFP) process, culminating in an actual research project.

During the autumn term, students were introduced to the researchers and their Arctic field projects through lectures and during a tour of the *USCGC Healy*. They were then given an RFP at the end of the term. During spring, teams of between one and four students wrote pre-proposals, and then met one-to-one with researchers to discuss the validity and practicality of their hypothesis and research plan. With this input, students then wrote full proposals, which were reviewed by leading US Arctic scientists. Two project teams were awarded funding.

Informal surveys following the project showed it motivated students to pursue science and technology courses after high school. Participation in the project also substantially improved students' scores in standardised tests of physics concepts. You can find more information on this project in the following article: Englert, K., B. Coon, M. Hinckley, and M. Pruis. 2009. Arctic Research and Writing: A Lasting Legacy of the International Polar Year. *Science Teacher*, 76.1, 20-26.

Contact: www.nwra.com, info@nwra.com

Searchable Keywords: Arctic, internship, research proposal, request for proposal

The Art of Science: an exhibition of children's artwork from the USA and Russia

Submitted by R. Max Holmes, Woods Hole Research Center, USA

Category: Exhibitions

Drawings, paintings and crafts created by students from schools participating in the National Science Foundation-funded Student Partners project were developed into a travelling exhibition. The artwork, the majority done by indigenous students from Siberia, depicts the children's environment and perceptions about environmental change. The collection, which demonstrates remarkable skill and awareness of their world, gives a glimpse of a remote part of the planet that most people know little about.

Although not originally planned as part of the Student Partners project, this growing exhibition has now been displayed at many outstanding venues including the United Nations (New York City), the American Association for the Advancement of Science (Washington, DC), the American Museum of Natural History (New York City), the New England Aquarium (Boston), the Vermont State House (Vermont), the Begich Boggs Visitors Center (Alaska), and the Flaten Museum (Minnesota), as well as at museums in Moscow, St. Petersburg and Yakutsk. These exhibitions, which feature the students' artwork as well as texts, photos and graphs related to global climate change and the Arctic, have been seen by hundreds of thousands of people and have allowed us to reach a much broader and diverse audience with the story of our research and education activities than would otherwise have been possible.

Figure 3.7 Student Partners project art exhibition, Flaten Art Museum, Minnesota, USA.

Contact: www.studentpartnersproject.org, rmholmes@whrc.org

Searchable Keywords: IPY, exhibition, Arctic, Siberia, student partners project

---

Beyond Penguins and Polar Bears: integrating literacy and IPY into primary school classrooms

Submitted by Jessica Fries-Gaither, Ohio State University, USA

Categories: Creating educational tools, Creative writing, Professional development for educators, Public presentations, Web-based

The goal of the Beyond Penguins and Polar Bears project, funded by the National Science Foundation, is to maximise IPY's impact on primary school classrooms by capturing student interest and fostering the ability of primary school teachers to integrate polar science concepts and literacy instruction.

Key features

Twenty issues of a free, online magazine connect topics from the primary school science curriculum, such as rocks and minerals, ecosystems and seasons to the polar regions. Each issue contains five areas of high-quality content: in the field/scientists at work, professional learning, science and literacy, across the curriculum, and polar news and notes. Regular columns help teachers increase their science and literacy content knowledge, target student misconceptions, and discover lessons and activities for classroom use. Each issue also contains science-themed nonfiction written for students in three age groups: six-year-olds, seven- to eight-year-olds, and nine- to ten-year-olds. The material is available in text, book and electronic book formats.

A blog provides updates on news, research, professional opportunities, and new project features. A companion podcast series, web seminars, and conference presentations provide opportunities for additional learning and project dissemination. Web 2.0 and social networking tools are used to disseminate project deliverables and provide opportunities for collaboration.

Keys to success
- Select a partner with an established network of projects and partners.
- Develop content well-aligned with education standards and curriculum.
- Use freely available technologies and tools to create and distribute content.
- Integrate multiple content areas (e.g., science and literacy).
- Support teachers as they build content knowledge and learn how to effectively use resources.

Impacts
Both the magazine and blog have been well received by teachers as well as education and outreach specialists. Emails, conversations at conferences and web seminars, and data from evaluations show that the magazine has increased primary school teachers' awareness and understanding of the polar regions and provided important resources to help them improve science instruction and effectively integrate literacy and science.

Contact: http://beyondpenguins.nsdl.org,
http://expertvoices.nsdl.org/polar

Searchable Keywords: science and literacy, elementary, cyberzine

Kiwis on Ice: talking to schoolchildren in New Zealand

Submitted by Shelley MacDonell, University of Otago, New Zealand; and CEAZA, Chile

Category: Classroom visits

During IPY and inspired by the local IPY Youth Steering Committee I gave a series of presentations to primary school children (between five and 12 years old) in rural New Zealand. My talks focused on my experience researching glaciers in Antarctica and working as a lecturer on a cruise ship. I prepared a slightly different presentation for each group, and talked to students based on their ability, attention span and the teacher's interest.

Polar animals, environmental impacts, and how and why people work and live in Antarctica were the topics that sparked the children's curiosity. The tricks that worked for me, and the things I learned, included: targeting each talk to students' age group; using lots of photos; asking them questions; having an in-depth knowledge of the film *Happy Feet*; and leaving lots of time for questions.

After the talks were completed, it was satisfying to know that as well as contributing to their understanding of polar environments, I was also able to trigger interest in the world of science. For me, the most rewarding part of the experience was the conversation after my presentation with a quiet eight-year-old boy who wanted to become an Antarctic scientist—it made it all worthwhile!

Contact: shelley.macdonell@ceaza.cl

Searchable Keywords: education outreach, scientists in schools, communicating with children

Teaching resource projects

Class Zero Emission: an educational workshop for students and teachers

Submitted by Isabelle Du Four, IPF, Belgium

Categories: Creating educational tools, Professional development for educators, Exhibition

Class Zero Emission (CZE) is a free interactive educational workshop centre in Brussels developed by the International Polar Foundation (IPF) and supported by the governments of Belgium's Flemish and French communities. It is open to students aged 10 to 18 and teachers from across Belgium. The material is available online in English, Dutch and French.

Key features

Built around a model of a giant iceberg, CZE has four areas covering four themes: climate change, polar regions, polar science and exploration, and sustainable development. Each area uses creative teaching tools (3-D puzzles of the Poles, digital flash animations, photographs, films, scientific experiments, games, etc.) to help students understand climate change. By taking part in experiments and interactive games, students learn about the fascinating world of polar science and realise the importance of adopting a sustainable way of life.

In addition, training sessions for teachers are held in CZE and online dossiers are meant to help teachers introduce polar-related issues like 'People in the Polar Regions,' 'Climate Change: What is it?' or 'Sustainable Development: What is it?' in the classroom. The dossiers are intended for late primary school (or middle school) teachers (10- to 12-year-old students) and secondary school science and geography teachers (12- to 18-year-old students).

The Class Zero Emission hands-on package for classroom usage includes an exercise booklet and a CD-ROM produced both in Dutch and French for classes of 10- to 14-year-olds. The exercise booklet deals with polar science from the angle of climate change. Students complete worksheets, short games, experiments, text analysis, and activities on climate change, polar regions, polar science, and sustainable development. Teachers can copy exercises for their students, and the key to exercises makes the booklet easy to use in the classroom.

The Class Zero Emission CD-ROM targets students aged between 10 and 18 years old. Teachers can use it in combination with the booklet or separately. The CD-ROM gives teachers a chance to discuss polar regions, polar science, the impacts of climate change on oceans as well as the role of humans for current climate change in an interactive, flexible and multi-media way.

Impacts

CZE's first year was a huge success: 1,700 pupils attended the workshop between March and June 2009. Feedback from teachers and students showed they appreciated the interactivity and diversity of the tools and the professionalism of the animators. Teachers also benefited from training sessions and an educational package, developed by IPF.

Figure 3.8 Exploration area at the workshop centre where children learn about the extreme polar environment and how to survive at the Poles.

Contact: info@polarfoundation.org, www.educapoles.org

Searchable Keywords: Class Zero Emission, International Polar Foundation, dossiers

The PoleS project in France: creating worksheets for students

Submitted by Thierry Touchais, IPF, Belgium

Categories: Creating educational tools, Professional development for educators

PoleS is a national project created by the Education Nationale Française (Centre régional de documentation pédagogique [CRDP] de l'académie d'Amiens), IPF and the Young Reporters for the Environment Association in France. The goal is to provide high school teachers with new tools and guidelines for teaching topics related to sustainable development.

IPF contributed to this project by creating 25 knowledge sheets to help teachers prepare lessons in sustainable development and climate change from a different angle—a polar perspective.

Each knowledge sheet addresses one topic and relates it to current teaching material in physics, chemistry, economics and languages. Topics include paleoclimates of the polar regions, plate tectonics, present polar climates, ecosystems, ice sheet dynamics, Arctic and Antarctic geopolitics, pollutants, the economic impacts of climate change in the polar regions, and how climate change is affecting indigenous peoples. These knowledge sheets compliment pedagogical sheets created by CRDP of Amiens.

The PoleS project provides a novel way to teach sustainable development at the same time as helping students and teachers to better understand the polar regions.

Contact: info@polarfoundation.org

Searchable Keywords: International Polar Foundation, education for sustainable development (ESD), polar regions

INTERNATIONAL **POLAR** FOUNDATION

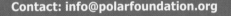

Ice, Ice, Baby: activities about polar ice sheets

Submitted by Cheri Hamilton, CReSIS, USA

Categories: Creating educational tools, Professional development for educators

Ice, Ice, Baby is an inquiry-based science programme created by the education team at the Center for the Remote Sensing of Ice Sheets (CReSIS), a National Science Foundation-funded science and technology centre based at the University of Kansas.

The 24 hands-on activities which constitute the Ice, Ice, Baby curriculum were developed to help students understand the role of polar ice sheets in sea level rise. These lessons demonstrate the scientific principles of displacement, density, and properties of ice. Student journals are used with each lesson as a strategy for improving students' science process skills; they also help the instructor assess comprehension and identify students' misconceptions.

When the Ice, Ice, Baby activities are presented in classrooms by the CReSIS educational outreach coordinator over the course of the school year, the programme also serves as ongoing professional development for teachers by modelling best practices in science instruction. Science inquiry skills are taught while students actively engage in hands-on learning, through the unusual topics of ice sheets, glaciers, icebergs and sea ice.

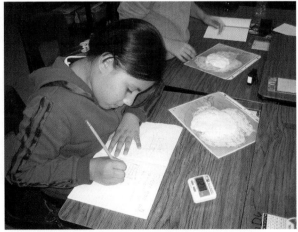

Figure 3.9 Students use 'glacier goo' to explore the characteristics of real glaciers while recording their measurements and findings in their science journals.

The Ice, Ice, Baby activities use everyday items that are easy to prepare and simple to teach, and the entire Ice, Ice, Baby curriculum is freely available online from the project's website.

Contact: www.cresis.ku.edu/education/iceicebaby.html

Searchable Keywords: CReSIS, ice sheets, sea level, teacher workshops

Bamboozle: Hot Puzzles, Cold Experiments

Submitted by Sandra Vanhove, IPF, Belgium

Categories: Creating educational resources, Mentoring, Public presentations, Science Fairs, Professional development for educators

The knowledge that young people, educators, teachers and the general public have about the North and South Poles is tested during a one-hour workshop that uses 3-D jigsaw puzzles, and allows participants to conduct experiments. By assembling two 3-D puzzles (each 1.2 m x 1.2 m x 20 cm) participants discover that while the two polar regions are similar in many ways they are also fundamentally different.

The puzzles are made up of different layers representing the continents, open oceans, sea ice and ice sheets superimposed on top of one another. A picture booklet with facts and figures along with a set of pieces representing indigenous people, polar explorers and local animal species can be used to start a discussion about people in the Arctic and Antarctic or biodiversity issues.

The project proved an ideal tool for explaining problems related to climate change to both young people and educators. Initially part of the Flemish government's programme to promote interest in science, the puzzle project was popular during IPY 2007–08, attracting thousands of students. The project remains in great demand for science outreach and public awareness events, in both Belgium and neighbouring countries.

Figure 3.10 Discovering the polar regions with Bamboozle.

Contact: info@polarfoundation.org, www.educaPoles.org

Searchable Keywords: International Polar Foundation, puzzle, polar experiments

Discovering Antarctica: an online educational resource

Submitted by Linda Capper, BAS, UK

Categories: Creating educational tools, Web-based

This award winning, online interactive resource is produced in partnership with the Royal Geographical Society and is funded by UK Foreign and Commonwealth Office Polar Regions Unit. Widely used across the UK by geography students and their teachers, this is British Antarctic Survey's (BAS) flagship educational resource.

Designed to link directly with the UK national science and geography curriculum, *Discovering Antarctica* provides free lesson-based resources and fun interactive activities. It is primarily for teachers to use in class or for homework but is equally rewarding for students to explore and research all things Antarctic. Content covers food webs, Antarctic tourism and politics, marine and terrestrial resources, Antarctica's rich history of exploration and discovery, as well as questions over its future.

A new science area on the website was launched in summer 2008. The long-term vision for *Discovering Antarctica* is to enhance its science content and create sections that are relevant and engaging for primary school students and teachers. Supplementary content on the BAS website is linked to www.discoveringantarctica.org.uk. The website routinely has 7,000 unique visitors per month, and about 33,000 unique visitors during exam period.

Contact: www.discoveringantarctica.org.uk

Searchable Keywords: British Antarctic Survey, Antarctica, teaching resources

British Antarctic Survey
NATURAL ENVIRONMENT RESEARCH COUNCIL

Student expeditions and beyond

Students on Ice: education expeditions for students, scientists and educators

Submitted by Tim Straka, Students on Ice, Canada

Categories: Scientific expeditions

Students on Ice is an award-winning organisation offering unique educational expeditions to the Antarctic and Arctic. Our mandate is to provide students, educators and scientists from around the world with inspiring educational opportunities at the ends of the Earth and, in doing so, help them develop a new understanding and respect for the planet. Since 1999, Students on Ice has successfully organised 18 expeditions to the Arctic and Antarctica, involving more than 1,200 students from 40 countries.

Key features

Students on Ice—International Polar Year (SOI-IPY) educational expeditions to the Arctic and Antarctic were offered to high school and university students from around the world. Students travelled with teams of leading scientists, researchers, educators, artists and innovators. Each expedition involved around 70 participating youth and 35 staff.

During the expeditions, several different learning formats were used, including presentations, workshops, hands-on activities and research. Topics covered included geopolitics, cultural history, terrestrial ecology, marine

Figure 3.11 Students analyse data with glaciologist Luke Copland.

biology (from micro-organisms to cetaceans), flora and fauna, environmental issues facing the polar regions, ice and glaciology, oceanography and the history of exploration in the region.

Hands-on activities and workshops include, among others, wildlife identification and observation, working with education team members on ongoing scientific research (i.e., seabird surveys, measuring pollution levels in ice-core samples, plankton tows focusing on marine diversity), nature interpretation through various activities (i.e., photography, art, journal writing, music), technology and nature (i.e., cetacean vocalisation, GIS mapping), mentored discussions aligning educators with students' interests, youth forums on leadership and steps towards sustainable living, hiking and shore walks, zodiac cruising and visits to research stations.

Impacts

The SOI-IPY expeditions resulted in many positive outcomes and achievements. The expeditions provided life-changing experiences for youth from around the world through its six educational expeditions during IPY. The organisation helped inspire the next generation of polar scientists and researchers; developed polar curriculum and resources; created educational websites videos, and a documentary film was launched at the *International Polar Year Film Festival* in September 2009. SOI-IPY received significant media attention around the world, serving as a tremendous IPY legacy project.

Figure 3.12 Student taking an ice core sample.

Three quarters of the participants received full scholarships or bursaries from public and private sources, and 80 aboriginal youth and staff from circumpolar countries participated in the expedition series.

Contact: www.studentsonice.com

Searchable Keywords: education outreach, career development, mentoring, workshop, polar education, youth expeditions, Students on Ice

STUDENTS ON ICE
·expeditions·
ANTARCTICA · ARCTIC

Schools on Board: bridging environmental science education and Arctic climate change research

Submitted by Lucette Barber, Schools on Board—ArcticNet/IPY-CFL, University of Manitoba, Canada
Categories: Events, Research expeditions, Youth forums

Schools on Board (SonB) is a scientific outreach programme of ArcticNet, a Canadian-led international network of Arctic climate change scientists and researchers. The programme provides authentic science experiences to secondary school students and teachers from across Canada. Each year a small team of students and teachers joins scientists on board the research icebreaker *CCGS Amundsen*, while it is in full research mode. Scientists give presentations and demonstrations, facilitate group discussions, oversee science experiments, and organise hands-on fieldwork experiences.

In addition to the field programme, every two years an Arctic Climate Change Youth Forum (ACCYF) is co-hosted with a secondary school and organised by a student planning committee, in conjunction with a national or international science conference. SonB also promotes scientific outreach in the ArcticNet science community, through education, outreach and communication sessions at science conferences, classroom visits and other events that bring students and teachers into contact with researchers, scientists and graduate students.

During IPY, SonB ran in conjunction with the IPY-Circumpolar Flaw Lead system study, the science team committing and funding a total of 14 berths for up to 21 days of the research programme. These programmes included teachers and students from Canada, USA, Spain, China, UK, Germany, Norway, and Sweden, as well as Inuit youth from Canada, Greenland, USA (Alaska) and Russia.

As well as the field programme, SonB promoted scientific outreach by: chairing an outreach session at the Arctic Changes 2008 science conference; joining the IPY Polar Day live from the *Amundsen;* participating in the Polar Perspectives forum; planning events such as the Arctic Science Days at FortWhyte Alive and planning Artists on Board IPY-CFL.

Figure 3.13 Schools on Board teacher drawing a water sample from a rosette.

Key features

SonB's key features include cross-curricular components linked to history, current affairs, political sciences, environmental education, mathematics, art and literature; daily dispatches posted on website, a conference call from the ship, emails and Skype correspondence with schools, interviews with the media, and blogs. The programme also facilitates Northern community visits including tours, cultural activities, and meetings with community leaders, Elders and local high school students.

Figure 3.14 Schools on Board student communicating her field and research experience at a science conference.

Keys to success
- Promoting full engagement of schools and participants in outreach by requiring schools to apply to the programme, partnering with schools to co-host ACCY Forums, and making outreach a required output for participants.
- Making schools responsible for student selection.
- Creating a flexible itinerary able of responding to changes in research plans, availability of scientists and weather.
- Giving attention to group dynamics to ensure strong group cohesion.
- Educating 'about', 'in' and 'for' Arctic climate change research by planning content linked to the curriculum and Traditional Knowledge, ensuring authentic settings.
- Planning a guiding or unifying question for each day related to the planned activities.
- Debriefing at the end of each day to gauge participants' understanding and allow reflection and sharing.
- Managing risk. When organising programmes for minors (students under legal age) in the field, it is important to demonstrate that you have identified possible risks, measures taken to address these risks, and necessary waiver forms. Depending on the nature of the programme, this may require legal advice from your research institution.
- Providing more than one option for scientists to become involved in scientific outreach, such as classroom visits, presentations, lab activities, demonstration of field practices, mentoring, organising events, sitting on youth forum committees, participating in conference calls.

Impacts

This programme continues to be transformational on an individual and professional level for students, teachers and scientists. The high level of involvement by schools has resulted in very creative outreach initiatives and events planned in conjunction with the field programme: Arctic Awareness Week, Climate Change Expo; around 60 presentations a year delivered by SonB participants to a wide range of audiences; schools agreeing to co-host youth forums; partnerships established between students and researchers after field programmes, resulting in mentoring and employment opportunities; partnerships established between researchers and teachers; students and scientists using this outreach experience in funding or scholarship applications.

Figure 3.15 Participants of the Schools on Board international field programme on the ice.

Contact: info@schoolsonboard.ca,
http://www.arcticnet.ulaval.ca/index.php?fa=SB.show

Searchable Keywords: Schools on Board field programme, ArcticNet, IPY-CFL, experiential learning, Arctic Climate Change Youth Forum, PromoScience, Polar Perspectives forum, Polar Weeks

Schools on Board, a great experience for teachers and students in Spain

Submitted by Josep Marlés Tortosa, Frederic Mistral/Tècnic Eulàlia School (Fundació Collserola), Spain
Categories: Educational expeditions, Events, Research partnerships between educators and scientists, Science Fairs, Scientific expeditions

To mark IPY, the University of Manitoba's Schools on Board offered eight schools in different countries—including Spain's Frédéric Mistral/Tècnic Eulàlia School in Barcelona—the chance to take part in the SonB programme.

Supervised by the Institute of Marine Sciences (ICM-CSIC), the aim of Spain's participation was to incorporate Arctic environmental issues into the curricula at various educational levels, and communicate this to other schools and educational institutions across the country.

The Spanish students and teachers joined the *CCGS Amundsen* for 15 days during March 2008, meeting Inuit communities in northern Canada as well as taking part in Arctic climate change research. As well

Figure 3.16 Teachers on the ice during the Schools on Board programme.

as contributing to the data collected during the expedition, information was collected that will be developed into teaching materials for Spanish-speaking students and teachers.

Through Spain's participation in SonB, over 2,000 students from secondary schools in Barcelona studied the Arctic food web, environmental issues affecting the Arctic, and changes in Mediterranean ecosystems due to the destabilisation of polar regions. There are plans that this work will be shared with schools across Spain.

Contact: info@schoolsonboard.ca

Searchable Keywords: Schools on Board, Spain, IPY

Canadian Network for Detection of Atmospheric Change: IPY Northern Experience Program

Submitted by Tara Cunningham, CANDAC, Canada

Categories: Contests and competitions, Educational expeditions

CANDAC's IPY Northern Experience Program contest was an essay competition for high school students aged from 15 to 18 years old and teachers from across Canada. In April 2009, the winners (15 students and six teachers) participated in an 11-day excursion to northern Nunavut to learn about the impacts of climate change.

The CANDAC IPY Northern Experience Program took place primarily in Resolute Bay, a community of approximately 250 people. Working with staff from Qarmartalik School, the CANDAC team provided a programme of lessons and activities on the atmosphere and the environment, the history and the geography of Nunavut, and Arctic flora and fauna.

Students and teachers gained first-hand knowledge of daily life in the High Arctic by meeting Elders and community members in Resolute Bay. They also spent one day at the Polar Environment Atmospheric Research Laboratory research station in Eureka, learning about the atmospheric research CANDAC is carrying out there.

This unique educational experience allowed participants to connect through their shared interest in climate change and its impacts, and led to new knowledge, new experiences and new friendships.

Contact: outreach@candac.ca,
http://candac.ca/candac/Outreach/Outreach.php

Searchable Keywords: CANDAC, IPY, essay competition, Northern Experience Program

Two Ways of Knowing: Inuit youth trained in scientific and Traditional Knowledge of Arctic char in Kugluktuk, Nunavut, Canada

Submitted by Heidi Swanson, University of New Brunswick, Canada

Categories: Mentoring, Engaging Audiences from Arctic Communities, Creating Curriculum, Classroom Visits

With a grant from Nasivvik Centre for Inuit Health and Changing Environments, researchers from the IPY project called 'Arctic Biodiversity of Chars' collaborated with a local consulting firm, the Kugluktuk Hunters and Trappers Association, and Kugluktuk High School to provide a one-week training course to Inuit high school students on 'two ways of knowing'.

Key features

Students received instruction on management, monitoring, and traditional uses of Arctic char from western scientists, community Elders and youth mentors. Through integration with a career and technology studies curriculum, participating students earned one high school credit for completing the course. Unique in its length, breadth, and incorporation of both western science and Traditional Knowledge, this project fostered cooperation and communication among community members, students and scientists.

Three scientists, three community Elders, and one youth mentor developed over 30 hours of hands-on curriculum designed to teach Inuit students about the ecological, social and nutritional importance of Arctic char. Students learned about effects of climate change on their community and their fisheries. They also learned field and laboratory techniques for monitoring fish populations and water quality, and practised fish preparation for pollutant analysis, drying and cooking. The course was designed to prepare students for community-based monitoring of local fisheries, and field and laboratory equipment purchased for the course was left in the community. Stories about the course were broadcast on a local radio show.

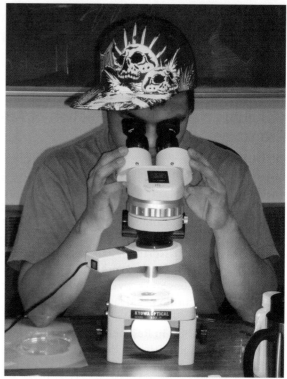

Figure 3.17 Student learning to age a fish using otoliths (ear bones).

Keys to success

This project would not have been possible without a dedicated liaison living in the community. They arranged logistics and secured participation of local Elders and youth mentors. Also, it was very important that instructors remained flexible and able to adapt their curriculum to changing student numbers and timelines. We found that students were eager to participate in hands-on activities and that a ratio of one instructor to four students was optimal.

Impacts

The project was an invaluable teaching and learning experience for instructors and students. Capacity-building outcomes included donations of equipment and training of students and teachers. All participants benefited from dialogue between Elders and scientists, and an emphasis on 'two ways of knowing'.

Contact: www.nasivvik.ulaval.ca

Searchable Keywords: mentoring, two ways of knowing, extended classroom visits, outreach

The 2008 Schools on Board Circumpolar Inuit Field Program (CIFP)

Submitted by Robin Gislason, University of Manitoba, Canada
Categories: Engaging audiences from Arctic communities, Scientific expeditions, Web-based

One of the IPY-Circumpolar Flaw Lead outreach programmes, CIFP saw eight circumpolar Inuit youth aged 17 to 25 years old from Canada, Alaska, Greenland and Russia take part in a Two Ways of Knowing Arctic climate change research field programme.

By combining Inuit Traditional Knowledge (TK) and western scientific research, the programme included activities in Inuvik and Sachs Harbour (Northwest Territories, Canada), plus work with Arctic climate change scientists on the Canadian icebreaker *CCGS Amundsen's* IPY-CFL scientific expedition.

Before joining the field programme, participants began their TK research in their own communities. Using tools supplied by the programme, they interviewed Elders and knowledgeable community members about regional climate change.

The field programme involved a series of interconnected knowledge exchange workshops to compare information between different regions, generations and between scientists and lay people. Participants learned how to analyse and disseminate their TK data, and presented their research to Elders and scientists at the end of the programme, which was marked by a community visit and feast in Sachs Harbour.

Throughout the programme, participants shared their experiences via daily web dispatches. They took part in workshops at the 2008 Arctic Climate Change Youth Forum and the 2008 Arctic Changes conference in Quebec.

Figure 3.18 Participants exchanging knowledge and observations of climate change as part of the Circumpolar Inuit Field Program.

Contact: www.ipy-cfl.ca

Searchable Keywords: CIFP, Inuit, Schools on Board, IPY

Teacher expeditions and beyond

ARISE: Educators from Germany, Italy, New Zealand and USA in Antarctica

Submitted by Louise Huffman, ANDRILL, University of Nebraska-Lincoln, USA

Categories: Correspondence from the field/lab, Creating educational tools, Professional development for educators, Scientific expeditions, Video, Web-based

ANDRILL (ANtarctic geological DRILLing), a multi-national, interdisciplinary science team provides research experiences for science educators. Eight educators from Germany, Italy, New Zealand and USA representing informal education and classrooms from primary school level (ages six to 11) to college level accompanied the ANDRILL scientists to Antarctica during IPY.

Key features

The ARISE (ANDRILL Research Immersion for Science Educators) programme grew out of earlier projects that sent one teacher into the field as a research assistant. ANDRILL created a programme that took a team of teachers to allow creative outreach collaborations during the immersion experience.

Teachers were selected on the basis of their proposed education outreach project that they would create to communicate the science. Some projects were completed in Antarctica and some after returning home. In the field, educators wrote blogs, and organised audio- and videoconferences with their classrooms.

Following the field experience, strong outreach programmes have been developed to communicate ANDRILL's climate change results. One educator developed a suite of climate change teaching resources, including a book of activities, posters and videos, accessible at www.andrill.org/flexhibit. Others wrote children's books or created photo and audio exhibits listed at www.andrill.org/education.

Figure 3.19 Scientist points out interesting layers in the core to ANDRILL educators.

Keys to Success

- Develop an application form and a rubric for evaluating and ranking the submissions.
- Create a list of expectations for the educators and the scientists.
- Be clear what the educator's roles will be.
- Bring the educator(s) to the institution before the field experience for an orientation; present the science and build background knowledge; explain equipment, procedures and jobs; talk about what a 'Day on Ice' will look like; prepare the educator(s) for the trip by discussing the details of travel and what to bring; do some team building before travelling so that the team is ready to work when they arrive in the field.
- Be sure to build time into the day for educators to ask questions—be sure scientists are aware of their role as 'teachers of teachers'.
- Develop an evaluation instrument to inform future immersion experiences.

Impacts

Both teachers and scientists profited from the immersion experience. Science educators gained an inside view of ANDRILL and authentic Antarctic geoscience, and they used their education expertise to implement innovative approaches to geoscience education, communication and public outreach. Educators and their students benefited from interacting with a world-class group of scientists. The project also built lasting relationships between educators, and between educators and scientists.

Project Circle: an online connection to teachers and scientists in the field

Project Circle is an interactive online ANDRILL outreach programme connecting teachers and students to authentic Antarctic research. Guided by an educator attached to a field team, classrooms ask scientists questions, and realise the excitement of science discovery as it happens. Project Circle offers both an 'inner circle' and an 'outer circle' for participation. In the 'inner circle' registered classrooms interact regularly through the group hub. There is no limit to the number of classrooms that can be involved, but experience shows that an international mix of less than 30 classrooms is optimum for good participation and ease of communication. In the 'outer circle' classrooms and individuals visit the website and interact with the activities there.

Project Circle offers various features for educators to involve students in learning about polar science, geological research, climate change, and living and working in an extreme environment. Students of all ages can communicate with Antarctica through blogs, phone calls and videoconferences. The group hub provides a password-protected environment for discussion and the sharing of resources. The website offers teaching materials and the *Sun Shadow Project* allows students around the world to compare local measurements. See the project at www.andrill.org/education.

Figure 3.20 Scientist conducting a videoconference with a classroom thousands of kilometres away.

Contact: www.andrill.org/education, www.andrill.org/flexhibit

Searchable Keywords: ARISE, ANDRILL, education, field experience

Coole Klassen (Cool School Classes) teachers' programme

Submitted by Rainer Lehmann, Freie Waldorfschule Hannover-Bothfeld, Germany

Categories: Contests and competitions, Correspondence from the field/lab, Professional development for educators

Coole Klassen (Cool School Classes) is a German IPY education project for teachers, started in 2006 to integrate new polar science questions, methods and results into school lessons. It is a nationwide, multidisciplinary network of interested geography, biology, physics, chemistry and social science teachers.

Teachers act as disseminators, and work on various polar projects with students. They learn from one another at conferences, in workshops and via the website. A very important subproject involves teachers working with

Figure 3.21 German students talk to their teacher in Antarctica.

scientists on polar expeditions, and taking an active part in the field or on research vessels, usually the *Polarstern*.

During their expedition teachers write blogs and participate in conference calls with school classes. Following their field experience they bring an in-depth understanding of polar research back into the classroom and develop new educational materials. Teachers also give talks at national and international conferences, and share their experiences with colleagues. Coole Klassen also carried out a number of national contests during IPY, such a drawing contest among schoolchildren. Moreover, with the help of Coole Klassen, teachers built partnerships between schools in Germany and in polar regions.

Beyond IPY, the initiative will continue to exist as part of the Polar Teachers Working Group, founded in 2008 by the German Society for Polar Research (DGP).

Contact: rainer.lehmann@gmx.net

Searchable Keywords: polarlehrer, interdisziplinäres netzwerk, expeditionslehrer, Coole Klassen, DGP

First joint US-Canada polar expedition for educators, Axel Heiberg Island, Nunavut, Canada

Submitted by Jason Clement and Marie-Claude Williamson, CSA, Canada

Categories: Creating curriculum, Educational expeditions, Professional development for educators, Research partnerships between educators and scientists

In 2008, six teachers from Canada and the US visited the McGill Arctic Research Station (MARS) in the Canadian High Arctic for two weeks, sponsored by the Canadian Space Agency (CSA), McGill University and NASA.

MARS was established in 1960 on western Axel Heiberg Island, a mountainous area dominated by ice caps, outlet and valley glaciers, polar desert, Arctic tundra and permafrost. The station's upper camp is one of the longest-operating seasonal field research facilities in the polar regions, and has an internationally recognised reputation for research on cold, perennial springs associated with evaporite domes.

Through fieldwork and hands-on demonstrations, the teachers joined a team of scientists and engineers to explore physical geography, geoscience, astrobiology and robotics. They discovered how planetary scientists use remote and extreme polar environments on Earth to better understand the evolution of the Moon and Mars.

When the teachers returned home, they brought back this experience to their classrooms, and used it to help develop a space curriculum. Two Canadian teachers, for example, developed a curriculum-relevant resource for secondary schools, as well as a professional development workshop for other educators held at the 2009 CSA National Space Educators Conference.

Contact: www.asc-csa.gc.ca, promo@asc-csa.gc.ca

Searchable Keywords: field experience, teachers, NASA, MARS

International Arctic expedition for teachers

Submitted by Elena B. Sparrow, University of Alaska Fairbanks, USA
Categories: Educational expeditions, Scientific expeditions, Professional development for educators

During this science cruise to the Eurasian basin of the Arctic Ocean, school teachers from Canada, France, Germany, Russia, the UK and the US spent 26 days on the icebreaker *Kapitan Drantizyn*.

The cruise gave the teachers a unique opportunity to take part in high-latitude Arctic climate change research by collecting and analysing data with the help of an international team of experienced polar researchers. The experience included lectures and laboratory work on oceanography, meteorology and Arctic paleo-ecology. Participants also learned about IPY, the Global Learning and Observations to Benefit, the GLOBE Program protocols and best teaching practices. Teachers also organised a panel discussion on climate change.

Figure 3.22 Teachers on the Arctic cruise with the icebreaker *Kapitan Drantizyn.*

A post-expedition survey found that teachers had not only gained knowledge of the Arctic and its role in the Earth system, but learned about real science and experienced different cultures. The teachers are now sharing their Arctic expedition experiences with their students, colleagues and the general public, and as part of IPY education and outreach activities.

The expedition was organised by the International Arctic Research Center, University of Alaska Fairbanks, the Alfred-Wegener-Institute for Polar and Marine Research in Germany, the Arctic and Antarctic Research Institute in St. Petersburg, and the A.M. Obukhov Institute of Atmospheric Physics in Moscow.

Contact: www.iarc.uaf.edu, info@iarc.uaf.edu

Searchable Keywords: teachers, expedition, international, Arctic

SIPEX: Australian teachers in Antarctica

Submitted by Sandra Zicus, formerly of ACE CRC, Australia

Categories: Correspondence from the field/lab, Creating educational tools, Scientific expeditions, Video, Web-based

The international Sea Ice Physics and Ecosystem eXperiment (SIPEX) explored the sea ice zone around Antarctica at the height of its winter extent, investigating relationships between the physical environment and Southern Ocean ecosystems. SIPEX included an extensive education and outreach programme through a specially created website that could be updated daily from the ship, despite lack of Internet access on board.

Key features

Two Tasmanian teachers, Jane Dobson and Caroline Lapworth, and the communications manager from the Antarctic Climate & Ecosystems Cooperative Research Centre (ACE CRC), Sandra Zicus, participated in the six-week voyage.

The three were out on the ice in all kinds of weather helping the scientists. They communicated their experiences to people around the world through the voyage website, writing daily science blogs, answering questions from students and creating educational resources for teachers. They were accompanied by Polar Knutsen, a toy polar bear from Rosetta Primary School in Tasmania, who wrote his own blog about the differences between the Antarctic and his home in the Arctic.

Many of the scientists and postgraduate students on board also wrote blogs. These, as well as a number of video interviews, were done in several languages, including English, French, German, Malay, Japanese, Chinese and Finnish.

Other web highlights included daily weather updates and an online Earth map showing the ship's location. There was also an art and poetry section, and a daily mystery photo, as well as comparative information about the Arctic and Antarctic environments and a link to similar Arctic research being done from the German research vessel *Polarstern*.

Figure 3.23 Teacher Caroline Lapworth and a researcher measuring temperature at the snow/ice interface.

Impacts

Eighty-five schools registered to follow the voyage via the website, representing every state and territory in Australia as well as the UK, USA, Canada, New Zealand and Singapore. Many more used the website, but did not register. The Education Network of Australia (EDNA) acted as an interface between the schools and the educators on board. EDNA updated an Earth map as schools registered, and forwarded student questions, poetry and artwork to the ship.

Coming back from Antarctica, Jane Dobson said: "Being part of SIPEX was a wonderful experience. We learned so much about Antarctica, how scientific research is carried out in such extreme environments, and what it takes to make a voyage like this possible. We especially enjoyed having the opportunity to communicate our experiences daily, in real time, to people all around the world via the SIPEX website."

Contact: www.sipex.aq

Searchable Keywords: Australia, sea ice, voyage

Scientific bi-literacy and the 2007 SIMBA expedition to Antarctica

Submitted by Ana L. Pallares-Weissling, Fabra elementary school, USA

Categories: Classroom visits, Correspondence from the field, Creating curriculum, Research partnerships between educators and scientists

The 2007 IPY SIMBA expedition to the Antarctic provided the context for a one-year educational outreach initiative in a bilingual classroom at Fabra elementary school in Boerne, Texas. The project focused on the development of scientific knowledge and language as well as academic linguistic abilities in English and Spanish among special needs and at-risk students aged between seven and eight.

Key features

The SIMBA education and outreach programme enhanced the primary education model at Fabra elementary by bringing polar science into the classroom.

The primary educational model at Fabra is that of creating a year-round learning environment and development of curricula that integrates science content with literacy activities. In this model, students study a thematic science unit through hands-on experimentation, research, reading, creative and guided writing, grammar and vocabulary activities to acquire knowledge and understanding of their environment as well as foster dual language development.

SIMBA provided a unique opportunity to integrate polar science in the curriculum, and thereby built a highly successful Antarctic sea ice study theme as the foundation for students' academic success. Part of the success lay in the multiple classroom visits and presentations by science personnel both before and after the expedition. These were coupled with interactive communications via satellite phone, blogs, email and data sharing between scientists and children during the two-month cruise on board the *Nathaniel B. Palmer*. Older students aged 11 to 12 took part in mentoring and teaching their younger schoolmates.

Figure 3.24 Young Scientists at work at Fabra elementary school.

Impacts

Student ownership of the specific science process and overall project was solidified through the naming of one SIMBA sea ice study station for the school, the Fabra site. Recent state testing of eight-year old children for essential knowledge and skills in the Texas Assessment of Knowledge and Skills (TAKS) confirmed both the academic success of this select group of special-needs students with a 100% pass rate in both language and mathematics, and of the outlined educational model. The children's success constitutes a feat unprecedented in this school's history.

> **Contact: www.polartrec.com**
>
> **Searchable Keywords: scientists in schools, bi-lingual, science education and outreach**

Forums, Science Fairs, Internships

The 2008 Arctic Climate Change Youth Forum

Submitted by Marc Dallaire, Le Petit Séminaire de Québec, Canada
Categories: Engaging students in doing outreach, mentoring

During the 2007–08 and 2008–09 school years, the high school Le Petit Séminaire de Québec organised and co-hosted an Arctic Climate Change Youth Forum (ACCYF) with Schools on Board and Arctic Changes 2008—a major international science and policy conference on Arctic climate change.

The organising committee included 30 students, a school administrator, four teachers, and three ArcticNet graduate students from the Université Laval acting as advisers. Using the Schools on Board model for an ACCYF, the student committee organised a day focused on environmental, political and social issues, and science related to climate change in the Arctic.

ArcticNet scientists who were attending the conference were also invited to participate in the youth forum, an event planned for the day before the conference. They delivered interactive presentations on the role of oceans in the climate system, the Arctic marine ecosystem, sea ice reduction, sea-level rise, permafrost and erosion, the Arctic landscape and Traditional Knowledge as well as Arctic sovereignty and resources, carbon taxes and communicating climate change.

As well as learning more about Arctic climate change research and associated issues, both students and teachers gained valuable skills in organising and hosting this major event.

Contact: http://www.psq.qc.ca/fjcca/index_en.htm, www.arctic-change2008.com, fjcca@psq.qc.ca

Searchable Keywords: Arctic, climate change conferences, polar youth, youth forums

Alaska Native Science Fairs for students

Submitted by Ray Barnhardt, UAF, USA
Categories: Creating curriculum, Engaging audiences from Arctic communities, Science Fairs

The project provides support for a statewide network of Alaska Native Science Fairs, where students present the results of their research with projects linking local knowledge with western science. Practising scientists judge the projects on their scientific merit and local Elders on their cultural merit. Awards are presented in both categories: science and cultural merit.

Key features

The Alaska Native Knowledge Network (ANKN) has formed a coordinated educational enrichment programme with secondary school students that uses projects prepared for local and regional science fairs as a way of analysing and comparing standard science subject matter with local, that is, indigenous observations and applications.

To take advantage of the diverse knowledge base of Alaska native communities, this initiative partners with school districts in each of the five major cultural regions in Alaska (Inupiaq, Yup'ik, Aleut, Tlingit/Haida and

Figure 3.25 A science instructor explains the experiment testing the audio amplification of a traditional Aleut bentwood hat.

Athabascan). ANKN provides resources and support in identifying and connecting science mentors and Elders with students and teachers preparing Native Science Fair projects. Using the twin judging criteria, outstanding projects advance to the Alaska Statewide Science Fair held in early spring in Anchorage. Winning projects are then documented for curricular use and distributed to all Alaska schools in a variety of multimedia formats (web, CD, calendar, publications, curriculum guides, etc.) to enrich and enliven the school curriculum.

Figure 3.26 Traditional seal oil lamps involve many variables for proper burning; Unalaska students test those variables to determine the cleanest and most efficient combination.

Keys to success

ANKN staff works directly with school districts and teachers, including helping participating school districts to sponsor a local or regional science fair, providing workshops for participating teachers, developing ideas for Native Science Fair projects, and organising and implementing a native science theme for the annual Alaska State Science Fair. Support is also available to help schools develop and implement culture- and place-based curricula, drawing on the science projects developed for the Native Science Fairs.

Contact: www.ankn.uaf.edu/publications/Alaska_Science/Fairs.html

Searchable Keywords: Indigenous knowledge, science fairs, Alaska Native, science education

Polar Perspectives: youth forums and speakers series in Canada

Submitted by Elizabeth McCrea, Canadian Museum of Nature, Canada
Categories: Engaging audiences from Arctic communities, Events, Exhibitions, Public presentations

The Alliance of Natural History Museums of Canada (ANHMC) and Students on Ice organised and delivered Polar Perspectives. This pan-Canadian programme of IPY speakers and youth forums took place from spring 2008 to winter 2009 at 15 venues across the country, reaching each of Canada's provinces and territories.

The speaker series consisted of evening presentations delivered to a general audience by prominent scientists—including oceanographers, paleobiologists and fisheries experts—as well as writers, artists, film-makers and adventurers. Presenters shared the latest knowledge on Arctic issues, including their impact on both the northern and southern Canadian population, and each evening programme also featured special presentations, competitions, and IPY-related displays.

The youth forums were unique full-day educational programmes for youth to learn about the polar regions, northern people, IPY and climate change. Videoconferencing across the Canadian Arctic enabled northern aboriginal youth to share thoughts on health, culture, conservation, sovereignty, stories and perspectives with other northerners and southern youth. More than 750 students participated across Canada and Greenland, including 150 aboriginal youth representing many different Arctic communities.

Polar Perspectives has left an IPY legacy of new knowledge, understanding and interest in the polar regions, and has captured the interest of Canadians of all ages.

Contact: http://nature.ca/nature_e.cfm, questions@mus-nature.ca

Searchable Keywords: polar perspectives, Canada, ANHMC, students on ice, IPY

Training Arctic youth: the Circumpolar Young Leaders Program (CYLP)

Submitted by Carolee Buckler, International Institute of Sustainable Development, Canada

Categories: Engaging audiences from Arctic communities, Engaging students in doing outreach, Posters, Public presentations, Web-based

In response to the need for leadership skills among northern youth to address the critical environmental, social and economic challenges facing their region, the CYLP was designed to build capacity among northern youth through training in Arctic issues, communication and leadership. In the programme these skills were combined with practical peer networking and work experience with organisations active in circumpolar affairs and northern issues. CYLP equipped young northerners with the skills, networks and knowledge to build future careers in sustainable development in their home regions.

Interns engaged in a range of outreach activities, including writing articles for the *Arctic Future Newsletter*, contributing to the circumpolar youth website Ookpik (www.ookpik.org), and presenting at conferences such as ArcticNet and the Jokkmokk Winter Conference. They also contributed to the publication *Securing a Sustainable Future in the Arctic: Engaging and Training the Next Generation of Northern Leaders*, which was distributed to over 1,000 individuals and organisations.

Each of the interns worked on IPY projects with their respective host institutions. At Students on Ice, for example, the students collected valuable experience on the IPY Polar Perspectives Forum, and at Schools on Board, an intern helped document and market their Inuit field school programme and Traditional Knowledge collection kit.

> **Contact: www.iisd.org, intern-info@iisd.ca**
>
> **Searchable Keywords: Arctic, circumpolar young leaders, IPY**

Students at home on land and sea: Inuit internships in Torngat Mountains National Park, Canada

Submitted by Mandy Arnold, kANGIDLUASUk, Canada

Categories: Educational expeditions, Engaging audiences from Arctic communities

In 2006, Parks Canada and the Nunatsiavut Government established kANGIDLUASUk base camp at the southern boundary of Torngat Mountains National Park. Run by local Inuit, the camp gives local Inuit youth the opportunity to participate in an experiential education and outreach initiative funded by IPY, ArcticNet and Nasivvik.

During the four-week intern programme students work alongside Inuit contractors, Elders, Parks Canada staff, artisans and scientists. Each season, Inuit youth assist different scientists working from the base camp, on shore-based longliners and in remote research camps.

Students are exposed to hands-on scientific fieldwork, including marine, freshwater, terrestrial and atmospheric research programmes, with research conducted in an environment familiar to Inuit with logistical support provided by Inuit from their communities, allowing students to explore questions and concerns about their environment through the dual lens of science and Inuit culture, experience and knowledge.

The kANGIDLUASUk student programme is a way of expanding science in northern ecosystems, blurring borders and cultural boundaries, and sharing the results with a wider world. It is also building capacity, confidence and skills amongst local Inuit youth as they develop into leaders and ambassadors for Nunavik (Northern Quebec), Nunatsiavut (Northern Labrador) and Torngat Mountains National Park of Canada.

> **Contact: www.kangidluasuk.com, students@kanguidluasuk.com**
>
> **Searchable Keywords: Arctic, Inuit, IPY, competence building, student programme**

University Level Initiatives

Field Courses and Expeditions

The Polaris Project: Rising Stars in the Arctic, USA and Russia

Submitted by R. Max Holmes, Woods Hole Research Center, USA
Categories: Creating curriculum, Web-based, Video

The Polaris Project includes a field course and research experience for undergraduate students in the Siberian Arctic; several new Arctic-focused undergraduate courses taught by project scientists at their home institutions in the USA and Russia; the opportunity for those scientists to initiate research programmes in the Siberian Arctic, and a wide range of student science projects and outreach activities.

Key features

The guiding scientific theme of the Polaris Project is the transport and transformations of carbon and nutrients as they move with water from terrestrial uplands to the Arctic Ocean—a central issue as scientists struggle to understand the changing Arctic. Undergraduate students develop their own research projects related to this theme, and complete the fieldwork during a one-month expedition to the Siberian Arctic.

Before the Siberian field course, all undergraduates take an on-campus course focusing on the Arctic as one of the collaborating institutions in the USA or Russia. During the field course, students work in groups to design and implement research projects that investigate some aspect of Arctic ecosystems and their likely responses to climate change.

To reach as broad an audience as possible, considerable effort is put into public outreach activities, including the project website and a blog that is frequently updated with text and photos from the field. Several videos have been produced about the student projects and the overall goals of the Polaris Project.

Keys to success

This project needs careful planning—taking 20 people to the Siberian Arctic for one month each summer is an ambitious undertaking. All participants live together in a collaborative environment on a barge along the Kolyma River in Siberia. Foreign scientists and staff of the Northeast Science Station in Siberia, and motivated, hard-working, engaged students and faculty members are fantastic partners in this endeavour.

Impacts

The Polaris Project is introducing exceptional early-career faculty members to Arctic research. It is involving many undergraduate students in research in Siberia, and a much larger number of them in the on-campus Arctic-focused courses. Finally, outreach activities are bringing the story of the Arctic and climate change to a broad public audience. The website received almost 70,000 views during the month-long expedition in 2008.

Figure 3.27 The Siberian home of the Polaris Project: a barge on the Kolyma River near the Arctic Ocean.

Contact: www.thepolarisproject.org, www.whrc.org

Searchable Keywords: Siberia, Russia, climate change, undergraduate education, permafrost, hydrology, biogeochemistry

THE WOODS HOLE
RESEARCH CENTER

The twenty-fifth Indian Antarctic expedition

Submitted by Manish Tiwari and Rasik Ravindra, NCAOR, India
Categories: Engaging students in doing outreach, public presentations, scientific expeditions

India has mounted successful scientific expeditions to Antarctica since 1981. To further involve college students in Indian Antarctic expeditions, two graduate students (selected through a nationwide competition) were sent to Antarctica by NCAOR during the twenty-fifth Indian Antarctic Expedition under the Students Participation Programme between December 2005 and March 2006.

On their return, one of the students presented a series of lectures on Antarctica in more than twenty rural and urban schools and colleges in her home state of Maharashtra. The lectures attracted hundreds of students and members of the general public, and introduced people from many walks of life to polar regions.

Contact: www.ncaor.gov.in, info@ncaor.org

Searchable Keywords: Indian IPY activities,
education and outreach, soccer competition, college

IPY Summer Institute

Submitted by Elena B. Sparrow, UAF, USA
Categories: Professional development for educators

The IPY summer institute was held in Russia and organised by the International Arctic Research Center at the University of Alaska Fairbanks with the A.N. Severtsov Institute for Ecology and Evolution of the Russian Academy of Sciences in Moscow, Russia, and the Central Forest State Nature Biosphere Reserve in Fedorovskoe, Russia. The institute provided a unique opportunity for participants to learn about IPY and the climate and environment of northern Eurasia from leading scientists and educators in a wide variety of disciplines, including meteorology, biology, chemistry and earth system modelling.

Thirty-one graduate students and early career scientists

Figure 3.28 Field work and 'classroom' in the Central Forest State Nature Biosphere Reserve, Fedorovskoe, Russia.

from six countries and eight Russian school teachers took part. During two weeks, the two groups worked together in workshops and during fieldwork, which focused on land-atmosphere interactions and wetland studies in the boreal forest zone.

Field trips in and outside the forest reserve highlighted different aspects of wetland studies and management in the European taiga environment. School teachers learned and practised protocols to study interannual variability of seasons in their own biomes. These teachers learned how to engage their students in Earth system scientific research and how to involve them in IPY.

Contact: www.iarc.uaf.edu, info@iarc.uaf.edu

Searchable Keywords: summer institute, IPY, Russia, forest

The international and interdisciplinary IPY polar field school

Submitted by Elise Strømseng, IPY Norway, UNIS and UArctic, Norway
Categories: Creating curriculum, Conferences, Educational expeditions, Mentoring

From 297 applicants, 24 students from 11 countries were selected for the interdisciplinary IPY field school in Svalbard during June and July 2009, providing them with a unique opportunity to receive polar experience in the high Arctic, engage in other disciplines and meet future colleagues. Admission was targeted at late undergraduate and early masters-level students. The field school was a collaboration between the Association of Polar Early Career Scientists (APECS), The University of the Arctic (UArctic), IPY Norway and The University Centre in Svalbard (UNIS).

Key features

The field school's main objective was to provide an opportunity for students to take part in IPY while learning new skills and fostering relationships with other young scientists. During the three-week course, students were exposed to a wide range of subjects, focussing on polar science such as glaciology, biology, permafrost studies, oceanography, climate change and sociology. Students attended lectures, carried out field work and engaged in group projects based either on samples collected during field excursions or from newly available IPY data.

The interdisciplinary nature of the field school helped students to discover how their disciplines fit into the broader picture of polar research. At the end of the field school, results were shared with fellow students, journalists and members of the local community in an oral presentation and poster session.

Figure 3.29 Students learning about ice wedges from Professor Hanne H. Christiansen.

In summary, key features of the initiative were:

- fostering interdisciplinary collaborations through experimental learning;
- developing an appreciation of polar regions through immersion in life in the High Arctic;
- improving science communication through interactions with journalists and the local community;
- enhancing communication through interdisciplinary project work;
- improving presentation skills through practical experience.

Keys to success

With support from IPY Norway and UArctic the field school enabled us to bring an energetic group of international students to the Arctic. Logistical support and teaching resources from UNIS, as well as the enthusiasm and experience of all lecturers and organisers, were vital in providing field-based learning and a valuable educational experience for all.

Impacts

A total of nine IPY project representatives attended the field school, giving a thorough presentation of IPY research, aims and results. Student evaluation was extremely positive with one describing the course as "a very exciting and interesting experience I will remember forever."

> **Contact: http://www.ipy.no, www.unis.no, post@unis.no**
>
> **Searchable Keywords: IPY, field school**

High Arctic Permafrost courses

Submitted by Hanne H. Christiansen, UNIS, Norway
Categories: Correspondence from the field/lab, Educational expeditions, Scientific expeditions

This international university course on High Arctic permafrost landscape dynamics in Svalbard and Greenland provided a unique field training for 10 internationally-recruited graduate students during IPY.

Students investigated landscape variability across the steepest High Arctic climatic gradient—from maritime Svalbard at Kapp Linné and at central Svalbard near Longyearbyen to continental northeast Greenland at Zackenberg. Working with a fieldwork permafrost project they studied the active layer and top permafrost by probing and coring, performed laboratory analyses, and collated data during a three-day workshop in Iceland.

Finally, students worked individually on analysing different parts of the collected data and prepared reports, which were evaluated by senior academics from the universities of Copenhagen and Oslo. Results were presented orally at a workshop held at University of Copenhagen in February 2009.

Participants used blogs for outreach and their data were also published internationally. Funding for the course was obtained from the TSP Norway IPY project, the Nordic Council Norden (Arctic Co-operation Programme 2006–08) and UNIS.

> **Contact: www.unis.no, post@unis.no**
>
> **Searchable Keywords: permafrost courses, field training, International University, Arctic, IPY**

IPY Arctic Observatory Network project: experiential learning and student contributions in ongoing research

Submitted by Anja Kade, Institute of Arctic Biology, UAF, USA
Categories: Creating curriculum, Educational expeditions, Scientific expeditions

Several excited students opted to forgo sleep and soaked in the Arctic scenery in the midnight sun. They were part of the new, hands-on field course in Arctic science created at the University of Alaska Fairbanks to expose undergraduate students to current hot topics in Arctic ecology in the light of climate change. This experiential course took place at the remote Toolik Field Station in northern Alaska, where students gained a firm background in the functioning of Arctic systems through morning lectures and scientific applied methods during afternoon field sessions.

One unique aspect of the course was the direct integration of students in our National Science Foundation-funded IPY Arctic Observatory Network project. After discussing Arctic carbon budgets,

Figure 3.30 Measuring CO$_2$-flux, Toolik Field Station, northern Alaska.

we introduced the students to CO_2-flux measurements with small chambers connected to an infrared gas analyser. Ultimately, we use the data collected by the students to assess terrestrial CO_2 fluxes at different scales as part of our project. We found that our innovative course curriculum effectively bridged classroom instruction and field experience while connecting students to an ongoing critical research project.

Contact: www.iarc.uaf.edu, info@iarc.uaf.edu

Searchable Keywords: summer institute, IPY, Russia, forest

UAF
UNIVERSITY OF
ALASKA
FAIRBANKS

Out of the Frying Pan and Into the Freezer: Students from the desert travel to Antarctica!

Submitted by Vanessa Lougheed, Jose Herrera, William Robertson and Craig Tweedie, University of Texas at El Paso, USA
Categories: Educational expeditions, Mentoring

IPY-ROAM (International Polar Year—Research and Educational Opportunities in Antarctica for Minorities) aimed to increase the number of under-represented minorities in science, and raise public awareness of the polar regions. Twenty-nine participants completed a field-research experience in Antarctica, and shared their experiences with others through formal and informal educational activities.

Key features

We recruited 16 undergraduates, eight graduate students and five teachers from across the US. Participants completed an online course in Antarctic system science; visited Washington, DC to learn about US environmental policy and the National Science Foundation; designed and completed research projects in terrestrial ecology, marine sciences, geosciences and tourism policy, and helped design educational products to take Antarctic system science into classrooms.

Data were collected during a 10-day expedition on board a tourist vessel. On their return, participants analysed data, presented research results at conferences, created educational resources and did outreach including visiting local schools. We also created an interactive museum exhibit, where people of all ages could learn about the polar regions and global climate change.

Key to success

A detailed application questionnaire, including questions regarding career goals and plans for outreach, was blind reviewed by outside evaluators to help classify the applicants. Web-based resources, including coursework and discussion boards, facilitated participation of individuals nationwide, while pre-trip orientation and team-building activities in the US increased the effectiveness of the Antarctic trip. Pre-trip, post-trip and one-year follow-up surveys of the participants evaluated project strengths and weaknesses.

Impacts

IPY-ROAM directly impacted on individuals from groups traditionally under represented in

Figure 3.31 IPY-ROAM participants and staff at Cuverville Island, Antarctica.

science: more than 80% participants were from ethnic minorities and 70% were women. Pre- and post-programme surveys showed that participants perceived that IPY-ROAM increased their ability to think critically, be leaders, communicate effectively, and perform with confidence in unfamiliar situations. Fourteen of the 16 undergraduate participants have continued to graduate school, and more than 10,000 people of all ages have been exposed to IPY-ROAM outreach activities.

Promise Banners

IPY-ROAM Promise Banner outreach programme, as it became known, aimed to educate and stimulated the interest of local students about polar sciences and the vulnerability of the polar regions to climate change. Promise banners were personalised pledges, signed by students from each classroom, to reduce their footprint on the environment. In return, the promise banners were taken on the IPY-ROAM expedition, photographed in Antarctica by IPY-ROAM student researchers, and returned to the corresponding classroom. More than 600 students from 22 classrooms were visited.

Figure 3.32 Two students display a promise banner in Antarctica.

Contact: info@ipyroam.org, www.ipyroam.org

Searchable Keywords: education, outreach, field research, minority students, promise banner

Professional development

Association of Polar Early Career Scientists (APECS): professional development workshops

Submitted by Jenny Baeseman, APECS, Norway

Categories: Conferences, Mentoring, Posters, Professional development for scientists

Many graduate students are trained to do science but often lack opportunities to develop the additional skills necessary for a successful career in science. APECS workshops aim to provide 'soft-skill' training for young researchers, providing both career development and exposure to what career advancement is like in other countries and disciplines. Half, full, or multi-day workshops bringing young researchers and mentors together are an effective way of developing these skills. Here is how APECS organises these workshops.

Key features

Workshops consist of sessions with hands-on training on new research techniques, scientific publishing, science communication, funding, career alternatives, leadership training, and international science and policy. Experts from these areas and senior polar researchers are included to share their experience and advise participants. It is also important to include short research oral or poster presentations by participants at the start of the workshop to give everyone an idea of what people are working on, and how they present their work.

Using a slightly secluded location helps develop a sense of community, a professional facilitator might assist with icebreakers, and long lunches, breaks and evening meals are encouraged.

Keys to success

To cut costs, try to add these events to another conference that young researchers are already attending. Using senior researchers and polar professionals provides valuable real-life experiences and knowledge exchange critical to polar research—an experience that professional career development trainers often cannot provide. It is also useful to poll participants before the workshop to find out what they are most interested in learning.

Figure 3.33 IMPETUS 2008: Workshop participants take a tour of free equipments and facilities at the Otto-Schmidt Laboratory, a German-funded lab at the Arctic and Antarctic Research Institute in St. Petersburg, Russia.

Impacts

Participants gain skills, colleagues, and a broader understanding of career issues they otherwise would not have acquired. These efforts are creating a cohesive group of polar researchers that understand national, cultural and disciplinary differences. These workshops are one way of advancing our understanding of the polar regions through global participation.

Contact: www.apecs.is, apecsinfo@gmail.com

Searchable Keywords: young researchers, early career, mentor, APECS, professional development, networking, polar, workshop, skills, communication

APECS mentor panel discussions for polar early career professionals

Submitted by Jenny Baeseman, APECS, Norway
Categories: Conferences, Mentoring, Professional development for scientists

Mentor panels held at larger conferences create better mentoring opportunities than the somewhat intimidating conference-wide socials where people normally talk to only those they already know. At these panel sessions, senior experts share advice and knowledge through an open forum. It allows establishment of new relationships and younger colleagues can also benefit from older professionals' experience. Mentoring from those outside of one's home institution, research group, and country, is a very effective outreach tool as it exposes people to new ways of thinking and different institutional and international perspectives.

To host a panel, contact the conference organisers and ask for a room and a few

Figure 3.34 Receptions following the panels are a key feature to allow for continued discussion in smaller groups. Here students and mentors converse over pizza and refreshments after a panel on careers in polar law at the International Polar Law Symposium.

potential meeting times. Contact three to five mentors that would be willing to participate and provide a few key points that your particular audience would be interested in. On the day of the meeting, have each mentor introduce themselves and share a bit of advice, and then open the floor to audience questions. We also recommend creating an audio podcast of the event.

New Generation of Polar Researcher Symposium

Submitted by Sheldon Drobot, National Center for Atmospheric Research, USA
Categories: Mentoring

In the spirit of IPY, in May 2008, the New Generation of Polar Researchers Symposium brought together a group of 34 early career polar researchers from various personal and professional backgrounds across the spectrum of social, biological and physical sciences. This diverse and ambitious group spent an intensive week learning from each other and from mentors about past, current and future polar research, IPY history and planning, communication and outreach, and developing successful careers in interdisciplinary and international research. The young scientists were selected through a competitive application process. A select group of mentors was also invited to share insights, stories and expertise in overcoming obstacles young researchers face. This provided a continuum of polar science knowledge and a sense of history that will carry these young leaders forward to the next IPY. More information is available at http://arcticportal.org/apecs/ngpr.

Contact: www.apecs.is, apecsinfo@gmail.com

Searchable Keywords: young researchers, early career, mentor, APECS, professional development, networking, polar, workshop, skills, communication

Other outreach ideas

Women's Narratives from the Circumpolar North: a graduate level course

Submitted by Carolyn Redl, Athabasca University, Canada

Categories: Creating curriculum, Engaging audiences from Arctic communities, Professional development for educators

Women's Narratives from the Circumpolar North was a graduate level course in Athabasca University's MA Integrated Studies programme. The course explored Inuit, Sámi and other indigenous women's life stories through letters, memoirs, autobiographies and journals written by women who travelled to, or lived for extended periods, in the circumpolar north from the mid-1800s to the present.

The focus of these narratives ranged from exploration, settlement, adventure and work to travel, scientific and cultural discoveries, and life experiences. The critical framework for the course was based on current theories from anthropology, gender studies, post-colonialism and literary studies of life writings, as well as indigenous and northern studies.

During the course, students interacted via email with an Inuit woman whose story is told in Nancy Wachowich's *Saqiyuq*. Works following Wachowich's answer questions about changing attitudes towards intercultural relations and nordicity, the evolution of women's roles in the circumpolar north and their contributions to northern studies. Participants had a chance to explore indigenous people's original occupancy, post- and neo-colonial attitudes and meanings of 'north'.

> **Contact: www.athabascau.ca/mais, mais@athabascau.ca**
>
> **Searchable Keywords: Women's Narratives from the Circumpolar North, Athabasca University, circumpolar north**

Applying IPY DIS (Data Information Service) data sharing concepts to teaching in tropical field schools

Submitted by Falk Huettmann, University of Alaska Fairbanks, USA

Categories: Scientific expeditions

Sharing scientific data in a digital world is an inherent part of IPY and its Data Information Service (IPYDIS). The Data and Information Service is a global partnership of data centres, archives, and networks working to ensure proper stewardship of IPY and related data. The global advantages of the IPYDIS are obvious when conducting research in remote wilderness areas. While carrying out research in a tropical field school in the cloud forest of Nicaragua, we found that IPYDIS' data sharing processes were very helpful to determine distribution and habitats of tropical wildlife and plant species. Our experience showed that using WLAN, metadata web publication, online data sharing software and web-based Earth maps greatly improve the science, as well as the teaching and quality of students' work. Additional aspects of online initiatives include increased communication, e.g., via email and Skype. The digital Pole, jungle and global village becomes a reality, offering great opportunities for sustainability and world peace.

> **Contact: http://ipydis.org, ipydis@ipydis.org**
>
> **Searchable Keywords: IPYDIS, data sharing, WLAN, cloud forest, field school**

Sub-Zero Soccer Tournament

Submitted by Manish Tiwari and Rasik Ravindra, NCAOR, India

Categories: Contests and competitions, Engaging audiences from mid-latitude countries, Events, Posters, Public presentations

Indian IPY outreach aimed to involve students at all levels—from primary school to graduate students. To achieve this, and to engage college students, NCAOR organised a soccer tournament. Ten teams of graduate students participated in the innovative WWF-India, intercollegiate soccer tournament called 'Sub-Zero Soccer,' at St. Stephen's College, New Delhi in December 2008. The organisation of this five-day event took about one month.

Aimed at raising awareness of climate change and polar regions among young people by engaging them in sports and culture, the tournament began with a film on Antarctica and a briefing on IPY. Team names were based on polar biodiversity: the Musk Ox beat the Emperor Penguins to take the boys' title, and the Albatrosses beat the Arctic Terns for the girls'. Information on receding polar ice and India's presence in Antarctica was displayed around the pitch on banners and posters, and match commentary included information on IPY and polar environmental issues. During the five-day tournament college students and their professors also had the opportunity to visit a poster exhibition on the polar regions.

Contact: www.ncaor.gov.in, info@ncaor.org

Searchable Keywords: Indian IPY activities, education and outreach, soccer competition, college students

Public Level Initiatives

Multi-level initiatives

Cape Farewell

Submitted by Hannah Bird, Cape Farewell, UK

Categories: Communicating science with the media, Correspondence from the field/lab, Events, Exhibitions, Engaging audiences from mid-latitude countries

Cape Farewell pioneers a cultural response to climate change. Working internationally, it brings artists, scientists and communicators together to stimulate art founded in scientific research. Cape Farewell is the most significant sustained artistic response to climate change in the world.

Key features

Created by artist David Buckland in 2001, Cape Farewell has led a series of expeditions to the Arctic inviting artists to places of natural beauty and artistic inspiration to see first hand the effects of climate change. Over 50 artists have travelled to the Arctic with Cape Farewell alongside Arctic scientists. Voyagers include Jarvis Cocker, KT Tunstall, Martha Wainwright, Ian McEwan, Siobhan Davies, Antony Gormley, Gary Hume and Rachel Whiteread. From these expeditions has sprung an extraordinary body of ideas, imagery, artwork and media.

Cape Farewell's premise is that climate change will affect all communities globally. Our lifestyles have created a problem and the solution is therefore a cultural responsibility. The organisation collaborates with outstanding creative individuals, thinkers and opinion formers from across the arts and the sciences. It empowers people—through increased understanding—to play a part in effecting change and finding a voice. It celebrates the potential of the human mind to research, understand and communicate creatively.

Key to success

Cape Farewell delivers projects in collaboration with partners. This increases the impact and quality of the outcomes. Significant partners to date include the National Oceanography Centre, British Geological Survey, Natural History Museum, Eden Project, Southbank Centre, the Royal Academy and British Council. The organisation's success also depends on enhancing Cape Farewell's media presence through high profile events such as the Arctic expeditions and exhibition openings, and the fact that the programme is artist driven.

Impacts

From Cape Farewell's expeditions has sprung an extraordinary body of artwork. Over 10 million people have viewed the documentary Art from the Arctic, co-produced with the BBC in 2006. Cape Farewell has exhibited across the UK, Europe, North America, Russia, Australia and the Far East. By the end of March 2008, audience numbers at Cape Farewell exhibitions stood at 868,000. Education resources created by Cape Farewell have been used in the curriculum for GSCE level geography and science. Cape Farewell has distributed 1,700 copies of the book *Burning Ice*, and its website receives 100,000 unique visitors per year.

Figure 3.35 Exhibition Art and Climate Change at the Natural History Museum in 2006.

Contact: www.capefarewell.com

Searchable Keywords: climate change, Arctic, art, creativity, culture, artists

LATITUDE60!

Submitted by José Xavier, University of Coimbra and Gonçalo Vieira, University of Lisbon, Portugal
Categories: Classroom visits, Communicating science with the media, Creating educational tools, Events, Web-based

Portugal participated in IPY for the first time in its history, and to reach the whole country, young polar scientists and teachers decided that a strong education and outreach programme was essential.

LATITUDE60! was part of Portugal's education and outreach programme during IPY. It reached thousands of students, hundreds of educators and politicians and raised awareness of the polar regions. As a result of IPY and these efforts, a new Portuguese polar research programme was created. Portugal joined the Scientific Committee for Antarctic Research (SCAR), the European Polar Board, and is about to sign the Antarctic Treaty.

Key features

A web-based forum for polar scientists and educators was created to bring enthusiastic educators from across the country together. Lectures about LATITUDE60! were given at schools and universities in major towns, and links were established with public and private sector companies to help organise events and promote the project. In all, over 40 activities were organised.

LATITUDE60! included a set of very different activities: a TV advert—made by seven- to 11-year-old students—was produced; a polar calendar highlighting polar science was published and distributed through post offices nationwide; a Braille brochure was published; and polar science weeks organised for schools and universities with young scientists visiting schools across the country.

Figure 3.36 A young scientist demonstrates how to collect an ice core sample during the Students on Ice expedition to the Antarctic.

Impacts

LATITUDE60! had a tremendous impact nationally and internationally. Its legacy includes a web portal with regularly updated educational materials, new relationships between Portuguese polar scientists, schools and teachers worldwide and the inclusion of educational and outreach in all Portuguese polar science projects.

National Polar Contest in New Zealand and Portugal

This contest was a high impact event to promote polar knowledge in schools in New Zealand as well as in Portugal. The contest's top prizes were trips to Antarctica on Students on Ice expeditions. In Portugal, thousands of students entered and over 500 individuals and groups submitted work in various categories, including art, science essays, polar writing, audio and video, websites, and projects using recyclable materials—such as plastic bottles and milk cartons—to build igloos. Winning entries were displayed at a special event at Lisbon's science museum, the Pavilion of Knowledge.

Figure 3.37 Participant at the prize giving ceremony of the national polar contest in Lisbon.

Lisbon Oceanarium: Sleeping with sharks and penguins!

One of the top prizes in the National Polar Contest was a sleepover with sharks and penguins. Thirty students from kindergarden to high school spent the night at the Lisbon Oceanarium, sleeping close to the impressive 5,000 m³ central tank, which houses marine animals from sharks and tuna to rays and sunfish. Biologists gave guided tours, particularly highlighting the Antarctic section.

Field courses on polar science

To illustrate Portugal's relationship with the polar regions, and that all parts of the planet are inter-linked, field courses were organised in the Serra da Estrela—the highest mountains in continental Portugal. Over two weekends, 15 teachers, 60 students and polar scientists worked together comparing geomorphological characteristics of Portuguese and Antarctic mountains, giving students a unique opportunity to spend time with polar scientists. The weekends were another prize in the National Polar Contest.

Figure 3.38 Students and a young polar scientist during the field course comparing European and Antarctic environments in Portugal.

Zoomarine: Polar Bio-fact Show

Together with Zoomarine aqua park (a sea life centre with a strong conservation and environmental education programme), an educational bio-fact show was produced to raise awareness among visitors—mainly foreign tourists—of the importance of the polar regions and IPY. The fact show was hands-on, giving visitors the opportunity to handle Antarctic exhibits including giant squid beaks and ear bones from Patagonian toothfish.

Mundicenter: IPY Exhibitions

In collaboration with an important shopping centre company, a travelling exhibition linking polar science and IPY was designed for the general public, touring different parts of the country, particularly major cities such as Lisbon and Braga. The exhibition tackled questions such as: why are the polar regions important; what is the relevance of IPY science today; does Portugal have polar scientists and, if so, what do they do? The exhibition had strong visuals and used simple language to communicate with a non-expert audience.

Contact: www.portalpolar.pt,
projecto.latitude60@gmail.com

Searchable Keywords: Portal Polar, ciência polar, polar research Portugal

EALÁT-Network Study: reindeer husbandry and climate change

Submitted by Anders Oskal, ICR; and Svein D. Mathiesen, Sámi University College, Norway
Categories: Creating curriculum, Engaging audiences from Arctic communities

The IPY EALÁT-Network Study's goal is to prepare reindeer herding communities and local authorities for climate change by analysing their adaptability to environmental change, and focusing on reindeer herders' knowledge. The study examines Sámi reindeer herding in northern Norway and Nenets reindeer herding in Western Siberia, Russia, with outreach taking place in other parts of Russia, Finland, Sweden, Norway and Alaska. EALÁT has four components: research, education, outreach and information.

Key features

During IPY, the education component consisted of research-based education on reindeer husbandry, climate change and adaptation coordinated by the International Centre for Reindeer Husbandry (ICR). Sámi University College offered a Bachelor's degree course *Learning by Herding, a Reindeer Herders' Online Nomadic School,* and a teachers' course on the same themes. The University of the Arctic created a course on *Adaptation to Global Change in the Arctic.*

EALÁT outreach covered two main areas, a set of community-based workshops and the development of an interactive online information platform. The workshop involved reindeer herders in Fennoscandia (Scandinavian Peninsula, Kola Peninsula, Karelia and Finland) and Russia, scientists and local authorities, and focused on climate change and dialogue on Traditional Knowledge. The website was created on www.reindeerportal.org.

EALÁT-Information, an Arctic Council project, addressed reindeer herding, loss of pastures, Traditional Knowledge and adaptation to climate change with community-based workshops in local reindeer herding communities throughout Fennoscandia and the Russian north. EALÁT-Information wants to give reindeer herders a voice in climate change discussions on the Arctic Council.

Figure 3.39 IPY EALÁT community-based workshop with a Chukchi herding group in Kanchalan, Chukotka AO, Russia.

Keys to success

The challenge of the IPY EALÁT-Network Study is to translate reindeer herders' knowledge into action for sustainable development in the Arctic and, in particular, to involve circumpolar reindeer herders in this process. Local communities, educational and research institutions and local authorities work together to understand and address the complex and many-faceted challenges of climate change for reindeer husbandry. Reindeer herders are involved at every stage of this process of jointly producing new knowledge.

Impacts

The project increases knowledge and understanding of the consequences of climate

Figure 3.40 IPY EALÁT indigenous researchers, students, reindeer herders and authorities gathered at a consortium meeting in Kautokeino, Norway.

change and alterations of land usage for reindeer husbandry—knowledge that local adaptation strategies can be based on. It already strengthened networks and capacity of reindeer herding peoples and the Association of World Reindeer Herders, and left as a legacy of IPY, the University of the Arctic EALÁT Institute for Circumpolar Reindeer Husbandry.

(See Chapter 4 for more in-depth information on EALÁT, the Reindeer Portal and the role of Traditional Knowledge in polar research.)

Contact: http://icr.arcticportal.org/en/ealat, www.reindeerportal.org

Searchable Keywords: Reindeer herding, traditional knowledge, adaptation to climate change

Narwhal Tusk Research: discovering the function of the male tusk

Submitted by Martin T. Nweeia, Narwhal Tusk Research, Smithsonian Institution and Harvard University, USA
Categories: Communicating science with the media, Engaging audiences from Arctic communities, Exhibitions

Narwhal Tusk Research is an interdisciplinary collaboration of scientists, Inuit and Inughuit hunters describing the function of the narwhal tusk involving extensive education and outreach activities. Myriad fields of science including marine mammal and evolutionary biology, chemical and structural tissue biology, genetics and mathematics combine with Traditional Knowledge to describe this unique tooth organ system that has baffled investigators for more than 500 years. The multinational team from USA, Canada, Greenland, Denmark, South Africa and Russia analysed information and tissue specimens from nine field expeditions to the Canadian and Greenland High Arctic.

Key features
Elders and hunters from six High Arctic communities in northwestern Canada and northeastern Greenland completed an in-depth video interview on narwhal, compiled, recorded and translated by Narwhal Tusk Research. Public, academic and cultural outreach during this 10-year study have reached millions of people on six continents and included two documentaries from National Geographic, a National Science Foundation-funded 10-part radio series, museum exhibitions at the National Museum of Dentistry in Baltimore, numerous lecture series, print articles, blogs and websites, as well as a travelling exhibit from the National Geographic Society.

More innovative outreach occurred in High Arctic communities, where university students in evolutionary biology helped create questions used in the Traditional Knowledge interview and Arctic narwhal hunters served as co-presenters in social science conferences. A video library of these interviews is currently being developed. In the High Arctic, the project also involved children who painted shipping containers—a useful means of attracting media coverage. It was a simple idea that made a routine shipping of specimens an endearing art project to the community, the airline and participating research institutes.

Keys to success
* Envision how the topic of interest can relate to a wide audience, since this will have more appeal to media outlets.
* Deliver the research results to interested media contacts in a timely manner and understand that media interest is fleeting. Respond to any media interest promptly as new items fall on their desks hourly.
* Find sources that can help you to media outlets when distributing a story. At the same time, do not be afraid to contact a media source directly; this may have the perceived affect of being a 'fresh' story.
* Do not be discouraged by one source in a media outlet, as both the person contacted and the timing may be critical in the response to your story. Often reporters and media outlets can be on deadline or on a production schedule that does not permit conversation or communication.

- Having good quality related photographs and graphics of the research interest can often make the story more appealing for the media venue.
- For print articles, shape the content of information provided to the story that you would like told.
- For television outlets, be fully flexible with their schedule for filming or appearing 'in studio'. If you feel that you are part of a story that you do not find agreeable, the sooner you approach the producer, the better. Do not be afraid to ask the production staff about the overall content.
- Be innovative with your approach to a topic, and try to relate it to education. It is one thing to report a new research finding, it is another to link a child's fascination with it.
- Make research fun. In our work, we found shipping containers routinely constructed of plywood and involved a community to dress it up.

Impacts

Linking scientists, Inuit Elders and hunters to solve a significant biologic question has been a legacy of this work and its success has brought significant and broad-based media attention. The story ties together components of an unusual marine mammal; a mysterious and legendary spiralled tooth; Inuit Traditional Knowledge; a forbidding environment; scientific disciplines ranging from molecular biology to anatomy; and an evolutionary adaptation that challenges its own description.

Figure 3.41 Narwhal, monodon monoceros, during spring migration outside Pond Inlet, Nunavut, Canada.

Figure 3.42 Kaviaqanguak Kissuk from Qaanaaq, Greenland reveals unusual narwhal behaviours in an interview with Narwhal Tusk Research.

Contact: www.narwhal.org

Searchable Keywords: narwhal, tusk, ELOKA, unicorn, tooth, Inuit Traditional Knowledge

Ways of Greenland (Drumuri in Groenlanda): polar science outreach in Romania

Submitted by Teodor Gheorghe Negoita and Mihaela Cotta, Romanian Polar Research Institute, and Paul-Andrei Iordache, Romania

Categories: Conferences and workshops, Communicating science with the media, Creative writing, Engaging audiences from mid-latitude countries, Exhibits, Web-based

The Ways of Greenland project aimed at raising Romanian public awareness of the importance of the Arctic, and the need for its environmental and cultural protection. As part of the project, the Romanian Polar Research Institute organised three international polar symposia during 2007–08 to raise awareness of the impact of global warming on the polar regions. Specialists from 10 countries and 19 universities and research institutes in Romania were involved, as well as the European Science Foundation, and the Alfred-Wegener-Institute for Polar and Marine Research in Germany.

The project produced three volumes of abstracts, organised conferences at the Romanian Academy, Romanian Research and Education Agency, universities in Romania and abroad, as well as events at libraries and schools, which featured in radio and TV broadcasts on IPY. Teodor Gh. Negoita's book *The Romanian Embassy in Antarctica—Law-Racovizta Station,* published in 2007, demonstrated Romania's close cooperation with Australia and was also part of the outreach project.

In 2009, the Romanian Polar Research Institute organised a series of exhibitions based on the photographs of Romanian polar scientist Paul-Andrei Iordache in 10 Romanian cities. Paving the way for other projects and as a permanent future reference, the project included producing the photography book, *Ways of Greenland,* in Romanian, Danish and English, and a DVD in Romanian with English subtitles.

Figure 3.43 Dr Teodor Gheorghe Negoita involved in polar research in the Antarctic.

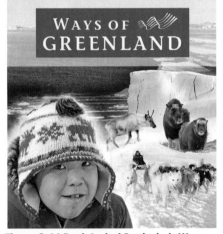

Figure 3.44 Paul-Andrei Iordache's Ways of Greenland logo and poster artwork.

Contact: www.groenlanda.paul-andrei.com, www.polar-institute.ro

Searchable Keywords: education, research, networking, mentoring, science, polar regions, outreach, Arctic research, public awareness, polar photography

IPY in Sweden

Submitted by Sverker Sörlin and Anders Clarhäll, Royal Institute of Technology, Sweden
Categories: Correspondence from the field/lab, Engaging audiences from Arctic communities, Exhibitions, Video

The Swedish Polar Year made outreach activities a core issue. The inauguration in Jukkasjärvi in March 2007 included the launch of a test balloon—widely covered in the media—and during the winter of 2009, IPY appeared on the milk cartons of Arla, the major supplier of milk to Swedish households.

An exhibition, *Cold Poles—Hot Stuff,* was held in October 2007 in the newly opened Swedish embassy in Washington, DC, after which it toured in Sweden. The same year, the Bildmuseet at Umeå University hosted an exhibition of Isaac Julien's artwork True North that was preceded by a two-day interdisciplinary symposium on polar research. Another exhibition, *Iskalla uppdrag,* at The Maritime Museum in Gothenburg, portrayed the history of Swedish polar research and the role of Gothenburg as the centre and starting point for expeditions past and present.

Stories and the images from explorers and adventurers travelling north in the nineteenth century became part of a travelling lecture series, *Främmande Nord (The Unknown North),* by seven humanities researchers from Umeå University. They have made more than 50 appearances—in venues ranging from a folk high school on the island of Tjörn in Bohuslän to a market in Lycksele in Lappland—arranged symposia, facilitated exhibitions and published books.

> **Contact: http://.ipyse.arcticportal.org**
>
> **Searchable Keywords: Sweden, lecture series, oral history of the North**

Exhibitions

Ice Stories: Despatches from Polar Scientist

Submitted by Mary Miller, Exploratorium, USA
Categories: Correspondence from the field/lab, professional development for scientists, web-based

Ice Stories: Dispatches from Polar Scientists is a collaboration between the Exploratorium in San Francisco and scientists working in the Arctic and Antarctic to showcase current polar research in a dynamic and interactive way.

Key features

With funding from the National Science Foundation, the Exploratorium gave scientists cameras, blogging tools, and training in media production and storytelling, and asked them to document their fieldwork on the museum's website. In addition, Exploratorium staff members travelled to the Arctic and the Antarctic to have conversations with glaciologists, biologists, climate scientists and astrophysicists during live webcasts originating at the museum and archived online.

The result is a pioneering use of digital media that lets the scientists present their

Figure 3.45 Scientists learn how to shoot an interview during an Ice Stories media production workshop.

work directly to the public in a lively, engaging, and immediate way. The blog format encourages visitors to post comments, ask questions, and create a dialog with scientists. Ice Stories offers Twitter and RSS feeds, live webcams, and video and audio dispatches from the 'deep field', as well as articles and videos by Exploratorium science writers and producers on topics like climate change, penguins and the history of Antarctic exploration. In addition, visitors can explore the dispatches in a geographic interface. This media-rich project features over 250 dispatches, over 100 videos and more than 1,000 photos taken by Ice Stories correspondents.

Keys to success

The scientists were in the field in remote settings where the public could not go. The Exploratorium provided an audience, production support and scientist media training. By combining forces, the Exploratorium's content curators, web designers and media producers relieved the scientists of web production and audience generation, so they could concentrate on communicating their research directly to a large public audience.

Impacts

The ability for scientists to relay their science directly to the public in collaboration with experienced media and web producers at a science museum provided a model for collaboration between informal and formal science institutions. Ice Stories showed the public an interactive and immediate way to a fuller understanding of current research—research that might otherwise have been difficult to convey for either partner working alone.

Contact: http://icestories.exploratorium.edu

Searchable Keywords: blog, webcast, media production training, polar science

---

The Sciencexpress: an exhibition travelling India and Germany by train
Submitted by Manish Tiwari and Rasik Ravindra, NCAOR, India
Category: Exhibitions

The *Sciencexpress* is a state-of-the-art free science exhibition on a train travelling India and Germany. The German Helmholtz Association developed the concept for this exhibition. The 16-coach train showcases cutting-edge science and technology. The exhibition strives to take modern research out of the lab, and to reveal just how relevant science is to everyday life. While the science train travelled India during IPY, NCAOR was asked to provide a few exhibits related to polar research. The exhibits included panels on climate change, Antarctica and information regarding the Indian Antarctic station, Maitri. The *Sciencexpress* recorded an astounding 2.25 million visitors during its journey in 57 cities. Today, it travels India for the third time and its progress can be viewed at www.scienceexpress.in, and in Germany as *ExpeditionZukunft* at www.expedition-zukunft.org.

CELEBRATE IPY Exhibition at the Ocean Institute, California, USA

Submitted by Sarah Wilson, formerly of the Ocean Institute and currently with National Geographic Society, USA
Categories: Events, Exhibitions, Creating curriculum, Creating educational tools

The Ocean Institute is an educational organisation in southern California that annually hosts over 90,000 school students in science and history programmes. At weekends its doors open to the public. Between October 2007 and February 2008 the institute highlighted IPY. In addition to the regular programming, there were a variety of activities every 30 to 60 minutes lead by staff for an audience of all ages.

We hosted scientists to speak about their studies, displayed original polar-themed paintings, and held children's storytimes with crafts. Our many lab rooms had tables with polar artefacts, ranging from pinniped pelts and walrus tusks to art and clothing from polar cultures.

Our mapping and imaging room had the addition of software to our interactive globe to view changes over time in sea ice and ocean temperatures. Hands-on labs had visitors comparing preserved Antarctic ocean invertebrates, collected by Scripps Institution of Oceanography, to local ocean creatures as well as a lab exploring climate change.

Even in sunny southern California dynamic programming can immerse visitors in the beautiful and elusive polar regions.

Contact: www.ocean-institute.org, oi@ocean-institute.org

Searchable Keywords: Ocean Institute, polar, exhibition, hands-on

ANDRILL photo exhibitions and outreach in France

Submitted by Lucia Simion, science writer and photographer, France and Italy
Categories: Classroom visits, Public presentations

During IPY, based on my visits to Antarctica, I engaged in several education and outreach projects. In November 2007 I was invited to Scott Base, Antarctica, to cover the IPY geological drilling project ANDRILL Southern McMurdo Sound. I photographed the international team of scientists working in the Crary Lab at McMurdo Station and the drilling operations at the camp. Back in Paris, I organised an exhibition at the Cité des Sciences et de l'Industrie de la Villette, a science museum similar to the Exploratorium in San Francisco. The exhibition, which ran for three months and attracted 90,000 visitors, featured large prints of the photographs and five text banners in French and Italian.

Figure 3.46 Primary school student's Antarctic story.

After eight expeditions to Antarctica, and following the publication of my book *Antarctica, White Heart of Our Planet,* I decided to share my knowledge and passion for the continent with others. In primary schools I gave talks on the exploration of Antarctica and asked students to write stories, and draw pictures set in this harsh environment. My aim was to raise awareness of Antarctica, and inspire young children and teenagers with the adventures of the nineteenth- and twentieth-century explorers and modern Antarctic expeditions.

Contact: www.luceantartica.com

Searchable Keywords: Lucia Simion Antarctique, Lucia Simion Antartide, Cité des Sciences

DAMOCLES Mobile Exhibition

Submitted by Nighat Amin, IPF, Belgium
Categories: Creating educational tools, Exhibitions, Video

Created by the International Polar Foundation and German museum designers Atelier Brückner, this mobile exhibition showcases the DAMOCLES project—the largest EU-funded research project in the Arctic Basin. Consisting of a seven metres square structure, its inside features an Arctic panorama. Through slits in this panorama, various Arctic themes are visible, reflecting the Arctic through history in terms of climate, science, and the nature of life during contrasting warm and cold periods. The questions raised by these themes—questions about the Arctic's importance in the global climate system, and the need to observe and understand it—are dealt with on the outside of the exhibit.

In the middle of the installation stands a circular desk displaying animations based on mathematical models of different parts of the Arctic climate system. These animations show how the system works, how data is collected, and how current and past experiences are used to predict future change.

Aimed at a wide public audience, the DAMOCLES Mobile Exhibition was first shown in 2007 at the Royal Belgian Institute of Natural Sciences in Brussels. Since then it has travelled to Bulgaria, Italy, France and Luxembourg, and has attracted more than 270,000 visitors.

Contact: info@polarfoundation.org,
http://www.polarfoundation.org/projects/P5/

Searchable Keywords: DAMOCLES, Arctic,
mobile exhibition

Ice Station Antarctica

Submitted by Linda Capper, BAS, UK
Category: Exhibitions

Ice Station Antarctica is a major interactive touring exhibition developed in partnership between British Antarctic Survey and the Natural History Museum (NHM) in London. Aimed at families with children aged seven and over, the exhibition challenges visitors to see if they have got what it takes to live and work in Antarctica.

The exhibition allows visitors to 'enlist' as an ice cadet and under the guidance of the *Ice Station* commander brave a variety of Antarctic challenges, from coping in sub-zero temperatures to riding a snowmobile. Visitors can explore the skills it takes to work in and preserve this frozen wilderness, and learn about this unique continent through a series of mini-environments including:

- Get out in the 'field': experience camping in a tent, where scientists have to melt ice for cooking and washing, and use basic toilet facilities for days on end.
- Have lunch in the dark: glimpse the 24-hour darkness winter residents have to cope with.
- Hold your nose: try the sights and smells of working in a penguin colony.
- Dress up: try walking in multiple layers of special Antarctic clothing.

Alex Gaffikin, one of the NHM exhibition developers of Ice Station Antarctica herself spent two and a half years working at BAS's Halley research station on the Brunt Ice Shelf.

Figure 3.47 Trying a snow mobile at Ice Station Antarctica.

The exhibition ran at the NHM from May 2007 to April 2008, attracting 183,634 visitors. *Ice Station Antarctica* then transferred to the Granada Science Centre in Spain, and is due to appear at the Space Center in Houston, USA from February to April 2010.

During its run in London, the exhibition ran alongside *Nature Live,* a series of public talks, in which the NHM featured researchers from BAS and speakers from the NHM.

Contact: www.nhm.ac.uk, www.antarctica.ac.uk

Searchable Keywords: British Antarctic Survey, Ice Station Antarctica, Natural History Museum

Polar Active Earth: a touch-screen museum display

Submitted by Kelly Carroll, Polar Earth Observing Network (PoleNET), USA
Categories: Exhibitions

PoleNET, the Incorporated Research Institutions for Seismology and UNAVCO collaborated to develop new outreach materials for the Active Earth Display. The Active Earth Display is a touch-screen web-based museum display available to museums, visitor centres, schools and libraries.

The polar Active Earth Display aims to engage users about the importance of polar-based research using a rich interactive multimedia environment. It highlights real-time data from Antarctica and Greenland, and provides a way for the public to learn about

Figure 3.48 Sample Page of the polar Arctic Earth Display.

PoleNET research. The pages are organised around four storylines: polar equipment, ice movement through time, life on the ice, and what ice in Antarctica has to do with us. The pages present complex scientific concepts in a way that is engaging and accessible to the general public by using simple text style, real-time data, videos, interactive games, and a set of coherent storylines.

The display's interactive and entertaining environment allows users to make themselves familiar with the challenges, reasons, and necessity of conducting research in some of the most inhospitable environments in the world.

Contact: www.Polenet.org, www.iris.edu

Searchable Keywords: Antarctica, Greenland, kiosk, display, multimedia, PoleNET

Science Events

Urban International Polar Weekends

Submitted by Margie Turrin, Lamont-Doherty Earth Observatory, USA

Categories: Creating educational tools, Events, Fairs and Festivals, Public Presentations, Professional development for scientists

Figure 3.49 Young visitors to an IPY Polar Fair.

Two urban communities (New York City and Baltimore) participated in IPY through four family-style events. To better engage urban families in current polar research a series of Polar Weekend events were organised and run at the American Museum of Natural History and the Baltimore Maryland Science Center.

IPY Polar Fairs focused on current IPY research and understanding the changing Poles. Activities for all ages included performances, short lectures, annotated film clips, and our signature Interactive Polar Fair. There scientists brought a human face to science research, meeting informally with the public while refining their outreach message as they explained their work through demonstration, hands on activities, posters, computer visualisations and curriculum support pieces.

These collaborative events had many sponsors—Columbia University, Barnard College, Museum of Natural History, Norwegian Consulate, Explorer's Club, Wings WorldQuest, with the National Science Foundation providing funding. A high profile museum setting assisted us in including indigenous peoples, engaging scientists from around the world and engaging over 12,000 visitors.

Contact: mkt@ldeo.columbia.edu

Searchable Keywords: education outreach, fairs, interactive learning

Seattle Polar Science Weekends

Submitted by Harry Stern, PSC, University of Washington, USA

Categories: Engaging audiences from mid-latitude countries, Events, Exhibitions, Public presentations

Polar Science Weekend is an annual four-day event featuring hands-on activities, demonstrations and exhibits about the polar regions and current polar research, presented by scientists from the University of Washington's Polar Science Center and other departments.

Held at Seattle's Pacific Science Center—Washington State's most popular museum—PSW lets students, teachers and families meet scientists who work in some of the most remote and challenging places on Earth, and learn first-hand about polar research in a fun and informal setting.

Activities and demonstrations include the salinity taste test, glacier flow, saltwater and freshwater ice, polar passport, oceanographic mooring, build an igloo and extreme cold. Exhibits range from an Arctic field camp and a Greenland ice core to measurement technology and the US Coast Guard. PSW also features popular IMAX films and slide shows.

A broad range of institutions participated in Polar Science Weekend 2009—which attracted more than 20,000 visitors—including Point Defiance Zoo and Aquarium, Earth and Space Research, US Coast Guard, Boy Scouts of America, Left Eye Productions, Chris Linder Photography, Expeditionary Art, and the University of Washington's Polar Science Center plus five other university departments. We also acknowledge NASA's support of future Polar Science Weekends.

Contact: http://psc.apl.washington.edu/psw, psw@apl.washington.edu

Searchable Keywords: science weekends, Seattle, hands-on, exhibition

Polar Science Weekend

Submitted by José Xavier, University of Coimbra and Gonçalo Vieira, University of Lisbon, Portugal

Categories: Classroom visits, Communicating science with the media, Creating educational tools, Events, Web-based

A wide range of activities was produced to promote polar science and IPY for schools and the general public in Portugal including a weekend to meet polar scientists and ask them questions. The weekend included general talks by polar scientists from Portugal and other countries, an exhibition on polar science, an exhibition of the best work on the Poles from students nationwide, hands-on science experiments, music and a computer game competition on polar regions. A touring children's play—*The Polar Regions of our Earth*—was also performed in Lisbon during the weekend. Before and during the weekend, interviews were given to TV, national radio and newspapers, and

Figure 3.50 Live music during Polar Science Weekend.

during the two days, 8,000 people visited Lisbon's Pavilion of Knowledge, double the museum's previous record attendance.

Contact: www.portalpolar.pt/index.php

Searchable Keywords: Portal Polar, ciência polar, science weekend, Portugal

Antarctica's Gamburtsev Province (AGAP) Project: creating a science event with new technology

Submitted by Margie Turrin, Lamont-Doherty Earth Observatory, USA

Categories: Communicating science with the media, Correspondence from the field/lab, Web-based, Creative writing

A project like AGAP that maps the deeply buried, subglacial Gamburtsev mountain range in East Antarctica while using airborne geophysics captures the imagination and easily appeals to the public. But the project's remoteness, the site's lack of access and bandwidth, and the need for infrastructure to support teachers and press created exciting challenges for establishing effective outreach work.

Social networking tools can be very effective when engaging the public, especially technology-loving teen and young adult audiences who do not traditionally read science journals and newspapers.

Through a series of outreach ventures new to IPY and polar science, the AGAP project team engaged a following through Twittering, an 'Xtreme South' Facebook Group, collaboration with the *Ice Stories* project at the Exploratorium

Figure 3.51 Fuelling the twin otter plane at AGAP's field camp.

in San Francisco, and a series of background and blogging dispatches. Other partners in the northern hemisphere allowed field scientists to send short pieces of information, and current images and data to people taking an interest in the project. Home base staff developed the material further into curriculum activities such as posters, classroom activities and public presentations, all available on the project's website.

**Contact: www.ldeo.columbia.edu/agap,
mkt@ldeo.columbia.edu**

Searchable Keywords: AGAP, education outreach, blogs, youth in science

---

University of Delaware Seminars

Submitted by Frederick E. Nelson, University of Delaware, USA

Categories: Events, Exhibitions, Public presentations

Named after William Samuel Carlson, glaciologist, Greenland explorer and former University of Delaware (UD) president, WS Carlson IPY events were developed to create a sense of community among UD's polar researchers and educators, promote knowledge about the polar regions in the State of Delaware, and raise the university's profile.

The events began when Captain Lawson W. Brigham publicly signed the American Geographical Society's Fliers' and Explorers' Globe, a globe previously signed by Amundsen, Nansen and Byrd. They ended with a ceremony honouring Peter Smith of the Phoenix Mars Mission, which recently found water ice in the Martian Arctic.

Featuring public lectures on everything from exploration history and Arctic material culture to climate change science and Antarctic astrophysical research, the project also used interdisciplinary seminars, a film series, two major photographic exhibitions (contemporary images of icebergs, and original photographs of nineteenth-century expeditions) in the UD museums, and public receptions to promote knowledge about the polar regions.

Outreach also included web-based blogs from polar researchers in the field, and a formal course from the UD's Academy of Lifelong Learning with classroom visits by UD polar researchers. A multi-disciplinary course, *The Polar World*, has been developed and will be offered periodically in the future.

> Contact: www.udel.edu/research/polar, udresearch@udel.edu
>
> Searchable Keywords: University of Delaware, seminars, IPY

Music

Arctic climate change through music—the WSO experience!

Submitted by Tanya Derksen, WSO, Canada
Categories: Music, Youth forums and student conferences

In 2008, the IPY-CFL Artists on Board programme invited the Winnipeg Symphony Orchestra's (WSO) composer-in-residence, Dr Vincent Ho, to spend one week on board the *CCGS Amundsen*, Canada's premier research icebreaker.

Dr Ho accompanied the Schools on Board Circumpolar Inuit Field Program and witnessed scientists at work. His experiences on board the ship and in northern communities inspired him to compose an orchestral work called *Arctic Postcards* that was premiered in February 2010 at the WSO's New Music Festival. The evening included a multimedia presentation highlighting the research and findings of the IPY-CFL project, and showcasing other aspects of the Artist on Board programme.

This partnership with the WSO also resulted in collaboration with the Schools on Board programme to combine the themes of music and science in their 2010 Arctic Climate Change Youth Forum. This event was organised the day before the premiere of *Arctic Postcards*. At the gala high school students and teachers met with climate change researchers and musicians. Collectively, they explored the science behind climate change research, the links between music and science, and the role of art and music as a means of communicating science to the public. The forum was co-hosted with a local high school and organised by a student committee.

Figure 3.52 Vincent Ho on the *CCGS Amundsen*.

> Contact: education@wso.mb.ca, www.wso.ca
>
> Searchable Keywords: Winnipeg Symphony Orchestra, New Music Festival, IPY-CFL, climate change and music, school outreach

Polar Synthesis: music for IPY

Submitted by James Bicigo, UAF, USA
Categories: Music, Web-based

James Bicigo, an associate professor at the University of Alaska Fairbanks (UAF) was commissioned by IPY Alaska to compose the *Polar Fanfare*. Performed by Borealis Brass, this 30-second piece for brass quintet had its premiere at IPY Alaska's opening ceremony in Charles Davis Concert Hall on the UAF campus.

The subsequent recording was used on the IPY Alaska website, converted to a mobile phone ringtone, and has been used by UAF scientists during several presentations at IPY conferences.

As a result of its success, IPY Alaska commissioned a longer work from the fanfare. The resulting piece—*Polar Synthesis*—is a five-movement work for brass quintet. The movements are *Polar Fanfare, Aurora, Break-up/Climate Change, Polar Bears and Understanding/Synthesis*. This work was premiered with Borealis Brass at the UAF IPY day at Fairbanks Ice Park in March 2008. Borealis Brass recorded the work, which was podcast internationally on www.brasscast.com in the summer of 2008. Since then, the work has been made available to other ensembles associated with IPY and will be submitted for publication by Wiltshire Music of Massapequa, New York, at the close of IPY.

Contact: www.borealisbrass.com, www.brasscast.com

Searchable Keywords: Polar Fanfare, Polar Synthesis, IPY, James Bicigo

Books

IPY Polar Books

Submitted by Joan Eamer, Polar Books, international
Categories: Communicating Science with the Media, Publishing

Polar Books is an IPY project featuring a collection of books about the Arctic and Antarctica that reflect IPY themes and are internationally endorsed by IPY.

The Polar Resource Library is a contribution from the United Nations Environment Programme (UNEP) to the legacy of the International Polar Year. It holds education and outreach materials from the books as well as materials developed through the IPY Education and Outreach Committee and the International Programme Office. Materials in this library include full books, book excerpts, posters, photos, artwork, poems, teachers' guides and activity sheets. Contents of this virtual library are freely available for education and outreach purposes.

Quality books slated for publication up to March 2011 (two years after IPY) will continue to be added to the Polar Books collection. Books must fit well within IPY themes, include information about IPY, and have a broad target audience. Children's books and teachers' resources are welcome. Project members cooperate on IPY promotion activities and provide resources from their books for free use in IPY education and outreach.

Polar Books is coordinated jointly by UNEP/GRID-Arendal and the IPY International Programme Office. The project operates as a collective: authors and editors of Polar Books review all submissions to ensure that candidate books for the collection reflect and advance IPY themes, have good mechanisms for review of scientific contents, and that the materials to be provided for public use will be useful as online education and outreach resources.

Antarctica, White Heart of our Planet

Submitted by Lucia Simion, science writer and photographer, France
Categories: Creative writing, Creating educational tools

Antarctique, Coeur Blanc de la Terre (Antarctica, White Heart of our Planet) is a book designed to raise awareness of Antarctica and polar science among the general public, teenagers and children. An IPY-endorsed project, selected for the IPY Polar Book Collection, it is published in French, Italian and German, and is used as an educational tool in elementary and secondary schools in France and Italy.

The book is illustrated with a selection of spectacular pictures taken by photographers from many different countries, including Yann Arthus-Bertrand, Frans Lanting, Ingo Arndt, George Steinmetz, Paul Nicklen and Lucia Simion. Historic images by Herbert Ponting and Frank Hurley are also featured.

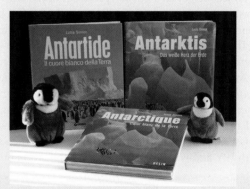

Figure 3.53 Cover: Antarctica, White Heart of our Planet

The book contains four main texts, an encyclopaedia and 10 interviews with scientists and other professionals, all from different countries involved with the Antarctic: ecologist David G. Ainley (USA); vulcanologist Philip Kyle (New Zealand and USA); glaciologist Claude Lorius (France); Rhian Salmon, Atmospheric Chemistry (UK and Germany); So Kawaguchi, a krill ecologist (Japan); and Yann Arthus-Bertrand (France), photographer and author of the best-selling book *The Earth from Above*.

Contact: www.unep.org/publications/polarbooks, polarbooks@grida.no

Searchable Keywords: polar books, UNEP, Antarctique, Lucia Simion

---

Children's book about the Arctic Fox

Submitted by Maarten J.J.E. Loonen, University of Groningen, Arctic Centre, The Netherlands
Categories: Creating educational tools, Engaging audiences from mid-latitude countries

Written by Stephen Person during IPY, this book features both the Arctic fox and a scientist studying it. The book is aimed at 10- to 14-year-old children, and teaches them facts about the animal and the Arctic. The author uses Maarten Loonen's research on the Arctic fox to describe the animal's survival techniques in the harsh polar environment and lure the readers into the fascinating world of the Arctic. The book works with catchy titles and full-colour photos, and is a good example of an educational narrative that teaches children about the Arctic and the consequences of climate change.

Contact: www.bearportpublishing.com

Searchable Keywords: children, book, Arctic Fox, Bearport Publishing

The Story of Antarctica

Submitted by Manish Tiwari and Rasik Ravindra, NCAOR, India
Category: Creating educational tools

Under the *Popular Book Series* initiative of the Ministry of Earth Sciences and the Geological Society of India, NCAOR published *The Story of Antarctica* in 2008 for free distribution among schoolchildren and the general public. NCAOR is the centre of polar research in India and its scientists were the obvious choice for authoring the new book.

The *Story of Antarctica* comprises information about polar science with a focus on Indian involvement in Antarctica. It describes early exploration and, for example, introduces its readers to the characteristics of Antarctic climate and landscape. The style in which it is written is easily comprehensible to its target audience of children aged between eight and 11 years old. The book was freely distributed among school libraries across India. Copies were also sent to major research institutes to inspire scientists to create similar books on their particular fields of expertise. A free copy of the book is also available for download on the NCAOR website.

Figure 3.54 Cover: The Story of Antarctica.

Contact: www.ncaor.gov.in, info@ncaor.org

Searchable Keywords: Antarctica, information, Indian polar research

Two Windows on our Planet

Submitted by Martha MacDonald, Labrador Institute of Memorial University, Canada
Categories: Creative writing, Creating educational tools, Engaging audiences from Arctic communities

This project aimed at creating a children's book showing two approaches to the creation of the Earth: traditional Inuit legends of Labrador, and a geologist's interpretation of the creation of a particular landform.

Two students who had been trained in interviewing techniques through introductory university courses in folklore spent time in their home community of Nain, Labrador collecting legends from Nunatsiavut. They collected several stories, and it was decided to use the story of the Polar Bear in the Rocks for the book project.

Using several oral accounts, a written version was compiled by Janet McNaughton, children's author and folklorist. Derek Wilton wrote the account of the polar bear's creation from a geologist's perspective, and Cynthia Colosimo, a southern Labrador artist, worked on the illustrations. The book was also translated into Inuktitut and launched in March 2010.

The purpose of the book is to give equal space to interpretations of landform creation, to promote interest among children in the study of geology; train students in ethnographic techniques; preserve and promote the place of traditional legends, and provide local material for educational resources.

Contact: www.mun.ca/labradorinstitute/, labrador.institute@mun.ca

Searchable Keywords: folklore, legend, Inuit, geology, Inuktitut

Using other media

Promotion of Arctic Science to Canadian News Media

Submitted by Ruth Klinkhammer, Arctic Institute of North America, Canada
Categories: Communicating science with the media

This project promoted Arctic research to the Canadian public through the news media. The project manager reviewed Arctic science articles from scholarly journals and rewrote the pieces as media releases. These releases were sent to an extensive network of print and broadcast journalists in northern and southern Canada. Journalists either ran the articles verbatim or, more often, interviewed scientists and wrote their own stories. As a second arm of the project, a freelance journalist was hired to work at the Arctic Institute's Kluane Lake Research Station (KLRS) in the Yukon for the 2009 field season. The writer spent 11 weeks at the station, interviewing scientists and then producing radio and print stories.

The Promotion of Arctic Science project was especially successful in the north. CBC North picked up many of our news releases and CBC Radio in Whitehorse ran a weekly column created by the KLRS journalist.

Media were more likely to pick up a story if the research was conducted in their community. Another key to the success of this project was that the releases issued by the Arctic Institute were written as news or feature stories using simple, non-technical language, a dominant story angle and quotes from scientists.

Contact: www.arctic.ucalgary.ca, arctic@ucalgary.ca

Searchable Keywords: journalists, media releases, CBC, news media

---

Polar Communications: the award winning *Ends of the Earth* radio show from Canada's Western Arctic

Submitted by Kirsten Murphy, CKLB Radio Station, North West Territories, Canada
Categories: Communicating science with the media, Engaging audiences from Arctic communities

The *Ends of the Earth* is an IPY-funded radio programme on CKLB radio in Yellowknife, Northwest Territories, Canada. The weekly show, hosted by William Greenland and Kirsten Murphy, highlights IPY-funded researchers and focuses on climate change from scientific, aboriginal, and even artistic perspectives.

Since 2008, the IPY Arctic Radio Project has hosted three ambitious live broadcasts for IPY Polar Days: one that connected listeners with scientists in Australia, Greece and Zambia; a second one that linked schools from across the North with IPY scientists in the high Arctic and Antarctic; and a third one with David J. Carlson, Chris Burn and Inuvialuit Elder Nellie Pokiak answering questions from students from the Northwest Territories, Brazil and the Yukon.

Figure 3.55 Kirsten Murphy and an Inuvialuit Elder, Nellie Pokiak during CKLB's Polar Week broadcast in October 2009 in Yellowknife, Northwest Territories, Canada.

Key features

The show raises awareness of the Canadian Arctic, its people and northern issues. The project's goal is to foster greater understanding of the polar regions and global climate change. Greenland and Murphy connect with leading scientists while including the Traditional Knowledge of Dene and Inuvialuit Elders. Within three months of being on air, the *Ends of the Earth* was named best syndicated radio show by the National Community Radio Association in Canada for 2009.

The Ends of the Earth is broadcast to more than 30 aboriginal communities in the Northwest Territories in Canada's Western Arctic. The show also streams live and as a podcast. For the past year, the programme has been in syndication with radio stations in British Columbia, Regina, Winnipeg and Thunder Bay. Northern schools are using the show as part of their climate change curriculum.

Keys to success

CKLB is part of a network of radio stations, the Native Communications Society of the Northwest Territories, which is part of an existing network of aboriginal radio stations. The IPY Arctic radio project built on and strengthened these connections.

Impacts

NCS's chair, Joachim Bonnetrouge, says CKLB radio continues to stretch the boundaries of radio: "The *Ends of the Earth* is another example of what we can do with a good idea and the support of a partner like the IPY Programme Office."

Ends of the Earth co-host William Greenland says Dene Elders often approach him with story ideas: "What I am hearing is that we are at a unique time in history where issues related to climate change, extreme weather patterns and animal extinctions threaten to change our way of life forever."

The show can be heard live at www.ncsnwt.com or as a podcast in the main webpage's audio library.

> **Contact: www.ncsnwt.com, kirsten@ncsnswt.com**
>
> **Searchable Keywords: Native Communications Society of the Northwest Territories, radio, aboriginal, ends of the earth**

The Netherland's Arctic station and an online sightseeing tour and weblog

Submitted by Maarten J.J.E. Loonen, University of Groningen, Arctic Centre, Netherlands
Categories: Correspondence from the field/lab, Engaging audiences from mid-latitude countries, Video, Web-based

Ny-Ålesund is an international research base on Spitsbergen, 79°N. With 200 people in summer and permanent stations from 10 countries, it is the biggest and most international science base in the Arctic. Rockets are fired from here to study the stratosphere, and quasars are used to position the Earth in space and to measure the movement of the continents. There is a large reference station for atmospheric research, and an impressive marine laboratory to study life in the fjord. NASA is using this site for testing new equipment for their Mars expedition, and they fly with an unmanned aircraft to the marginal ice edge of the North Pole. There is a small museum, an information centre with a science exhibition, a shop and a post office. Each summer, 30,000 tourists visit the town. The tourists

Figure 3.56 Scientist checking a nest of a barnacle goose.

walk the streets but cannot enter most of the buildings. Their stay is usually too short to learn about inhabitants and their science projects.

The Netherlands Arctic station in Ny-Ålesund focuses on biological research in the Arctic summer. Migratory birds (mainly geese) are studied in their environment with detailed measurements on goose behaviour, vegetation, predators and health. You can learn about the station on its website with features such as a weblog and a streetview of Ny-Ålesund.

The Arctic station weblog shows daily encounters with other scientists visiting the town. You can read about history and polar exploration, retreating glaciers and climate change, arctic foxes or imprinted goslings, which walk behind the researchers.

Using the idea of online streetviews, a web-based sightseeing tour of Ny-Ålesund guides you through the town's streets and lets you turn in all directions. Many views are accompanied by short videos explaining more about the buildings, the inhabitants and the science. Watching these videos allows you to enter buildings and learn more about practising science in the Arctic than you would during a real visit. The website is set up in such a way that it is constantly updated.

> **Contact: www.arcticstation.nl**
>
> **Searchable Keywords: Arctic station, Ny-Ålesund streetview, Arctic biological research, Netherlands polar research**

International Polar Foundation coverage of CHINARE 25

Submitted by Jean de Pomereu, IPF, Belgium

Categories: Correspondence from the field/lab, Research partnerships between educators and scientists, Scientific expeditions

In November and December 2009, polar writer and photographer Jean de Pomereu became the first foreign journalist to take part in a Chinese Antarctic research expedition.

During the two months he spent on the CHINARE 25 expedition at sea on board China's research icebreaker *Xue Long* (Snow Dragon), and at Zhongshan research station in East Antarctica, Jean witnessed and documented China's Antarctic activities and contributions to IPY.

These included the Xue Long's navigation and ice breaking operations; oceanographic work in the Southern Ocean; the renovation of Zhongshan station; scientific work as part of China's multi-year IPY research programme PANDA; and perhaps most importantly, the preparations and departure of the CHINARE 25 inland traverse team responsible for building the first phase of Kunlun Station at Dome Argus (Dome A), the highest and possibly coldest plateau in the Antarctic.

Reports, features and interviews from the trip were published on the International Polar Foundation's website, and in the French language magazine *Chine Plus,* which focuses on Chinese affairs. A booklet of Jean's photojournalism will be published by IPF in the near future.

> **Contact: info@polarfoundation.org, www.jeandepomereu.com**
>
> **Searchable Keywords: CHINARE 25, Antarctica, China, articles, journalism**
>
> INTERNATIONAL
> **POLAR**
> FOUNDATION

KRILL game: an adventure in the Antarctic

Submitted by Begoña Vendrell-Simón, Institut de Ciències del Mar (ICM-CSIC), Spain
Categories: Creating educational tools

The board game KRILL was developed by a multidisciplinary group of polar scientists, with help from an environmental education association, to increase interest and knowledge about polar science among the general public, especially children and young people, and also with the potential of favouring family dynamics. Designed for a wide age range of audiences, its rules vary according to age.

KRILL was a pioneering project that took on board feedback from educators during its first year of use. In schools, polar scientists used the game as an activity that added to their classroom presentation on Antarctic topics. KRILL was also used as one of the activities during open days at the Marine Science Institute (ICM-CSIC) in Barcelona.

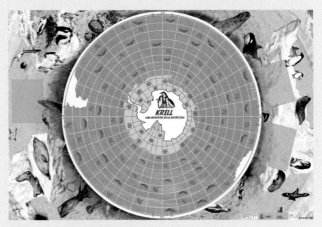

Figure 3.57 Illustrating the board game KRILL.

Contact: www.fundaciocollserola.cat/sotazero

Searchable Keywords: Antarctic, board game, Spain, Krill, penguin, Año Polar Internacional

During a travel by dog sledge, an Inuk from Clyde River, Baffin Island, Nunavut, Canada, is building from inside an igloo house on the sea ice because of an incoming storm. He is installing the last piece of the igloo's roof.

Authors: Ole Henrik Magga, Svein D. Mathiesen, Anders Oskal and Johan Mathis Turi

Introduction

For centuries, reindeer herding peoples have lived and worked across wide areas of Eurasia in extremely harsh environments. Today, reindeer herding communities across the Arctic and Subarctic are facing profound changes impacting on their societies and they are at the forefront of climate change induced transformations. The challenges of climate change, globalisation, and increased economical development are of such proportions that people around the world need to utilise available knowledge resources in order to prepare themselves for the future. Scientific research has been and will continue to be very important to meet these challenges and to sustain indigenous peoples' communities in the circumpolar north. Beyond scientific inquiry, however, knowledge embedded within reindeer herding communities— Traditional Knowledge—is also needed as a foundation for adaptation to changes in northern polar regions.

In the circumpolar north, Traditional Knowledge developed through centuries of close observation of reindeer, pastures and the environment, and was handed down from generation to generation. It is a rich and unique resource on the natural environment in which reindeer herding peoples live.

This essay explores the challenges reindeer herding peoples in the circumpolar north face today, and stresses the significance of Traditional Knowledge for adaptation processes to these challenges. We give you background information on reindeer herding communities, describe the IPY project EALÁT—a landmark initiative that gives a voice to indigenous communities in the Arctic—and finally, we address the need to preserve, develop and utilise Traditional Knowledge to be able to face future global climate variability and change.

The Voice of Reindeer Herding Communities during IPY

The Association of World Reindeer Herders (WRH) makes important long-term contributions towards capacity building in reindeer herding communities across Eurasia with a special focus on adaptation to the challenges of climate variability and change, and the pressing issue of loss of pastures. Today, changes taking place in polar regions might be the first indications of major global changes. The Association of World Reindeer Herders initiated IPY EALÁT to address climate change related issues and to develop and sustain robust reindeer herding societies. *(See the project description of IPY EALÁT in Chapter 3 for more information.)* As such, IPY EALÁT builds on and preserves Traditional Knowledge, which is closely connected to indigenous peoples' use of language.

The language of Sámi is spoken among the indigenous Sámi people of Norway, Sweden, Finland and the Kola Peninsula in Russia. The term 'Ealát' is Sámi for 'good pasture'. 'Ealát' is related to the term 'eallu,' which means 'herd'. The origin of these terms derives from the word 'eallin' or 'life'. In other words, the Sámi language shows how the land and its people are inseparably connected through reindeer herding: pasture is the foundation for reindeer herds, and reindeer herding constitutes the livelihood of over 20 indigenous peoples throughout the circumpolar north. Despite the number of different indigenous peoples, reindeer herding in the Arctic and Subarctic shows remarkably similar patterns of organisation. Reindeer husbandry can be seen as a circumpolar model for sustainable management of the barren areas of the North. It can also be seen as a system built on strong inter-linkages between people, reindeer and habitat— *a coupled human-environmental system* (Berkes et al., 2003)—with an original high resilience to climate variability and change.

We at EALÁT argue that Arctic indigenous peoples' insights and understanding have brought a new dimension to polar research during IPY; a dimension hitherto not recognised by 'western science'. IPY has engendered a paradigm shift towards more human, holistic and multidimensional perspectives in Arctic polar research. We hope that the results of IPY will generate new perspectives in sustainable research and education in Arctic societies.

IPY EALÁT: The Significance of IPY for Reindeer Herding Peoples

The IPY EALÁT consortium is a unique research, documentation, outreach and teaching initiative that places Traditional Knowledge on an equal footing with scientific knowledge. EALÁT aims to make indigenous peoples familiar with the effects of climate variability and changes on their societies and environment. The EALÁT-Network study also focuses on the question to what extent public institutions and local governance create or constrain opportunities to adapt to the effects of global change in the Arctic. In this context, adaptation is defined as adjustment in ecological, social or economic systems in response to actual or expected climatic stimuli and their effects or impacts. To meet these goals, EALÁT is structured around four components: research, education, outreach and information.

Students at the Bachelor, Master and PhD level learn to recognise that the ability to adapt to change is based on knowledge that is built into their languages and experiences, the structure of local institutions and the actions of individuals. Here, Traditional Knowledge is seen as more than a supplement to

Figure 4.1 Nenets and Sámi reindeer herding youth examine experience and Traditional Knowledge at the EALÁT workshop in Nadym, Yamalo-Nenets Autonomous Area, northwest Siberia, March 2007.

scientific knowledge. For example, at the Sámi University College in Norway, IPY EALÁT develops online forms of education particularly adapted to nomadic reindeer herders. The programme also created an MSc course entitled 'Adaptation to Global Change in the Arctic' as part of the University of the Arctic Thematic Network on Global Change.

In terms of EALÁT outreach, IPY made possible the development of the Reindeer Portal (www.reindeerportal.org), a web-based communication platform to the world of reindeer husbandry created in cooperation with the Arctic Portal (www.arcticportal.org). The website is important for the exchange of information and the collection of results from different IPY projects relevant to reindeer herders' societies. The Reindeer Portal

Figure 4.2 Nenets reindeer herders in Yamalo-Nenets Autonomous Area working with their herd, April 2007.

wants to be the focal point on reindeer herding for herders, indigenous peoples, students, administrators, politicians, businessmen and –women, and the general public. The Reindeer Portal also informs mainstream society about reindeer herders' knowledge related to pasture use, climate variability and climate change.

The IPY EALÁT-Information project in the Arctic Council has arranged a series of community-based workshops in local reindeer herding societies across the Arctic, where reindeer herders from different areas, scientists from various disciplines, and local authorities are brought together to address the challenges of climate variability and change and shifts in land usage while focusing on concepts of adaptation and Traditional Knowledge. Nine such workshops have been held between 2007 and 2009 in local reindeer herding communities in Norway, Finland and Russia. The central goal of EALÁT-Information is to become the voice of reindeer herders to the Arctic Council on issues of climate change, loss of pastures and adaptation, while promoting competence building for indigenous peoples locally.

Two examples illustrate reindeer herding communities' need to adapt to external changes: first, local food production in communities in the North, and second, increasing economic interests in Arctic territories of the oil and gas industry.

Socio-ecological adaptation to warming in the Arctic makes necessary the development of robust local societies—economies based on Traditional Knowledge that produce local food for human consumption. Arctic societies have very diverse food cultures, which are based on local natural resources of high nutritional values for humans, such as reindeer meat, fish and berries. Constraints on local food production, which do not respect indigenous peoples' rights to determine their own food sources, are a serious threat to their ability to adapt their diets to environmental changes happening around them. Indigenous societies have to be able to develop their own problem management strategies, including their right to generate their own set of knowledge through their own research institutions.

Recently, the territories of traditional reindeer husbandry have become economically attractive for the oil and gas industry. Even though oil and gas infrastructure development can severely disrupt the livelihoods of reindeer herders, these developments might also offer benefits for reindeer husbandry. In contrast to the direct impact of alternative energy systems such as windmills and hydroelectric power plants—technologies with potential widespread impact on land and animals—oil and gas development offers hope of a financial foundation that will leave a positive effect on reindeer herding communities. Trends to regard the Arctic as a source of energy will cause a 'tidal wave' for indigenous peoples' ways of life. "The tide lifts all boats," people say. It is important that indigenous peoples of the North are equipped with the necessary tools to face this tide, and continue to thrive when oil and gas development in these areas recede. Small, ill prepared indigenous communities risk being swamped by this onslaught of economic interest. Reindeer husbandry has been an important livelihood for people in these areas from time immemorial, and must be sustained during and after these resources might have been exploited. To this end, local capacity building in indigenous reindeer herding societies is essential to determine suitable approaches to these economic challenges.

IPY EALÁT faces the difficult task to transform, mould and catalyse reindeer herders' knowledge into action for sustainable development of the Arctic and, in particular, to actively involve circumpolar reindeer herders in this process. IPY provided new mechanisms for indigenous reindeer herders to reach this goal. The IPY EALÁT project contributes to the sustainable future management of reindeer husbandry by documenting Arctic reindeer herding peoples' Traditional Knowledge and by stimulating cooperation among reindeer herding peoples and international research, as well as educational institutions to create new knowledge. Moreover, IPY provided an opportunity for young reindeer herders to meet in workshops and lectures for cultural exchange and networking.

During IPY the IPY EALÁT consortium has established a unique institutional network in the circumpolar north, which should be preserved for the future cooperation between local peoples, science and larger political agencies. Therefore, as a continuation of these efforts, the Association of World Reindeer Herders, the International Centre for Reindeer Husbandry and the Sámi University College have taken the initiative in establishing, as a legacy of IPY, a University of the Arctic Institute for Circumpolar Reindeer Husbandry, the UArctic EALÁT Institute. It is envisaged that this institute will build and expand on the network already established, thereby further embedding the goals of the IPY and IPY EALÁT in future knowledge development and outreach.

Strengthening Traditional Knowledge in Polar Research

Capacity building among reindeer herding peoples should draw on available Traditional Knowledge in the circumpolar north. Traditional Knowledge is based on people's experience and is a form of knowledge that has been accumulated for generations in people's memories, stories and actions. A deep understanding of and insights into the sustainability and resilience of reindeer herders is also expressed in their languages. Therefore, it is knowledge that is actually validated in the same way that scientific empirical knowledge is found valid:

by trial and error. The difference between them lies in how they are obtained and over what length of time. From the beginning, human societies have accumulated holistic and long-term Traditional Knowledge—from the first settlements, to early barter systems, and the establishment of trading networks. As modern science developed and new knowledge brought extraordinary results in all aspects of life, a shift in people's attitude towards Traditional Knowledge occurred and it became gradually devalued.

Today, an appreciation of Traditional Knowledge evolves. Over the last decades, the global community has begun to demand the implementation of local and Traditional Knowledge, and even institutions such as the United Nations require and encourage that Traditional Knowledge be embedded into the management of the natural environment. This change in attitude is closely connected to the global challenges that we face. Both governments and citizens have begun to realise that we need more comprehensive perspectives regarding the management of our natural environment. This is a field where Traditional Knowledge and scientific knowledge have the potential to complement each other and to provide us with a more complete insight into our world.

Traditional Knowledge is characterised by the fact that it is oral and not preserved in written records. As a result, people often perceive it to be something very diffuse and difficult to use. Therefore, one of IPY EALÁT's main tasks is to make Traditional Knowledge available to more people.

Another major challenge that we face is to see the implementation of Traditional Knowledge in governance, public plans, or industrial development projects. Of course, there are a great number of specific challenges that have to be met in this process: issues of ownership, intellectual property and documentation, ethical considerations, storage questions, and the demand for an enhanced understanding of the handling of Traditional Knowledge from the academic and professional communities. As a result, we are continually seeking collaboration with academic institutions and all levels and disciplines of research.

In general, Traditional Knowledge needs to remain where it originates. This ensures that traditional skills are developed locally and not far from the communities that brought them forth. This is a guarantee that knowledge remains where it is needed, and that local communities have immediate access to the benefits from the knowledge developed. Herding peoples have a unique set of knowledge of the climate and ecology of their regions, and because they inhabit places where climate change is expected to be most dramatic, their knowledge is particularly valuable and has to continue to thrive in these particular communities. IPY EALÁT was able to create 'meeting places' for people at the grassroots and the relevant professional level. By establishing these 'communities' where local knowledge meets theory-based knowledge in an active manner, one can build up local expertise, strengthen the robustness of local communities and enhance the effectiveness of local adaptation strategies. The aim is to empower reindeer herders and the communities in which they live with the best technologies available combined with traditional skills and knowledge to further enhance sustainable reindeer husbandry. During IPY, this has been the essence of the IPY EALÁT project.

Conclusion: Adaptation to Change and Unpredictability

We conclude that adaptation to climate change demands the training of local Arctic leaders in long-term sustainable thinking in both indigenous peoples and mainstream society. This educational goal needs to be based on the best available knowledge about adaptation, that is, a combination of scientific, and experience-based traditional and local knowledge. We also recommend that national adaptation strategies must recognise minorities, indigenous peoples' Traditional Knowledge, cultural and linguistic rights. Johan Mathis Turi, chairman of the International Centre for Reindeer Husbandry (ICR), said on UN World Environmental Day in Tromsø in June 2007 that concepts of adaptation rather than stability are inherent in reindeer herding societies:

> We have some knowledge about how to live in a changing environment. The term 'stability' is a foreign word in our language. Our search for adaptation strategies is therefore not connected to 'stability' in any form, but is instead focused on constant adaptation to changing conditions.

We therefore conclude that IPY projects with indigenous perspectives to them have not only been important for indigenous peoples but also for scientific communities and have brought forth fresh insights and improved understanding into the possibilities of adaptation based on different world views and value systems. It is imperative that all available forms of knowledge are included when developing adaptation strategies to climate change in the Arctic.

Figure 4.3 Traditional Nenets reindeer herders' migration, crossing rivers on the Yamal Peninsula, part of the Yamal-Nenets Autonomous Area, July 2009.

In the Bering Sea: A CTD sensor is lowered through a hole in the sea ice to determine the temperature, salinity, light and algal concentrations in the sea water immediately below the sea ice.

For each institution and organisation we give you the acronym, full name, country and website. This list is not complete and if you are looking for an acronym not listed here, you might want to consult IASC's list at http://web. arcticportal.org/iasc/services/polar-acronyms, or APECS collection of polar institutions in their 'Resource' section at www.apecs.is.

ACE CRC
Antarctic Climate & Ecosystems Cooperative Research Centre
Australia
www.acecrc.org.au

AINA
Arctic Institute of North America
University of Calgary
Canada
www.arctic.ucalgary.ca

ANDRILL
Antarctic Geological Drilling
United States
www.andrill.org

APECS
Association of Polar Early Career Scientists
International
www.apecs.org

Arctic Centre
University of Groningen
Netherlands
www.let.rug.nl/arctic/

ArcticNet
Network of Centres of Excellence of Canada
Canada
www.arcticnet.ulaval.ca

AWI
Alfred-Wegener-Institut für Polar- und Meeresforschung
Alfred Wegener Institute for Polar and Marine Research
Germany
www.awi.de

BAS
British Antarctic Survey
UK
www.antarctica.ac.uk

Government of Canada IPY Program
Canada
www.http://www.ipy-api.gc.ca

CANDAC
Canadian Network for Detection of Atmospheric Change
Canada
www.candac.ca

Cape Farewell
Art, Polar Science and Climate Science
International
www.capefarewell.com

CReSIS
Center for Remote Sensing of Ice Sheets
USA
www.cresis.ku.edu

DAMOCLES
Developing Arctic Modelling and Observing Capabilities for Long-term Environmental Studies
European
www.damocles-eu.org/

DGP
Deutsche Gesellschaft für Polar Forschung
Germany Society for Polar Research
Germany
www.dgp.de

Geophysical Institute
University of Alaska Fairbanks
USA
www.gi.alaska.edu

IARC
International Arctic Research Centre
University of Alaska Fairbanks
USA
www.iarc.uaf.edu

IASC
International Arctic Science Committee
International
http://web.arcticportal.org/iasc

ICM-CSIC
Institut de Ciències del Mar—Consejo Superior de Investigaciones Científicas
Institute of Marine Science
Spain
www.icm.csic.es

ICR
International Centre for Reindeer Husbandry
International
http://icr.arcticportal.org

ICSU
International Council of Science
International
www.icsu.org

Institutul Român de Cercetari Polare
Romanian Polar Research Institute
Romania
www.polar-institute.ro

IPF
International Polar Foundation
International
www.polarfoundation.org

IPY
International Polar Year and Legacy
International
www.ipy.org

Labrador Institute
Memorial University
Canada
www.mun.ca/labradorinstitute/

LDEO
Lamont-Doherty Earth Observatory
Columbia University
USA
www.ldeo.columbia.edu

NASA
National Aeronautics and
Space Administration
USA
www.nasa.gov

NCAOR
National Centre for
Antarctic & Ocean Research
India
www.ncaor.gov.in

NOAA
National Oceanographic and
Atmospheric Administration
USA
www.noaa.com

NSIDC
National Snow and Ice Data Center
USA
http://nsidc.org

PSC
Polar Science Center
University of Washington
USA
www.psc.apl.washington.edu

Sámi University College
Sámi allaskuvla
International
www.samiskhs.no

UArctic
University of the Arctic
International
www.uarctic.org

UAF
University of Alaska Fairbanks
USA
www.uaf.edu

UNIS
The University Centre in Svalbard
Norway
www.unis.no

WHRC
Woods Hole Research Centre
USA
www.whrc.org

WMO
World Meteorological Organisation
International
www.wmo.int

WRH
Association of World Reindeer Herders
International
http://icr.arcticportal.org

Glossary

Active layer: The uppermost layer of soil in *permafrost* areas that freezes and thaws on a seasonal basis.

Adsorption: The adhesion of a substance on the surface of a solid or liquid.

Aerosols: Gaseous suspensions of fine liquid or solid particles.

Albedo: Fraction of electromagnetic radiation from sources such as the Sun that is reflected by a surface.

Altitude: In astronomy, the vertical distance of an object above the horizon.

Anemometer: Device for measuring wind strength and velocity.

Anisotropic: Refers to an object that has variable properties depending on the direction in which it is measured.

Antarctic Bottom Water (AABW): A high *density water mass* in the Southern Ocean around Antarctica. AABW is formed when surface water enriched in salt from sea ice formation cools and, due to its increased density, flows down the Antarctic continental margin and onto the sea floor.

Antarctic Circle: An imaginary line that consists of the parallel of latitude approximately 66.33°S. South of this latitude, the sun is above the horizon for 24 hours on the summer *solstice* and does not rise at all on the winter solstice.

Antarctic Circumpolar Current (ACC): A powerful ocean current that flows from west to east completely encircling Antarctica.

Antarctic Treaty System: The Antarctic Treaty and related agreements, collectively called the 'Antarctic Treaty System', regulates international relations in Antarctica. Ratified in 1961, the treaty now has 47 signatories, and designates Antarctica as a continent for peace and science.

Anthropology: The scientific study of the origin, behaviour, and physical, social and cultural development of humankind.

Archimedes' Principle: The principle that states the net fluid force on a submerged or floating body in a stationary fluid is an upward force equal to the weight of the fluid displaced.

Arctic Circle: An imaginary line that consists of the parallel of latitude approximately 66.33°N. North of this latitude, the sun is above the horizon for 24 hours on the summer *solstice* and does not rise at all on the winter solstice.

Arctic Council: A high-level intergovernmental forum that addresses issues faced by the Arctic governments and the *indigenous* peoples of the Arctic.

Atmosphere: A layer of gases, droplets, and particles that surrounds a celestial body of sufficient *mass*, such as the Earth, due to gravitational attraction.

Aurora borealis/aurora australis: Sometimes called the northern and southern lights, auroras are natural light displays in the sky, usually observed at night. They are formed when charged solar wind particles interact with the upper *atmosphere* (usually the *ionosphere*) particularly in the polar regions. The aurora borealis is only visible in the sky from the Northern Hemisphere, and the aurora australis is only visible in southern latitudes.

Azimuth: In astronomy, the angle measured from the meridian (line of reference such as the horizon) to a celestial object. In navigation, the angle measured clockwise from a line of reference to the object of interest.

Basal sliding: The movement of a glacier over bedrock due to the lubricating effects of a thin layer of water under the glacier.

Beta decay: A type of radioactive decay in which a *beta particle* is emitted.

Beta particle: An *electron* or positron emitted, or an electron captured, during radioactive *beta decay*.

Bioaccumulation: The total build-up of pollutants in an organism from any environmental source when the rate of uptake exceeds the rate at which the organism can remove it.

Bioconcentration: The build up of pollutants in an organism from water when the rate of uptake exceeds the rate at which the organism can remove it. Often used synonymously with *bioaccumulation*.

Biological pump: In *oceanography*, the process by which carbon dioxide and other gases and nutrients are removed from the upper layers of the ocean by the sinking of organic matter.

Biomagnification: The increase in concentration of substances such as pesticides or other contaminants in one line in a *food chain* to another. Also known as bioamplification or biological magnification.

Biosphere: All of the living organisms on Earth and the environments in which they live.

Birefringence: Double refraction; the splitting of a ray of light into two rays that are polarised perpendicular to each other.

Blubber: The thick layer of insulating fat between the skin and the muscle layers of whales and other marine mammals.

Buoyancy: The ability of an object to float on a liquid because of the greater *density* of the liquid.

Carbon cycle: The biogeochemical cycle by which carbon is exchanged among the *biosphere*, *pedosphere*, geosphere, *hydrosphere* and *atmosphere* of the Earth through processes such as photosynthesis, decomposition and respiration.

Cherenkov radiation: Light emitted when a charged particle such as an electron passes through a medium where the particle is moving faster than the speed of light through that medium.

Chlorofluorocarbons (CFCs): Organic compounds containing carbon, chlorine and fluorine. Many have been widely used as refrigerants, aerosol propellants and solvents and their use is now slowly being phased out.

Climate: The composite or generally prevailing weather conditions of a region encompassing *temperature*, humidity, atmospheric pressure, wind, rainfall, atmospheric particle count and numerous other meteorological elements in a given region over 30 years—the classical period defined by WMO.

Climate change: A statistically significant variation in the mean state of climate, or in its variability, persisting for an extended period (typically decades or longer). It can be a change in the average *weather* or a change in the distribution of weather events around an average and may either be limited to a specific region, or may occur worldwide. In recent usage, especially in the context of environmental policy, *climate change* refers to particular changes in modern climate.

Climate variability: Fluctuations in *climate* on all temporal and special scales resulting from internal atmospheric processes as well as from interactions among different components of the climate system, such as between the *atmosphere*, the oceans and/or the land.

Climatology: The science that studies *weather* conditions over extended periods of time using statistics based on at least 30 years of readings.

Community (ecological): An assemblage of two or more populations of interacting, different species occupying the same specific habitat.

Community (human): A group of people who share a particular environment, and have common goals, beliefs, resources, preferences, needs, risks and other conditions.

Conduction (heat): The transfer of thermal energy between neighbouring molecules in a substance due to a temperature gradient. It always takes place from a region of higher *temperature* to a region of lower temperature, and acts to equalise temperature differences.

Conjugate auroras: Mirroring of northern and southern auroras, observable from spacecraft.

Constructive interference: A process that occurs when two waves that are in phase with each other combine to form a larger wave.

Convection (heat): The transfer of heat by the movement of molecules within fluids, including gases. In *meteorology* this generally applies to vertical transport of atmospheric properties, especially upwards.

Coriolis effect: The tendency of moving objects when on the surface of the Earth to be deflected to the right in the Northern Hemisphere and to the left in the Southern Hemisphere because of the rotation of the Earth.

Cosmic rays: Energetic particles, predominantly *protons,* from outer space that impinge on the Earth's *atmosphere.*

Creep: Internal flow in the interior of a glacier or *ice sheet* where the downslope component of the weight of the ice deforms the crystal structure.

Cryosphere: The collective description for the portions of the Earth's surface where water is in solid form. This includes not only *sea ice,* lake ice and river ice but also snow cover, glaciers, ice caps and *ice sheets* and frozen ground, such as *permafrost.*

Crystal lattice: A systematic, symmetrical, three-dimensional arrangement of atoms in a crystal.

CTD sensor: An acronym for Conductivity, Temperature, and Depth sensor. It is the primary tool for determining essential physical properties of sea water giving a precise and comprehensive charting of the distribution and variation of water *temperature, salinity* and *density.*

Decomposers: Organisms that feed on other dead organisms from all levels of the *food chain,* causing mechanical and chemical breakdown of dead organisms and recycling nutrients in the environment.

Density: The *mass* per unit volume of a material.

Dependent variable: A factor whose value depends on one or more other variables in an experiment or equation.

Destructive interference: A process that occurs when two waves that are out of phase with each other meet and partially or completely cancel each other, resulting in either a smaller wave or no wave at all.

Diatoms: A major group of eukaryotic algae that have silica-based skeletons and are one of the commonest types of *phytoplankton.*

Ecological niche: The role or function of an organism in an ecosystem.

Ekman spiral: A theoretical model to explain the overall movement of a mass of water with depth as a consequence of the *Coriolis effect.* For example, if there is a steady wind blowing over the surface of the ocean in the northern hemisphere, the water

surface is deflected to the right. The water mass below is further deflected to the right, creating a downward spiral movement.

Electrical conductivity: A measure of a material's ability to conduct an electric current. When an electrical potential difference is placed across a conductor, its movable charges flow, giving rise to an electric current.

Electrical resistance: A measure of the degree to which a material opposes an electric current passing through it; the reciprocal quantity of *electrical conductivity.*

Electron: A fundamental subatomic particle that carries a negative electrical charge. Electrons are found within atoms surrounding the nucleus of *protons* and *neutrons* in a particular electron configuration.

El Niño: A periodic warm phase event in the Pacific in which sea surface *temperatures* are above normal. The event is defined by the difference of warm waters and high rainfall in the costal regions of Peru and Ecuador and cool waters and dry conditions in eastern Australia and Indonesia.

El Niño-Southern Oscillation (ENSO): Switch in the *atmosphere* and ocean system of the tropical Pacific region. El Niño is the warm phase of this oscillation and La Niña is the inverse event.

Equinox: The moment in time when the centre of the Sun can be observed to be directly above the Earth's equator, occurring roughly around 21 March and 23 September each year. At the equinox, all parts of the planet have 12 hours of daylight and 12 hours of darkness.

Exosphere: The uppermost layer of the *atmosphere.* Exosphere is sometimes used synonymously with 'outer space'.

Food chain: The transfer of energy from primary producers through a linear sequence of consumers.

Food web: A complex network of interlocking *food chains.*

Geophysics: The study of geological structures by the quantitative observation of its physical properties.

Glacial plucking: An erosional process caused by friction between the base of a moving glacier and the rock floor that causes the base of the glacier to melt. When meltwater seeps into cracks in the bedrock and freezes, it bonds pieces of rock to the base of the glacier. As the glacier continues moving, it takes some of the rock with it.

Glacial polish: The smoothing of a rock surface by fine-grained sediments embedded in the base of a glacier as it passes over the rock.

Glacial striations: Scratches or gouges cut into bedrock by glacial abrasion. Glacial striations usually occur as multiple straight, parallel grooves representing the movement of the sediment-loaded base of the glacier.

Glacial till: Unsorted glacial sediment deposited directly by the glacier. It may vary from clays to mixtures of clay, sand, gravel and boulders.

Glaciology: The study of natural forms of ice, particularly glaciers, and phenomena related to ice. It includes the study of how glaciers are formed and depleted, how they move, and how they affect the physical landscape, the *climate* and living organisms.

Global distillation: The process in which certain chemicals are transported from warmer to colder regions of the Earth through alternating events of chemical vaporisation at higher *temperatures*, and condensation at lower temperatures.

Gravity: The force that attracts objects to Earth's surface. The force of gravity per unit volume of air is directly proportional to *density*.

Greenhouse effect: The process in which short wave from the Sun passes through Earth's *atmosphere* while outgoing long wave heat *radiation* is trapped, increasing global surface *temperatures*.

Greenhouse gas: The major atmospheric gases causing the *Greenhouse effect,* which are water vapour, carbon dioxide, methane, *ozone* and nitrous oxide.

Gyres: The circular motion of major global ocean surface currents caused by a combination of prevailing wind patterns, the *Coriolis effect* and the shape of the ocean basins.

Heterotrophic: Describes organisms that obtain energy from consuming organic substances rather than directly from inorganic materials or the Sun.

Hydrometer: An instrument used to measure the specific gravity of liquids—i.e., the ratio of the *density* of the liquid to the density of water.

Hydrosphere: In physical geography, the combined mass of water found on, under and over the surface of a planet including surface water, groundwater, snow cover, ice and water in the *atmosphere*.

Hygrometer: An instrument for measuring relative humidity.

Hypothesis: A testable conjecture about the cause of an observation or scientific problem.

Iceberg: A massive body of ice that has broken off from a snow-formed glacier or *ice shelf* and is floating in open water.

Icehouse climate: One of two types of global Earth climates, the other being Greenhouse or Hothouse. Icehouse is characterised by frequent continental glaciations and severe desert environments. We are currently in a warm phase of an Icehouse, known as an *interglacial period.*

Ice sheet: A mass of glacier ice that covers its surrounding terrain.

Ice shelf: The floating extension of a grounded *ice sheet* that is fed by land-derived ice.

Ice wedge: A near-vertical sheet of ice tapering downwards to 12 m deep found in a periglacial environment, such as *permafrost*. Formed by repeated contraction of the ice, filling of the gap with melt water and refreezing.

Independent variable: The factor that is manipulated or changed in an experiment and is not affected by changes in the other variables in an experiment or equation.

Indigenous: Here we refer to First Nations, Dene, Métis, Inuit, Inuvialuit and Sámi as 'indigenous' thus including many distinct cultures and frameworks of knowledge in the term.

Insolation: Solar *radiation* entering the Earth's atmosphere (from Incoming solar radiation).

Interglacial period: An interglacial is a comparatively short, geological interval of warmer global average *temperature* lasting 10,000–15,000 years separating longer glacial periods (90,000–100,000 years). We are presently living in the most recent interglacial called the 'Holocene', which began about 11,500 years ago.

Internal flow: Occurs in the interior of a glacier where the downslope component of the weight of the ice deforms the crystal structure, also called *creep*.

Ionosphere: The ionosphere is the uppermost part of the *atmosphere* (80 to 500 km) where charged particles (ions) are relatively abundant.

Isotropic: Having properties that are identical in all directions.

Linguistics: The scientific study of the general and universal properties of language.

Lipid: A broad group of naturally occurring molecules which are insoluble in water, but soluble in organic solvents.

Lipophilic: Having the ability to dissolve in or is attracted to fats, oils and other lipids.

Lithosphere: The hard and rigid outer portion of the Earth consisting of the crust and upper mantle, approximately 100 km thick.

Magnetic field: A vector field surrounding magnetic materials and electric currents that is detected by the force it exerts on other magnetic materials and moving electric charges.

Magnetism: Attraction or repulsion that arises between electrically charged particles in motion.

Magnetosphere: A magnetosphere is a highly magnetised region around an astronomical object. The Earth's magnetosphere was discovered in 1958 by Explorer 1 during the International Geophysical Year.

Mass: The total quantity of matter in a body regardless of any forces acting on it.

Meridional overturning circulation: The north-south flow of water that brings warm water from the equator towards the Poles along the surface and cold, dense water from the Poles towards the equator along the bottom.

Mesosphere: The middle layer of Earth's *atmosphere*, lying above the *stratosphere* and below the thermosphere, at *altitudes* of 50–80 km. It is characterised by decreasing *temperature* with increasing altitude.

Metabolism: The physical and chemical processes in a living organism that maintain the body and produce energy.

Meteorology: The branch of science that deals with the *atmosphere* of a planet, particularly that of the Earth, the most important application of which is the analysis and prediction of *weather*.

Montreal Protocol: Entering into force on January 1st 1989 and adjusted and amended since then, the Montreal Protocol on Substances That Deplete the *Ozone Layer* is an international treaty designed to protect the ozone layer by phasing out the production of a number of substances believed to be responsible for ozone depletion.

Moraine: Material (rock and soil) transported by a glacier and then deposited.

Multimeter: An electronic measuring instrument that combines several measurement functions (typically voltage, current and resistance) in one unit.

Muon: An elementary particle with negative electric charge heavier than an *electron* but lighter than *other particles having nonzero rest mass.*

Neutrino: An elementary particle with no electric charge and a very small *mass*.

Neutron: An uncharged elementary particle of slightly greater *mass* than the *proton*. The nuclei of stable isotopes of all elements except hydrogen and helium contain a number of neutrons equal to or greater than the number of *protons.*

North Atlantic Deep Water (NADW): A *water mass* that forms primarily in the regions around Labrador and Greenland. It is found in the Atlantic

Ocean at depths of 1,000–4,000 m and can be traced into other ocean basins.

Nucleons: The *protons* and *neutrons* that make up the nucleus of an atom.

Ocean acidification: The ongoing decrease in the pH of the oceans that has increased since pre-industrial times and will continue to increase in coming decades due to human-generated carbon dioxide (CO_2) emissions.

Ocean currents: Continuous, directed movements of ocean water generated by forces acting on the water, such as winds, the *Coriolis effect,* differences in *density* and tides caused by the gravitational pull of the Moon and the Sun.

Oceanography: The science that studies the ocean, using the sciences of biology, chemistry, physics and geology.

Ohm: A unit measuring the resistance of the passage of an electrical current through a conductor.

Optimal foraging theory: States that organisms forage in such a way as to maximise their energy intake per unit of time.

Ozone (O_3): A powerfully oxidising allotropic form of the element oxygen. The ozone molecule contains three atoms.

Ozone hole: Found in the *ozone layer* over Antarctica and the smaller area over the North Pole in the spring of each year.

Ozone layer: A region of the upper *atmosphere*, between about 15 and 30 km in altitude, which contains a relatively high concentration of *ozone*.

Palaeolimnologist: A scientist who reconstructs the palaeo-environments of inland waters and especially changes associated with such events as climatic change, human impact, and organisms' internal development processes.

Parallelism: In geography, refers to the fact that the tilt of the Earth's axis remains parallel to the same plane throughout its revolution around the Sun, giving rise to the Earth's seasons.

Pedosphere: The outermost layer of the Earth where soil-forming processes occur.

Permafrost: Any rock or soil that remains at or below 0°C for two or more years.

Persistent: Taking a long time to break down into less dangerous substances, describing certain pollutants.

Persistent organic pollutants (POPs): Harmful organic compounds that do not break down easily in the environment and accumulate in the fatty tissues of living organisms.

Physical pump: The physical process where carbon dioxide is dissolved in ocean water and carried by sinking water to the deep ocean where it may remain for hundreds of years before being returned to the *atmosphere* by upwelling.

Physiology: The biological study of the functioning of living systems and their parts.

Phytoplankton: Mostly autotrophic microscopic algae, which inhabit the illuminated surface waters of the oceans, lakes, estuaries and ponds and are responsible for the photosynthetic activity in the oceans.

Plane of the ecliptic: The plane of the Earth's orbit around the Sun. It is the primary reference plane when describing the position of bodies in the Solar System.

Plasma: A partially ionised gas, in which a proportion of *electrons* are free rather than being bound to an atom or molecule.

Plate tectonics: The theory that the Earth's crust is composed of large, rigid plates that move relative to one another on top of the more fluid mantle.

Polarisation: The direction of vibration of the electrical field vector of electromagnetic radiation.

Polar stratospheric clouds: Form in the winter polar *stratosphere* at *altitudes* of 15–25 km, when the *temperature* drops below –75°C. They play a central role in the formation of the *ozone hole* in the Antarctic and Arctic by providing surfaces upon which heterogeneous chemical reactions take place. Also known as nacreous clouds.

Polar vortex: A circumpolar cyclonic wind that forms above the Antarctic continent during the cold months of the austral winter.

Positive feedback loop: A process where a change in one part of a system causes further changes in another part, leading to increased changes in the first part of the system.

Practical salinity unit (psu): Units used to measure water salinity based on water conductivity rather than total dissolved salts.

Primary producer: Organisms in an ecosystem that produce biomass from inorganic compounds. In almost all cases these are photosynthetically active organisms.

Proton: A stable, positively charged subatomic particle having a *mass* 1,836 times that of the *electron*. It is found in the nucleus of each atom, along with *neutrons*.

Protozoan: A group of primarily unicellular microorganisms that exist singly or in colonies and are usually non-photosynthetic. They include flagellates, ciliates, sporozoans, amoebas and foraminifers.

Proxy data: Data that can provide indirect evidence about something that cannot be measured directly. *Temperature* proxies, such as tree ring widths and ice core layering, are used by climatologists to create a temperature record.

Qualitative data: Data that gives information about things that are difficult or impossible to measure numerically. It provides information by being rich in detail and description and is placed in a contextual framework. It is often used in social science research.

Quantitative data: Information that is measurable and is represented in numerical figures.

Radiation (also **Heat Transfer Mechanism**): A term applied to the emission and transmission of energy through space or through a material medium and also to the radiated energy itself. Commonly radiation refers to emission and transmission of the electromagnetic spectrum.

Refractive index: A measure of how much the speed of light or other waves (e.g., sound) is slowed down by the medium through which it passes.

Remineralisation: In biogeochemistry, this refers to the transformation of organic molecules to inorganic forms, typically mediated by biological activity.

Remote sensing: The acquisition of information about an object or phenomenon by the use of either recording or real-time sensing devices that are wireless, or not in physical or intimate contact with the object.

Request for Proposal (RFP): The procedure that invites different interested parties to join a competitive selection process for public works, service contracts, research funding, etc. In most countries, RFP follows a legal protocol.

Rookery: A colony of breeding animals, commonly applied to the nesting place of birds, such as crows and rooks, seabirds and marine mammals.

Salinity: The technical term for saltiness of a liquid.

Satellite (Earth-observing): A satellite specifically designed to observe Earth from orbit, intended for non-military uses such as environmental monitoring, *meteorology*, map making, etc.

Sea ice: Ice formed by the freezing of sea water. Because the oceans consist of salt water, this occurs at about −1.8°C (28.8°F).

Seismology: An area of geophysics involving the study of seismic waves that are released as the result of disturbances within Earth's interior.

Solar wind: The continuous outward flow of ionised solar gas and a 'frozen-in' remnant of the solar magnetic field through the solar system. This flow arises from strong outward pressure in the solar corona carrying away from the Sun about one million tons of gas per second.

Solstice: During the solstices, one pole (as far north or south as 66½°) has 24 hours of light, while the other pole has 24 hours of darkness. At two points in the year (around 21 June and 22 December), because of the tilt of the Earth's axis, the noon sun falls directly at 23½°N latitude in June (known as the Tropic of Cancer) and at 23½°S in December (the Tropic of Capricorn).

Stratification: In *oceanography*, when waters of different densities form layers that prevent vertical mixing of the water.

Stratosphere: The second major layer of Earth's *atmosphere*, just above the *troposphere*, and below the *mesosphere*. The stratosphere extends up to approximately 50 km above the surface at moderate latitudes, while at the Poles it begins at an *altitude* of around 8 km. It is characterised by constant *temperature* or rising temperature with increasing height.

Temperature: One of the principal parameters of thermodynamics, temperature is a physical property of a system that underlies the common notions of hot and cold. In scientific terms, it describes the average speed per molecules of all the molecules in a substance.

Thermal expansion: The increase in volume resulting from an increase in *temperature*, contraction being the reverse process.

Thermohaline circulation: The part of the large-scale ocean circulation driven by global *density* gradients created by surface heat and freshwater fluxes.

Thermosphere: The biggest of all the layers of the Earth's *atmosphere* directly above the *mesosphere* and directly below the *exosphere*, beginning at 80 km. It is characterised by increasing *temperature* with increasing *altitude* and by extremely low *density*.

Traditional Knowledge (also Traditional Ecological Knowledge): Knowledge about the environment, its resources and its history traditionally connected with *indigenous* communities. It stands for a different way of looking at the natural world and the Earth system, and exists parallel to the scientific perspective on natural phenomena. It is often holistic and passed on orally.

Trophic level: The position an organism occupies in a *food chain*.

Troposphere: The lowermost layer of the *atmosphere*. It extends up to approximately 8 km at the Poles and to approximately 17 km at the equator.

Van Allen Radiation Belts: Two doughnut-shaped zones of highly energetic charged particles *(plasma)* around the Earth, which are held in place by Earth's magnetic field. On the sunward side, it is compressed because of the *solar wind*, while on the other side it is elongated to around three Earth radii.

Virga: Precipitation that evaporates before reaching the ground, appearing as wisps descending from the clouds.

Water mass: An oceanographic water mass is an identifiable body of water which has physical properties distinct from surrounding water. Such properties might include *temperature, salinity* and chemical or isotopic ratios.

Weather/Weather systems: The state of the *atmosphere* at a given time and place, with respect to variables such as *temperature*, moisture, wind velocity and barometric pressure. Weather occurs due to *density* (temperature and moisture) differences between one place and another.

Zooplankton: An important constituent of the ocean's *food chain,* zooplankton include a wide variety of microorganisms such as copepod and larval forms of higher animals.

Abbreviations and Acronyms

See *Contributing Polar Institutions* for more information on acronyms in italics.

AABW	Antarctic Bottom Water
AAIW	Antarctic Intermediate Water
ACC	Antarctic Circumpolar Current
ACCYF	Arctic Climate Change Youth Forum
ACE CRC	Antarctic Climate & Ecosystems Cooperative Research Centre
AGAP	Antarctica's Gamburtsev Province
AHDR	Arctic Human Development Report
AINA	Arctic Institute of North America
ALISON	Alaska Lake Ice and Snow Observatory Network
ANDRILL	*ANtarctic geological DRILLing*
ANHMC	Alliance of Natural History Museums of Canada
ANKN	Alaska Native Knowledge Network
APECS	*Association of Polar Early Career Scientists*
AR4	Fourth Assessment Report
ArcticWOLVES	Arctic Wildlife Observatories Linking Vulnerable EcoSystems
ARISE	ANDRILL Research Immersion for Science Educators
AWI	*Alfred-Wegener-Institut für Polar- und Meeresforschung/Alfred-Wegener-Institute for Polar and Marine Research*
BAS	*British Antarctic Survey*
BBC	British Broadcasting Corporation
°C	degrees Celsius
^{14}C	Carbon-14
CANDAC	*Canadian Network for Detection of Atmospheric Change*
CBC	Canadian Broadcasting Corporation
CCGS	Canadian Coast Guard Ship
CCNY	City College of New York
CEAZA	Centro de Estudios Avanzados en Zonas Áridas
CERES	Clouds and the Earth's Radiant Energy System
CFCs	Chlorofluorocarbons
CFL	Circumpolar Flaw Lead system study
CH_4	Methane
CIFP	Circumpolar Inuit Field Program
ClO	Chlorine monoxide
cm	centimetres
CO_2	Carbon Dioxide
CRDP	Centre regional de documentation pédagogique
CReSIS	*Center for Remote Sensing of Ice Sheets*
CSA	Canadian Space Agency
CTD	Conductivity, Temperature and Depth
CUNY	City University of New York
CYLP	Circumpolar Young Leaders Program
CZE	Class Zero Emission
DGP	*Deutsche Gesellschaft für Polarforschung/ German Society for Polar Research*
EALÁT	'good pasture' (Sámi)
EDNA	Education Network of Australia
e.g.	for example (exempli gratia)
EISCAT	European Incoherent Scatter Scientific Association
ENSO	El Niño-Southern Oscillation
EOC	Education, Outreach and Communication
EQ	equator
ESA	European Space Agency
etc.	et cetera
g	gram
GCSE	General Certificate of Secondary Education (UK)
GIIPSY	Global Interagency International Polar Snapshot Year
GIS	Geographic Information System
GLOBE	Global Learning and Observations to Benefit the Environment
GPS	Global Positioning System
GRID	Global Resource Information Database
H_2O	Water
IARC	*International Arctic Research Centre*
IASC	*International Arctic Science Committee*
ICM-CSIC	*Institut de Ciències del Mar—Consejo Superior de Investigaciones Científicas*
ICR	*International Centre for Reindeer Husbandry*
ICSU	*International Council of Science*
ICT	Information and Communication Technology
i.e.	that is (id est)
IGCSE	International General Certificate of Secondary Education
IGY	International Geophysical Year
IPCC	Intergovernmental Panel on Climate Change
IPF	*International Polar Foundation*
IPY	*International Polar Year*
IPYDIS	International Polar Year Data Information Service
IQ	Inuit Qaujimajatuqangit

kg	kilogram	PSC	Polar Stratospheric Clouds
KLRS	Kluane Lake Research Station	*PSC Washington*	*Polar Science Center Washington*
km	kilometres	psu	practical salinity units
km²	square kilometres	PVC	Polyvinyl Chloride
KPT	Keep Planting Trees		
		RFP	Request for Proposal
LandSat	Land Satellite	ROAM	Research and Educational
LCD	Liquid Crystal Display		Opportunities in Antarctica for
LDEO	*Lamont-Doherty Earth Observatory*		Minorities
m	metres	SCAR	Scientific Committee for Antarctic
m²	square metres		Research
m³	cubic metres	SIPEX	Sea Ice Physics and Ecosystem
mm	millimetres		eXperiment
MA	Master of Arts	SonB	Schools on Board
MARS	McGill Arctic Research Station	SOY-IPY	Students on Ice—International Polar
MIW	Mediterranean Intermediate Water		Year
mL	millilitres	SPARC	Sensitivity of Permafrost in the
MODIS	Moderate Resolution Imaging		Arctic
	Spectroradiometer		
MSc	Master of Science	TAKS	Texas Assessment of Knowledge and
			Skills
NACSW	North Atlantic Central Surface Water	TK	Traditional Knowledge
NADW	North Atlantic Deep Water	tsp	teaspoons
NASA	*National Aeronautics and Space*		
	Administration	*UAF*	*University of Alaska Fairbanks*
NAVSTAR	Navigation Signal Timing and Ranging	*UArctic*	*University of the Arctic*
	Global Positioning System	UD	University of Delaware
NCAOR	*National Centre for Antarctic & Ocean*	UNAVCO	University NAVSTAR Consortium
	Research	*UNEP*	*United Nations Environment*
NCS	Native Communications Society		*Programme*
NGO	non-governmental organisation	UNESCO	United Nations Educational,
NHM	National History Museum (UK)		Scientific and Cultural Organisation
NILU	Norwegian Institute of Air Research	*UNIS*	*The University Centre in Svalbard*
NOAA	*National Oceanographic and Atmospheric*	UV	ultraviolet
	Administration		
NSIDC	*National Snow and Ice Data Center*	VBL socks	vapour barrier liner socks
NWRA	NorthWest Research Associates		
		WLAN	Wireless Local Area Network
O₂	Oxygen	*WMO*	*World Meteorological Organisation*
O₃	Ozone	*WRH*	*Association of World Reindeer*
OSCAR	Ocean Surface Analyses Real Time		*Herders*
		WSO	Winnipeg Symphony Orchestra
PANDA	Program of Antarctic Nova Disciplines	WWF	World Wildlife Fund
	Aspect		
pH	power of hydrogen	YAWA	Yayasan Anak Warisan Alam/
PhD	Doctor of Philosophy		Children's Environmental Heritage
POLENET	Polar Earth Observing Network		Foundation
POPs	persistent organic pollutants		
ppb	parts per billion		
ppm	parts per million		
ppt	parts per trillion		

References

Prelude
Parts of this chapter were published in:
Salmon, Rhian A., David J. Carlson. 2007. International Polar Year – the Poles and the Planet. In *EcoScience. The 34th Professor Harry Messel International Science School,* Stewart, Chris, and Anne Green, eds. 146–61. Sydney: Science Foundation of Physics within the University of Sydney.

Arktowski. 1931. First IPY commentary. In National Oceanic and Atmospheric Administration (NOAA) Arctic Research. 2008. *Office: The First International Polar Year: The Arctic Environment in Historical Perspective.* http://www.actic.noaa.gov/aro/ipy-1 (accessed 26 December 2009).

Barr, William. 1983. Geographical Aspects of the First International Polar Year, 1882–83. *Annals of the Association of American Geographers,* 73.4, 463–84.

Behrendt, John C. 1998. *Innocents on the Ice: A Memoir of Antarctic Exploration, 1957.* Niwot, Colo.: University Press of Colorado.

Enterrés Volontaires au Cœur de l'Antarctique, DVD, directed by Djamel Tahi (Terra Incognita and the CNRS, 2008).

NOAA, Images and Dates of the First IPY (1881–84): www.arctic.noaa.gov/aro/ipy-1/ (accessed 26 December 2009).

Allison I., N.L. Bindoff, R.A. Bindschadler, P.M. Cox, N. de Noblet, M.H. England, J.E. Francis, N. Gruber, A.M. Haywood, D.J. Karoly, G. Kaser, C. Le Quéré, T.M. Lenton, M.E. Mann, B.I. McNeil, A.J. Pitman, S. Rahmstorf, E. Rignot, H.J. Schellnhuber, S.H. Schneider, S.C. Sherwood, R.C.J. Somerville, K. Steffen, E.J. Steig, M. Visbeck, A.J. Weaver. 2009. *The Copenhagen Diagnosis, 2009: Updating the World on the Latest Climate Science.* The University of New South Wales Climate Change Research Centre (CCRC), Sydney, Australia. http://www.copenhagendiagnosis.org/ (accessed 26 December 2009).

Chapter 2
Anderson, Lorin W., David R. Krathewohl, eds. 2001. *A Taxonomy for Learning, Teaching, and Assessing: A Revision of Bloom's Taxonomy of Educational Objectives.* New York: Longman.

Bloom, Benjamin S., David R. Krathwohl, eds. 1975. *Taxonomy of Educational Objectives. Handbook 1: Cognitive Domain.* New York: David McKay Co Inc.

Marzano, Robert J., John S. Kendall. 2007. *The New Taxonomy of Educational Objectives.* Thousand Oaks, CA: Corwin Press.

Wiggins, Grant P., Jay McTighe. 2005. *Understanding by Design.* Alexandria, VA: Association for Supervision and Curriculum Development.

Chapter 4
Berkes, Finkret, Johan Colding, Carl Folke, eds. 2003. *Navigating social-ecological systems. Building Resilience for Complexity and Change.* Cambridge: Cambridge University Press.

Nuttall, M., P.A. Forest, S.D. Mathiesen. 2008. Background Paper on Climate Change in the Arctic. In *Joint Seminar of the UArctic Rectors' Forum and the Standing Committee of Parliamentarians of the Arctic Region.* Snellmann, O., L. Kullerud, G. Lindstrom, and B.W. Ropstad, eds. 17–21. UArctic Publication Series No.2.

Oskal, A., J.M. Turi, S.D. Mathiesen, P. Burgess. 2009. EALÁT Reindeer Herders' Voice: Reindeer Herding, Traditional Knowledge and Adaptation to Climate Change and Changed Use of the Arctic. In *Arctic Council SDWG EALÁT-Information Ministerial Report, International Centre for Reindeer Husbandry and Association of World Reindeer Herders.* International Centre for Reindeer Husbandry Report 2.

Vistnes I., P. Burgess, S.D. Mathiesen, C. Nellemann, A. Oskal, J.M. Turi. 2009. Reindeer Husbandry and Barents 2030. Impacts of Future Petroleum Development on Reindeer Husbandry in the Barents Region. In *Report for StatoilHydro Barents 2030 Scenario Programme.* International Centre for Reindeer Husbandry Report 1.

CD-ROM
The authors of 'Negotiating Research Relationships with Inuit Comunities' have made every effort to ensure that its content is accurate and up to date. However, information pertaining to research regulatory requirements may have changed. Newer versions of this document can be found and downloaded at: www.inuitknowledge.ca and www.nri.nu.ca.

Credits

Table of Contents
Images: Douglas Yates

Introduction
Chapter Opener: Christian Morel, www.ourpolarheritage.com.

Prelude
Chapter Opener, P.2, P.7, P.10, P.14: Christian Morel, www.ourpolarheritage.com; Atmosphere, Ice, Oceans, Land, People heading; P.1, P.4, P.9, P.12: Douglas Yates; Space heading: Merrick Peirce; P.3, P.11, P.15, P.19: Sandra Zicus; P.5: Courtesy of WMO "The State of Polar Research" (2009) and CCNY/CUNY; original figure in Tedesco, Marco, Xavier Fettweis, Michiel van den Broeke, Roderik van de Wal and Paul Smeets, 2008: "Extreme snowmelt in northern Greenland during summer 2008." Eos, 89 (41): 391.; P.6: Simon Marsland; P.8: DAMOCLES; P.13: Courtesy of WMO "The State of Polar Research" (2009); original figure in: Young, T. K. and W. Dallmann, 2008: Circumpolar health indicators: sources, data and maps. Circumpolar Health Supplements 2008; 3. International Association of Circumpolar Health Publishers.; P.16: Courtesy of IPY Norway, "Visual Profile Guide," Bjørn Jørgensen/NN/Samfoto.; P.17: Courtesy of IPY Norway, "Visual Profile Guide," Torfinn Kjærnet.; P.18: Adrian Boyle, www.wildlifeimages.com.au.

Chapter 1
Chapter Opener, 1.1: Christian Morel; Atmosphere, Ice, Oceans, Land, People heading, 1.75: Douglas Yates; Space heading, 1.68: Merrick Peirce; 1.2, 1.8, 1.9, 1.17, 1.19, 1.20, 1.21, 1.22, 1.23, 1.25, 1.26, 1.28, 1.31, 1.33, 1.35, 1.42, 1.43, 1.44, 1.45, 1.46, 1.71: Sandra Zicus; 1.3: BAS and Geographical Information Centre; 1.4; 1.7: NOAA/Department of Commerce; 1.5, 1.6, 1.18, 1.64, 1.65: IPF; 1.10, 1.12, 1.14, 1.72: NASA; 1.11: Rob Webster; 1.14, 1.30: Hugo Ahlenius, UNEP/GRID-Arendal, Climate change - ice and snow and the albedo effect, UNEP/GRID-Arendal Maps and Graphics Library, http://maps.grida.no/go/graphic/climate-change-ice-and-snow-and-the-albedo-effect (accessed 2 January 2010); 1.15, 1.16, 1.24, 1.57, 1.58: Louise Huffman; 1.27: Peter Wasilewaski; 1.29: Jean Pennycook; 1.32: Pidwirny, M. (2006). "Surface and Subsurface Ocean Currents: Ocean Current Map". Fundamentals of Physical Geography, 2nd Edition. http://www.physicalgeography.net/fundamentals/8q_1.html (accessed 2 January 2010); 1.34: Steve Rintoul, courtesy of Royal Society of Tasmania; 1.36, 1.37, 1.38:

The Maury Project, Density-Driven Ocean Circulation, American Meteorological Society; 1.39: Patty Virtue; 1.40, 1.41: Josep Marlés Tortosa; 1.47, 1.48, 1.49, 1.50, 1.51: Mieke Sterken; 1.52: US Antarctic Program; 1.53: José Xavier; 1.54, 1.55, 1.56: Torsten Sachs; 1.59, 1.60: Frank Doyle; 1.61, 1.69: Lars Poort; 1.62: Sigurður St. Helgason, Grunnskóli Bláskógabyggðar, Laugarvatn, Iceland; 1.63: Elizabeth Hodges Snyder and Nancy Nix; 1.66, 1.67: Andrea Kaiser, courtesy Unilab of Humboldt University, Berlin; 1.70: Clip art compilation; 1.73, 1.74: IceCube collaboration, www.icecube.wisc.edu (accessed 2 January 2010).

Chapter 2
2.1: Louise Huffman; 2.2: Anica Brown; 2.3: Elke Bergholz (PolarTREC 2007), courtesy of ARCUS; 2.4: Joanna Hubbard.

Chapter 3
Chapter Opener: Christian Morel, www.ourpolarheritage.com; 3.1: College André Lahaye, France; 3.2: Barbara Parker, Delta Cyber School; 3.3, 3.13, 3.14: Courtesy of Schools on Board; 3.4: Kenji Hoshikawa; 3.5: Elena B. Sparrow; 3.6: Cornelia Zaharia; 3.7: R. Max Holmes; 3.8, 3.10: Courtesy of IPF; 3.9: Cheri Hamilton; 3.11, 3.12: Courtesy of Students on Ice; 3.15, 3.18, 3.52: Doug Barber; 3.16: Patrícia Álvarez; 3.17: Heidi Swanson; 3.19, 3.20: Louise Huffman/ANDRILL; 3.21: Steven Michelbach; 3.22 Mike Dunn; 3.23: Sandra Zicus; 3.24: Ana L. Pallares-Weissling; 3.25, 3.26: Ray Barndardt; 3.27: Tyler Llewellyn; 3.28: Vladimir Alexeev; 3.29: Liz Thomas; 3.30: Anja Kade; 3.31: Sarah Robertson; 3.32: Jose Herrera; 3.33, 3.34: Jenny Baeseman/APECS; 3.35: David Buckland; 3.36: Ana Salomé David; 3.37: Madalena Mota; 3.38, 3.50: José Xavier; 3.39: A. Kuytskiy; 3.40: Svein D. Mathiesen; 3.41: Glenn Williams; 3.42: Joe Meehan; 3.43: Teodor Gheorghe Negoita; 3.44: Paul-Andrei Iordache; 3.45: Kate O'Donnell; 3.46, 3.53: Lucia Simion; 3.47: BAS; 3.48: Kelly Carroll; 3.49, 3.51: Robin Bell; 3.54: Courtesy of NCAOR; 3.55: William Greenland; 3.56: Elise Biersma; 3.57: Courtesy of Ministerio de Ciencia e Innovación.

Chapter 4
4.1, 4.3: Svein D. Mathiesen, EALÁT/ICR 2007; 4.2: Ellen Inga Turi, EALÁT/ICR 2007.

List of Contributing Polar Institutions
Chapter Opener: Christian Morel, www.ourpolarheritage.com.

Index